W9-BSZ-011

SCIENCE COMICS

FLYING MACHINES
How the Wright Brothers Soared

FLYING MACHINES
How the Wright Brothers Soared

ALISON WILGUS   MOLLY BROOKS

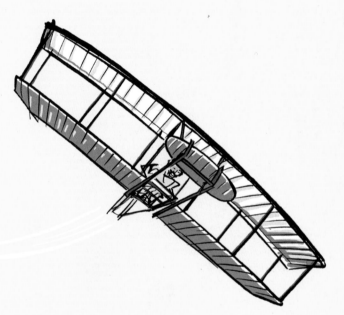

First Second

New York

For my family, who got me here
—Alison

To Kix, Barbara, and Eric Brooks
♥ Molly

First Second

Text copyright © 2017 by Alison Wilgus
Illustrations copyright © 2017 by Molly Brooks

Drawn on 96 lb Canson Recycled Bristol with a Pentel Pocket Brush Pen and Deleter G-Pen nibs dipped in Koh-i-Noor Rapidograph Universal ink. Colored on a MacBook Pro and Cintiq 22HD with a Wacom Art Pen using Chisel Felt Nibs, Adobe Photoshop CS6, and a combination of several custom PS brushes and Kyle T. Webster's ULTIMATE MegaPack.

Published by First Second
First Second is an imprint of Roaring Brook Press,
a division of Holtzbrinck Publishing Holdings Limited Partnership
175 Fifth Avenue, New York, New York 10010
All rights reserved

Library of Congress Control Number: 2016945553

Paperback ISBN 978-1-62672-139-5
Hardcover ISBN 978-1-62672-140-1

Our books may be purchased in bulk for promotional, educational, or business use. Please contact your local bookseller or the Macmillan Corporate and Premium Sales Department at (800) 221-7945 ext. 5442 or by e-mail at MacmillanSpecialMarkets@macmillan.com.

First edition 2017
Book design by John Green
Edited by Casey Gonzalez

Printed in China by Toppan Leefung Printing Ltd., Dongguan City, Guangdong Province
Paperback: 10 9 8 7 6 5 4 3 2 1
Hardcover: 10 9 8 7 6 5 4 3 2 1

Your guide in this delightful retelling of the story of flight is Katharine Wright, little sister of Wilbur and Orville Wright, inventors of the airplane. As you will learn, the Wright brothers had plenty of competition, and the story of their improbable success is a gripping tale of hairbreadth escapes, blind alleys, and brilliant breakthroughs.

Along the way, you will meet a little boy named Frank Whittle, who grew up during the early days of flight and dreamed of making airplanes go impossibly fast. Together, the Wrights and Whittle laid the foundation for the modern jet plane that takes us wherever we want to go in the world.

But let me tell you about Katharine. She was the youngest in the family and the only girl. When she was fourteen, her mother died, and little Katie took over managing the household. Her father, a church bishop, was on the road much of the time, and she also served as his secretary, managing his correspondence while he was away. A few years later, she was the only one of his five children to earn a college degree.

Katharine was teaching high school Latin when her bachelor brothers, Wilbur and Orville, plunged into a problem that had frustrated the world's greatest, smartest, and richest inventors—building a flying machine.

She observed this crazy quest with great interest and unflagging support. And when it came time for Wilbur and Orville to market their airplane, she was what we would now call their public relations director. Since the first sales were in Europe, she had to deal with the kings, queens, counts, countesses, and other aristocrats who flocked to the flight demonstrations, often angling for free rides. I guess kings and queens never grow up!

Back to the brothers. How did they do it? Their genius was that they broke the problem down into manageable parts. (This is good advice for anybody.) Other inventors had simply attached a motor and a crude propeller to a bird-like contraption and then started the engine. They invariably crashed. Had they gotten into the air, they would have had no idea what to do.

By contrast, Wilbur and Orville realized that control was the most crucial problem of all, and they set about solving it first. That's why they went to Kitty Hawk on the North Carolina coast, where steady winds allowed them endless experience perfecting the controls of their gliders. When they could finally glide as expertly as the gulls (well, almost), they designed and built an efficient set of propellers and had their mechanic, Charlie Taylor, construct a lightweight gasoline engine. Then, on December 17, 1903, they made history: the world's first powered, controlled, heavier-than-air flight.

You may think I have just told you the story of flight. But you haven't heard anything yet. Fasten your seat belts, bring your seatbacks and tray tables to their upright positions, turn off all electronic devices, and keep reading, for you are about to have the ride of your life!

—Richard Maurer,
Author of *The Wright Sister*

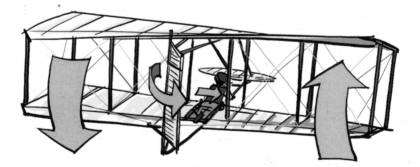

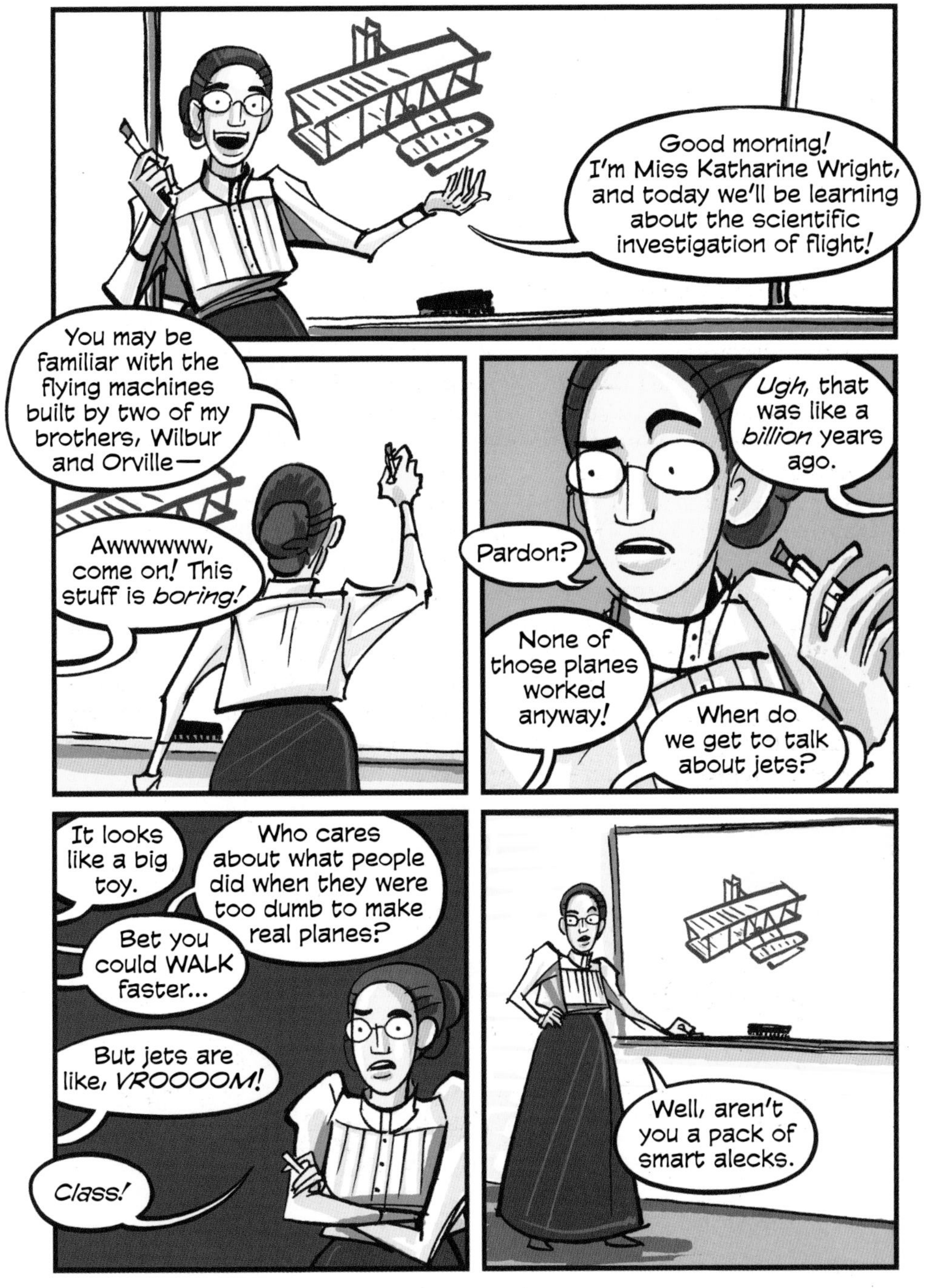
Good morning! I'm Miss Katharine Wright, and today we'll be learning about the scientific investigation of flight!
You may be familiar with the flying machines built by two of my brothers, Wilbur and Orville—
Awwwwww, come on! This stuff is *boring!*
Ugh, that was like a *billion* years ago.
Pardon?
None of those planes worked anyway!
When do we get to talk about jets?
It looks like a big toy.
Who cares about what people did when they were too dumb to make real planes?
Bet you could WALK faster...
But jets are like, *VROOOOM!*
Class!
Well, aren't you a pack of smart alecks.

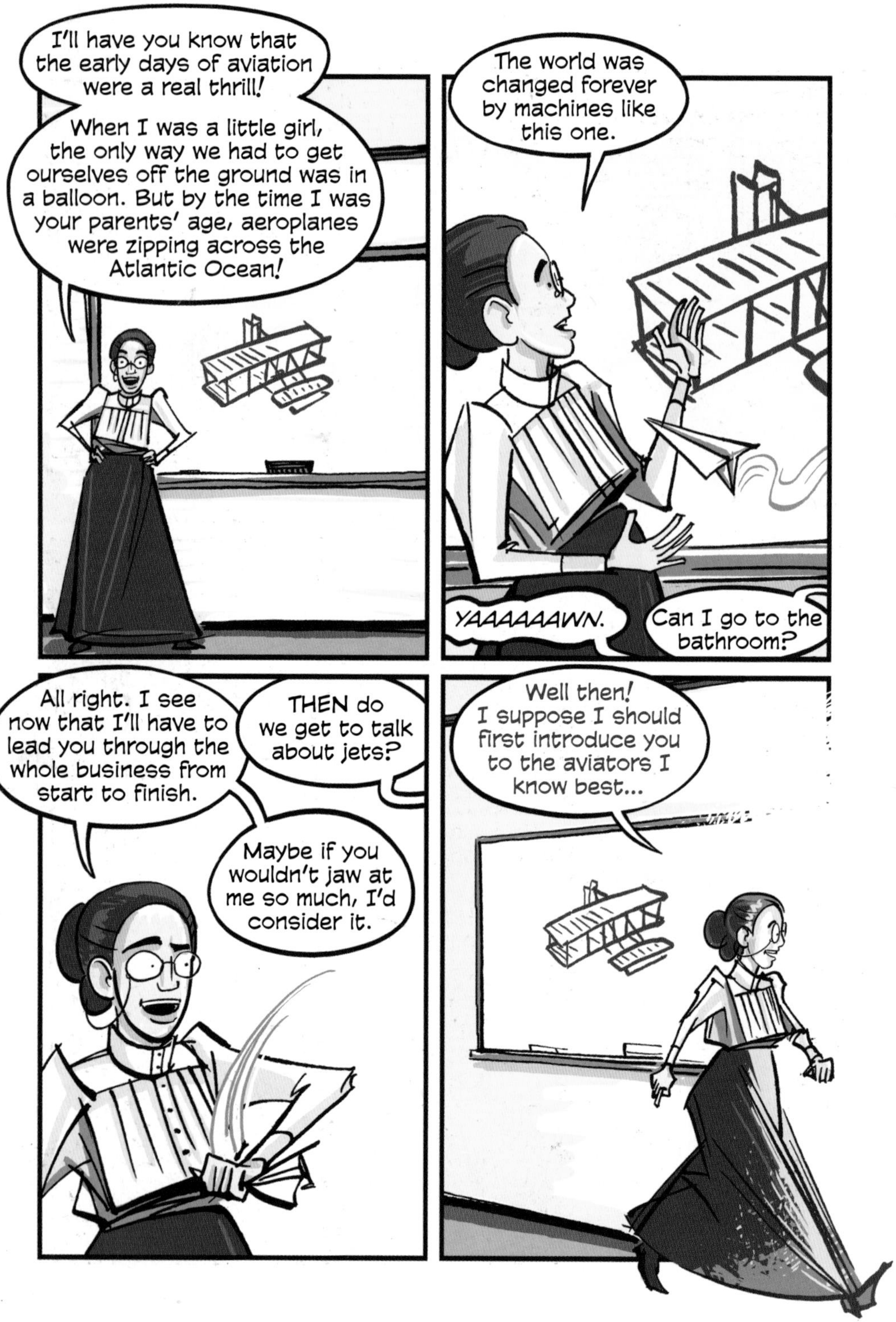

I'll have you know that the early days of aviation were a real thrill!
When I was a little girl, the only way we had to get ourselves off the ground was in a balloon. But by the time I was your parents' age, aeroplanes were zipping across the Atlantic Ocean!
The world was changed forever by machines like this one.
YAAAAAAWN.
Can I go to the bathroom?
All right. I see now that I'll have to lead you through the whole business from start to finish.
THEN do we get to talk about jets?
Maybe if you wouldn't jaw at me so much, I'd consider it.
Well then! I suppose I should first introduce you to the aviators I know best...

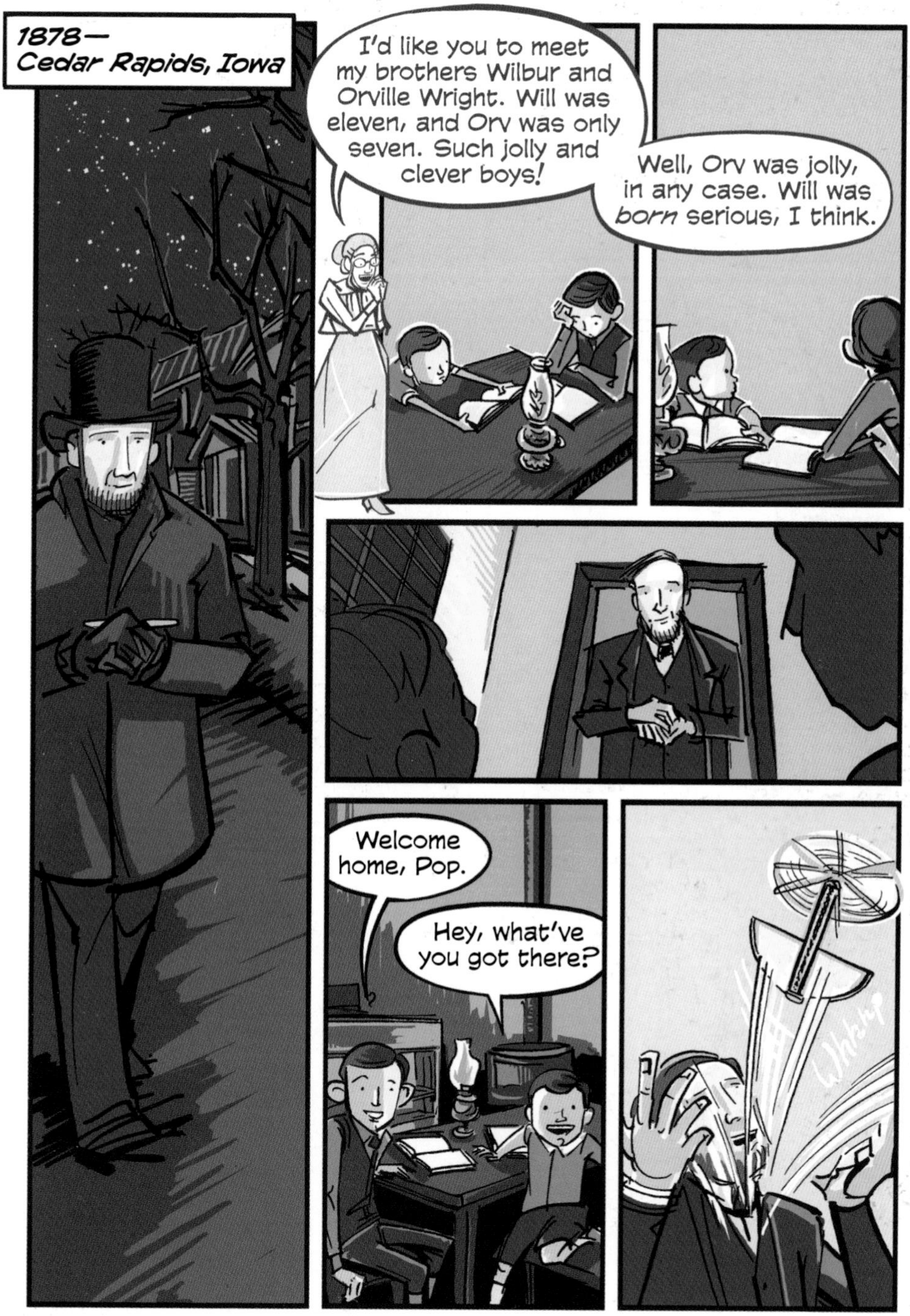
1878—
Cedar Rapids, Iowa
I'd like you to meet my brothers Wilbur and Orville Wright. Will was eleven, and Orv was only seven. Such jolly and clever boys!
Well, Orv was jolly, in any case. Will was *born* serious, I think.
Welcome home, Pop.
Hey, what've you got there?

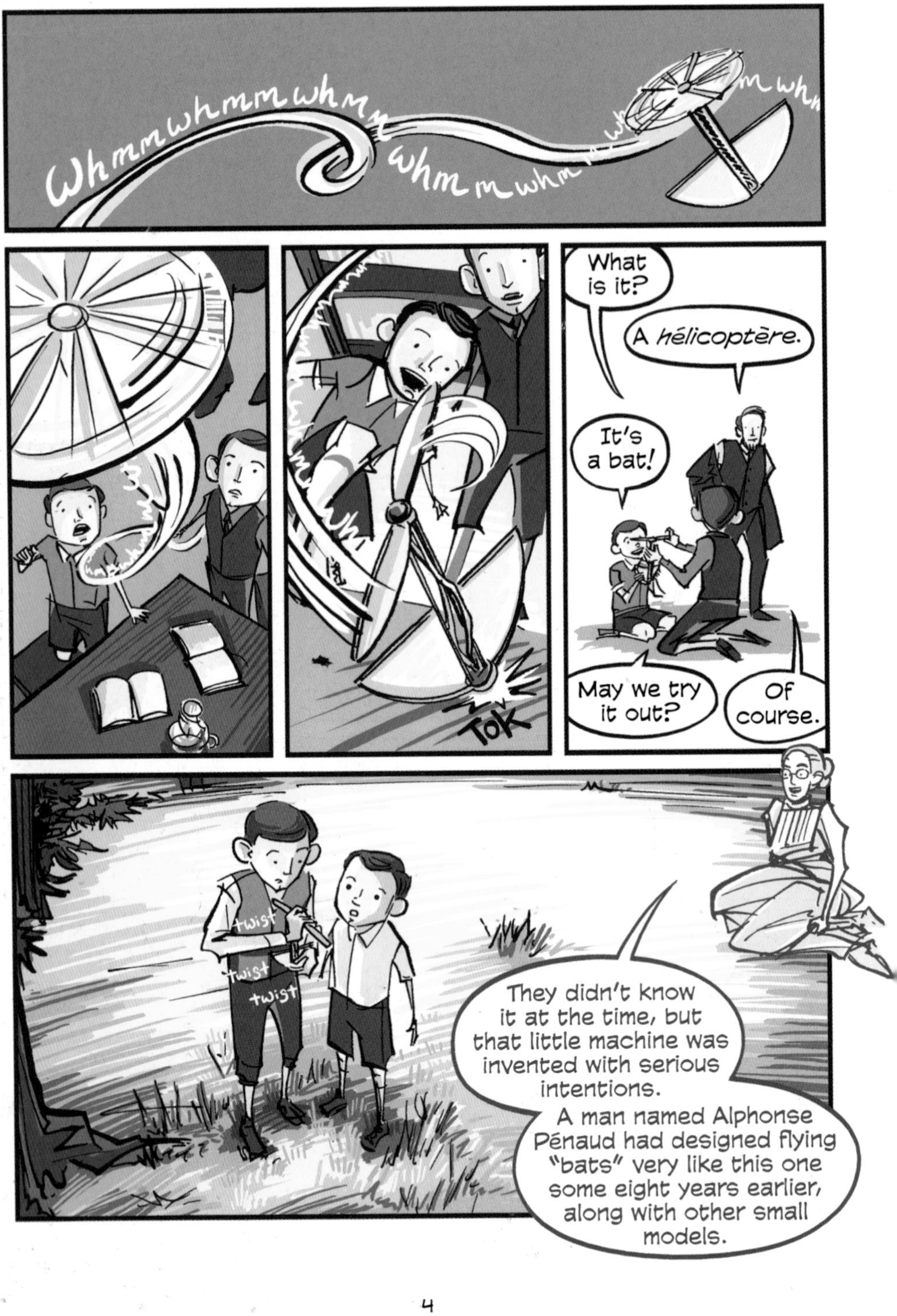

Whmmwhmmwhmm
What is it?
A *hélicoptère*.
It's a bat!
TOK
May we try it out?
Of course.
twist
twist
twist
They didn't know it at the time, but that little machine was invented with serious intentions.
A man named Alphonse Pénaud had designed flying "bats" very like this one some eight years earlier, along with other small models.

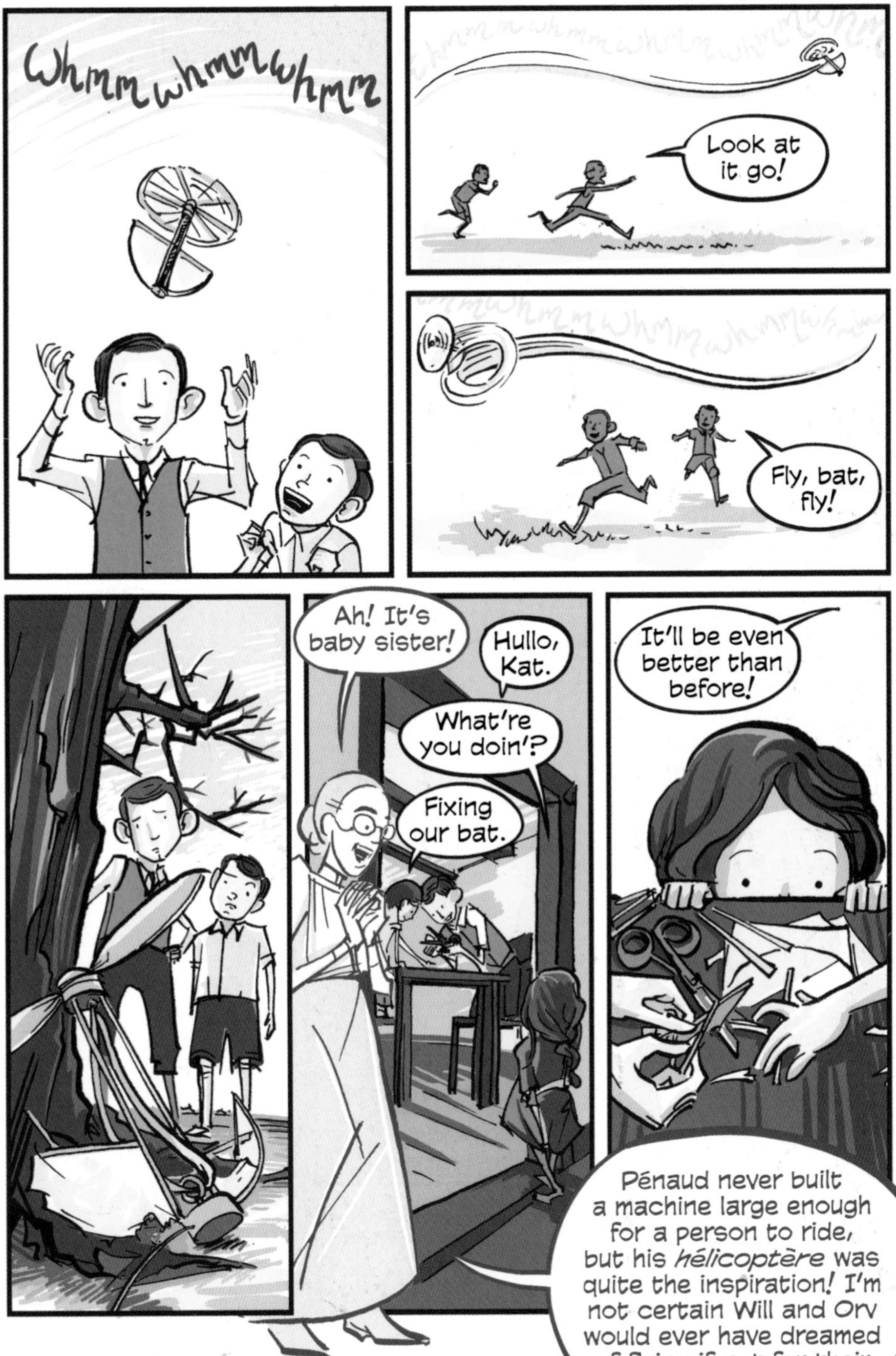
Whmm whmm whmm
Look at it go!
Fly, bat, fly!
Ah! It's baby sister!
Hullo, Kat.
What're you doin'?
Fixing our bat.
It'll be even better than before!
Pénaud never built a machine large enough for a person to ride, but his *hélicoptère* was quite the inspiration! I'm not certain Will and Orv would ever have dreamed of flying if not for their little "bat."

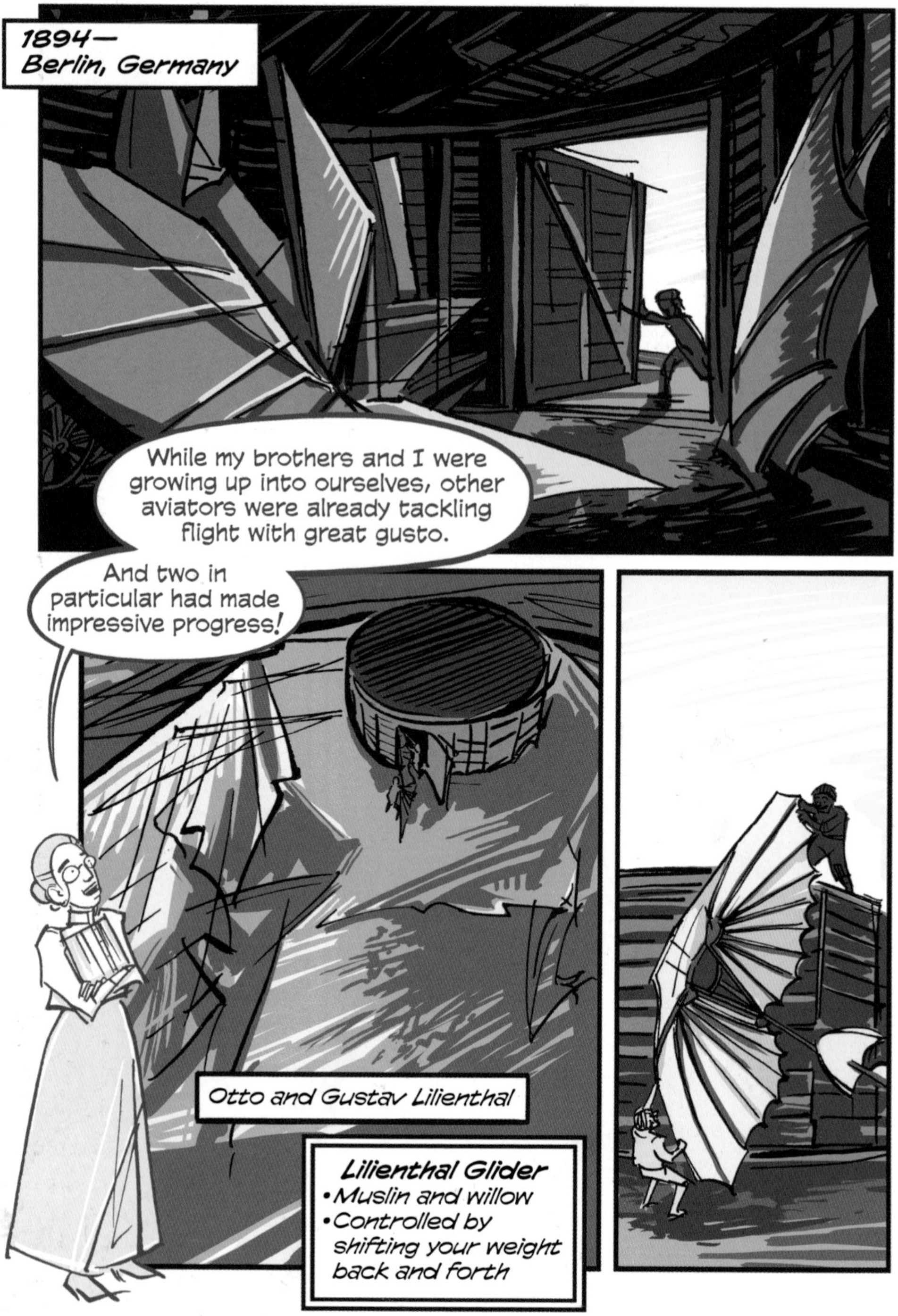
1894—
Berlin, Germany
While my brothers and I were growing up into ourselves, other aviators were already tackling flight with great gusto.
And two in particular had made impressive progress!
Otto and Gustav Lilienthal
Lilienthal Glider
•Muslin and willow
•Controlled by shifting your weight back and forth

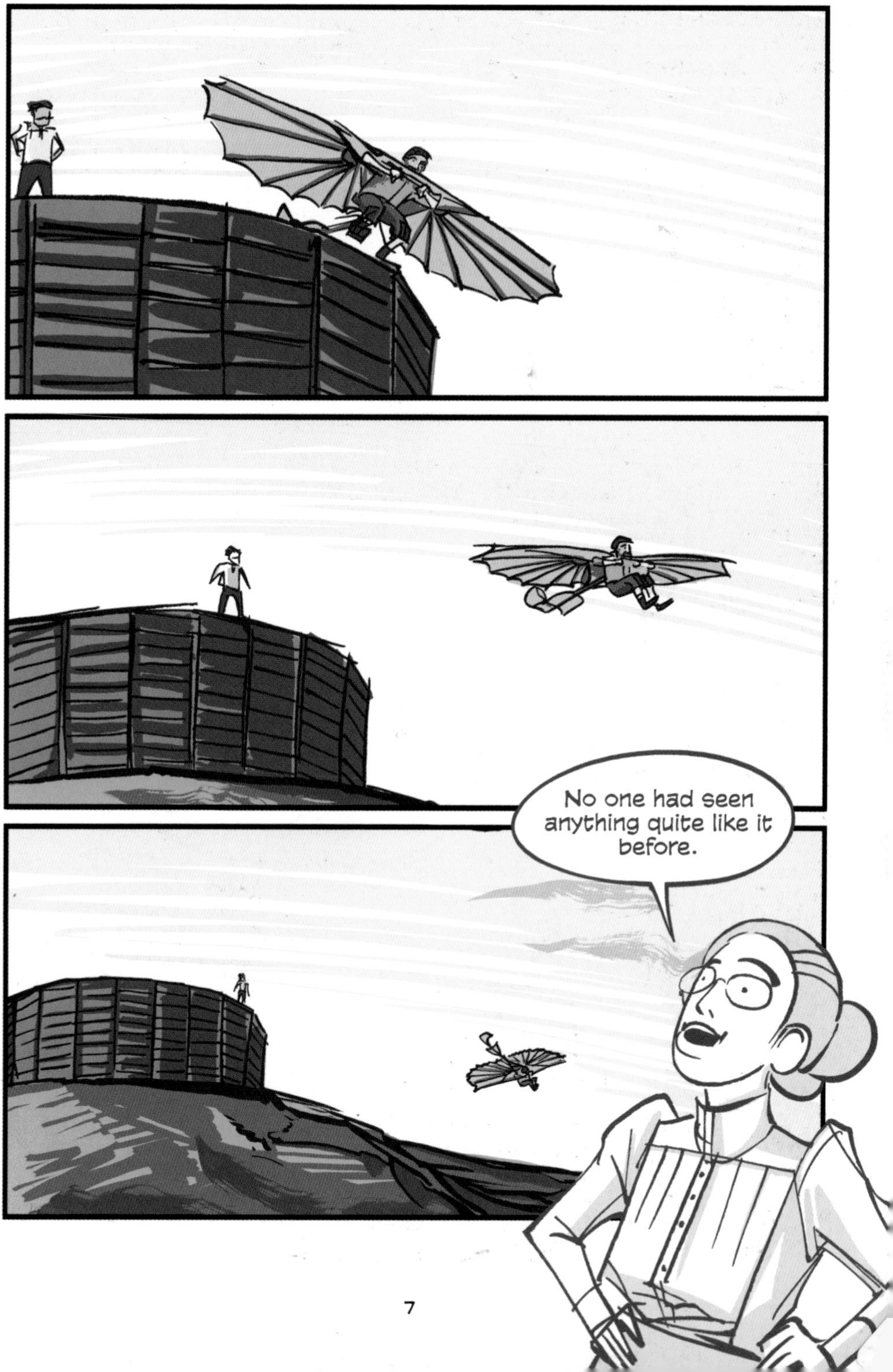
No one had seen anything quite like it before.

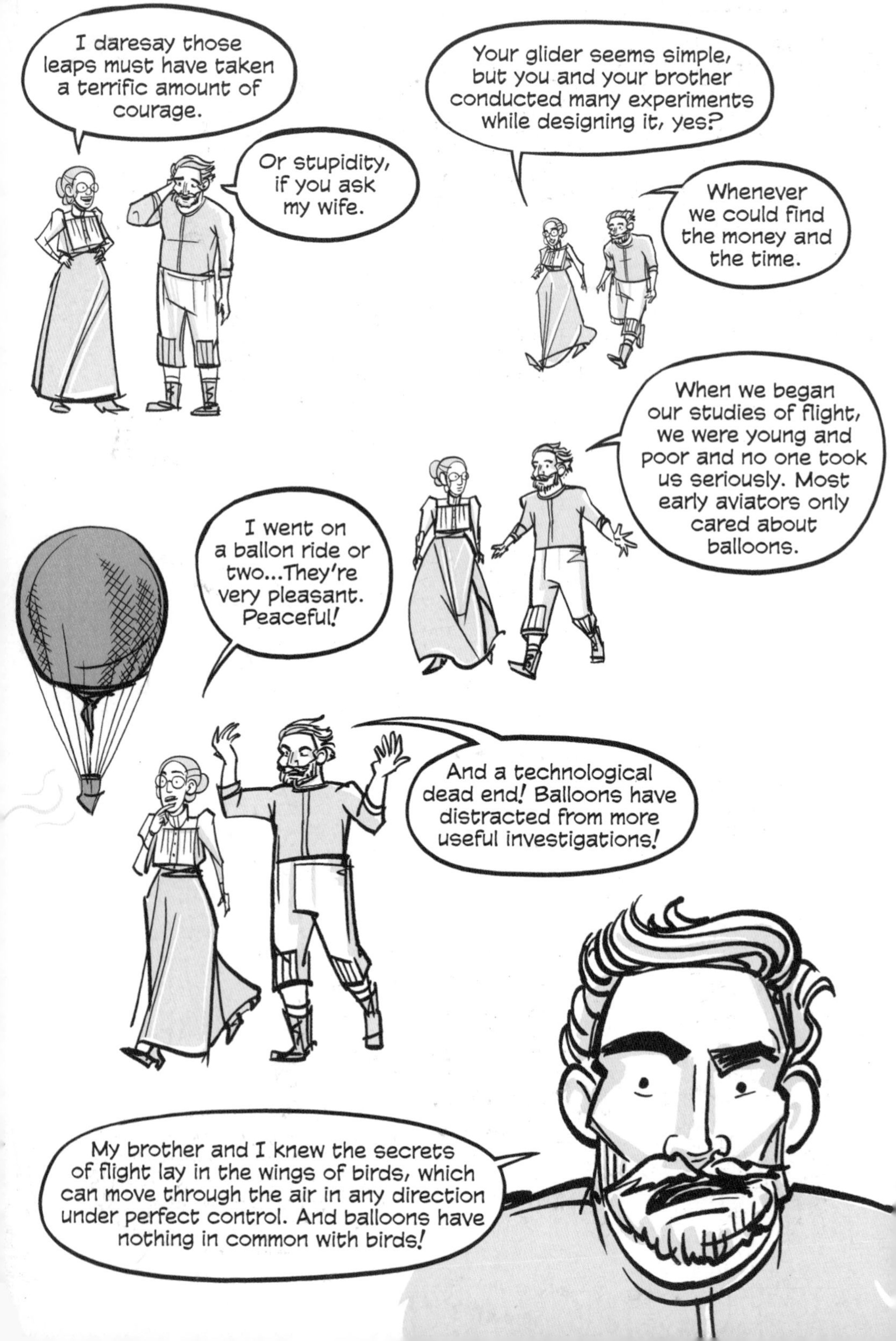
I daresay those leaps must have taken a terrific amount of courage.
Or stupidity, if you ask my wife.
Your glider seems simple, but you and your brother conducted many experiments while designing it, yes?
Whenever we could find the money and the time.
When we began our studies of flight, we were young and poor and no one took us seriously. Most early aviators only cared about balloons.
I went on a ballon ride or two...They're very pleasant. Peaceful!
And a technological dead end! Balloons have distracted from more useful investigations!
My brother and I knew the secrets of flight lay in the wings of birds, which can move through the air in any direction under perfect control. And balloons have nothing in common with birds!

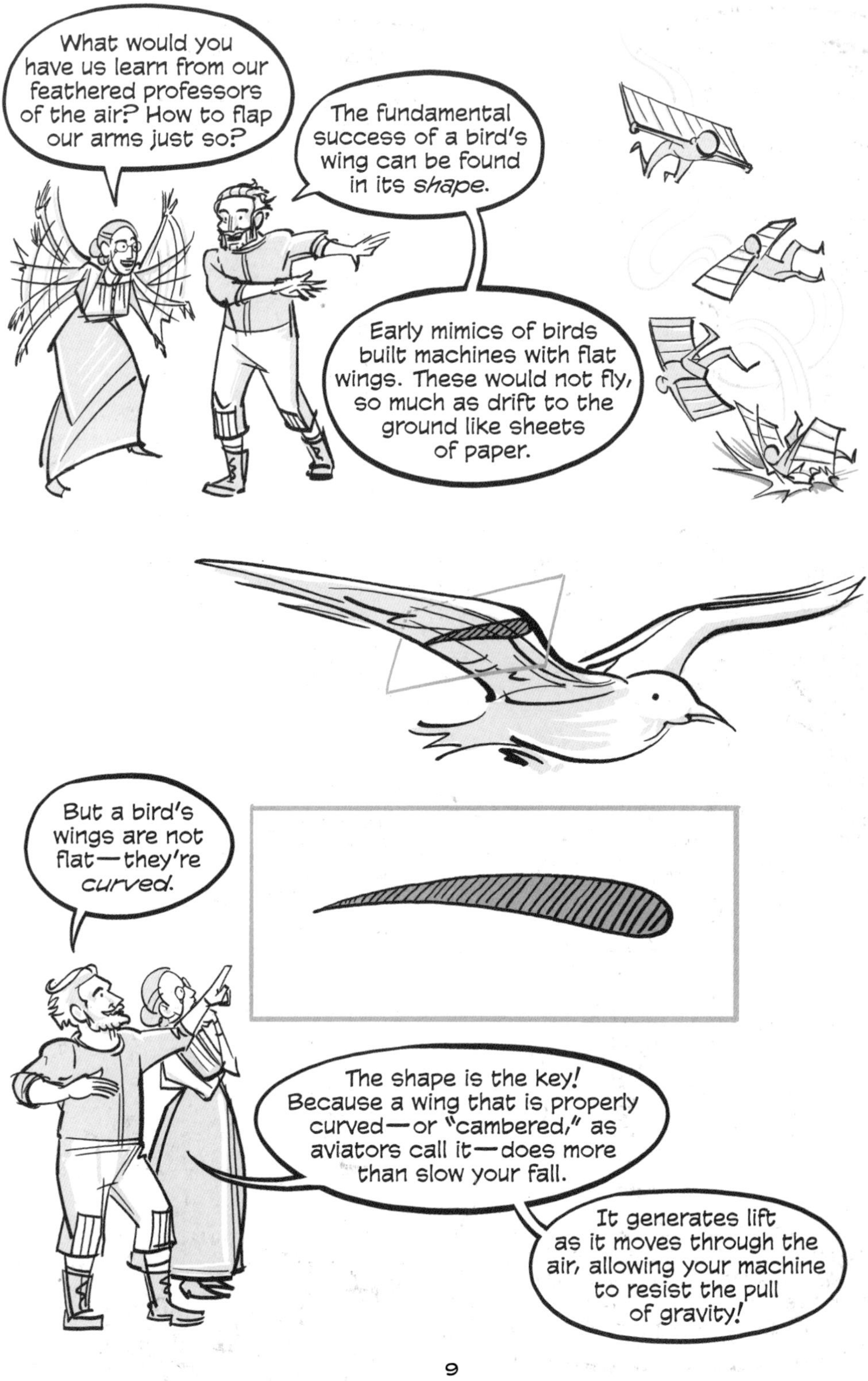
What would you have us learn from our feathered professors of the air? How to flap our arms just so?
The fundamental success of a bird's wing can be found in its *shape*.
Early mimics of birds built machines with flat wings. These would not fly, so much as drift to the ground like sheets of paper.
But a bird's wings are not flat—they're *curved*.
The shape is the key! Because a wing that is properly curved—or "cambered," as aviators call it—does more than slow your fall.
It generates lift as it moves through the air, allowing your machine to resist the pull of gravity!

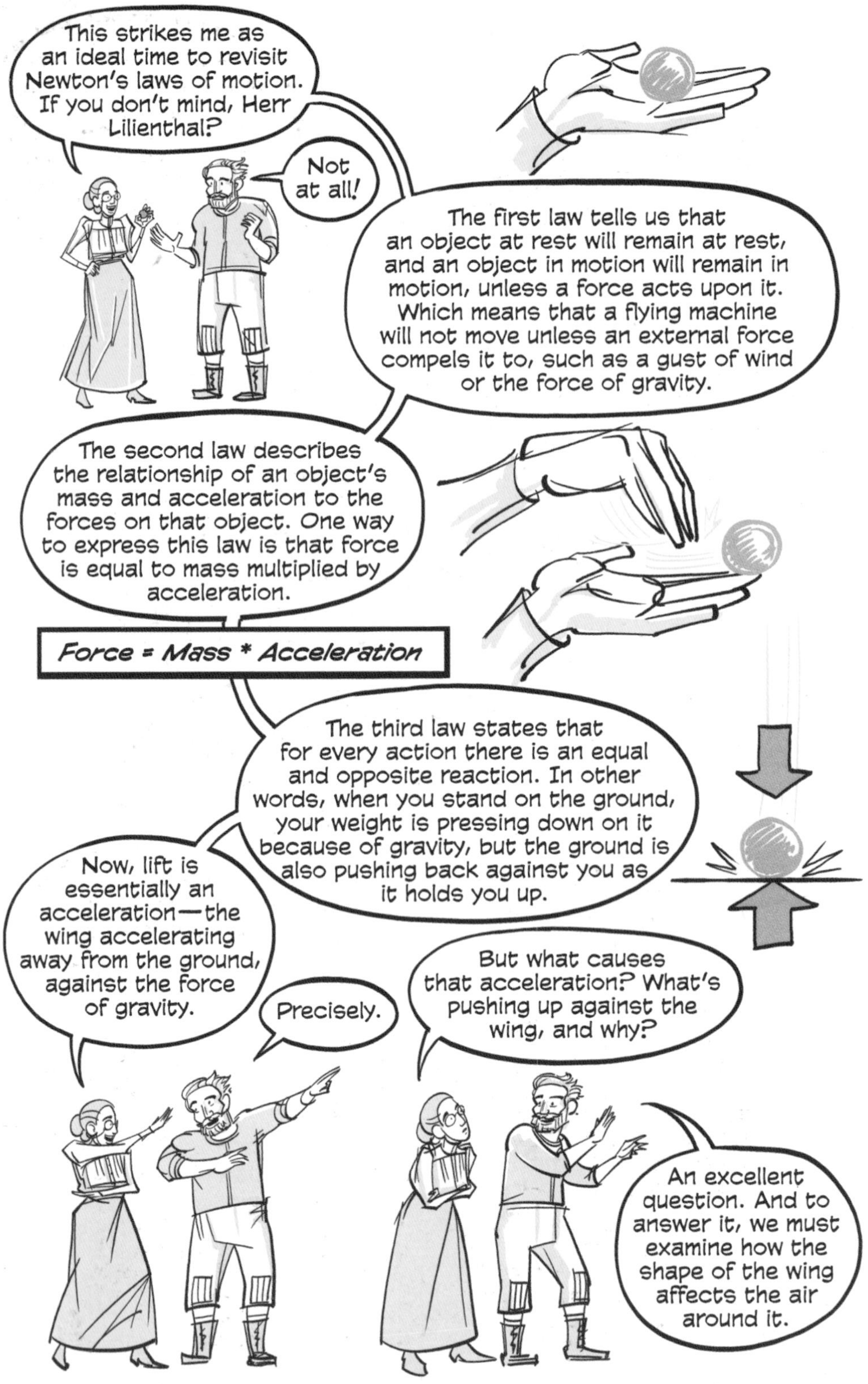
This strikes me as an ideal time to revisit Newton's laws of motion. If you don't mind, Herr Lilienthal?
Not at all!
The first law tells us that an object at rest will remain at rest, and an object in motion will remain in motion, unless a force acts upon it. Which means that a flying machine will not move unless an external force compels it to, such as a gust of wind or the force of gravity.
The second law describes the relationship of an object's mass and acceleration to the forces on that object. One way to express this law is that force is equal to mass multiplied by acceleration.
Force = Mass * Acceleration
The third law states that for every action there is an equal and opposite reaction. In other words, when you stand on the ground, your weight is pressing down on it because of gravity, but the ground is also pushing back against you as it holds you up.
Now, lift is essentially an acceleration—the wing accelerating away from the ground, against the force of gravity.
Precisely.
But what causes that acceleration? What's pushing up against the wing, and why?
An excellent question. And to answer it, we must examine how the shape of the wing affects the air around it.

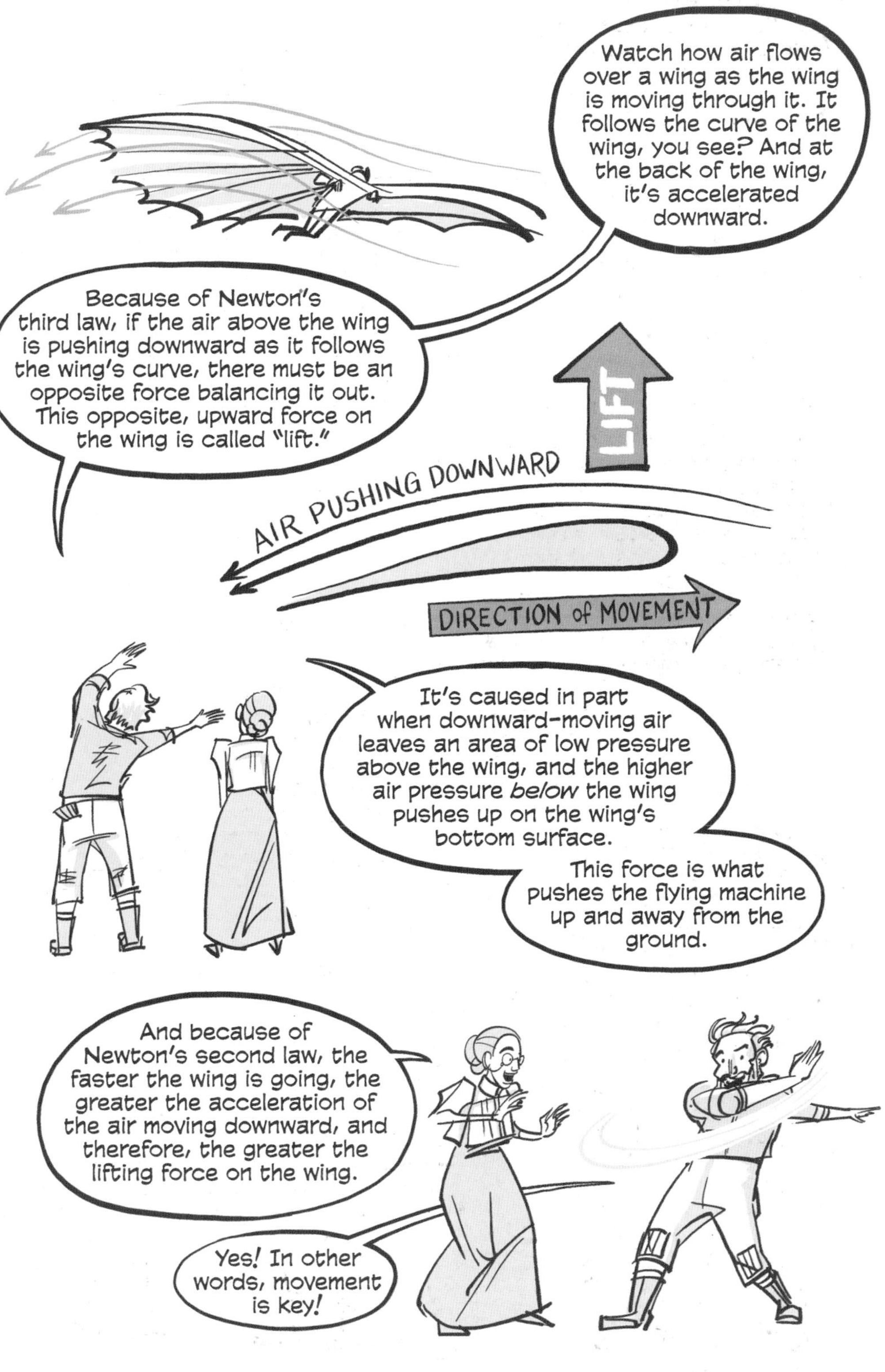
Watch how air flows over a wing as the wing is moving through it. It follows the curve of the wing, you see? And at the back of the wing, it's accelerated downward.
Because of Newton's third law, if the air above the wing is pushing downward as it follows the wing's curve, there must be an opposite force balancing it out. This opposite, upward force on the wing is called "lift."
LIFT
AIR PUSHING DOWNWARD
DIRECTION of MOVEMENT
It's caused in part when downward-moving air leaves an area of low pressure above the wing, and the higher air pressure *below* the wing pushes up on the wing's bottom surface.
This force is what pushes the flying machine up and away from the ground.
And because of Newton's second law, the faster the wing is going, the greater the acceleration of the air moving downward, and therefore, the greater the lifting force on the wing.
Yes! In other words, movement is key!

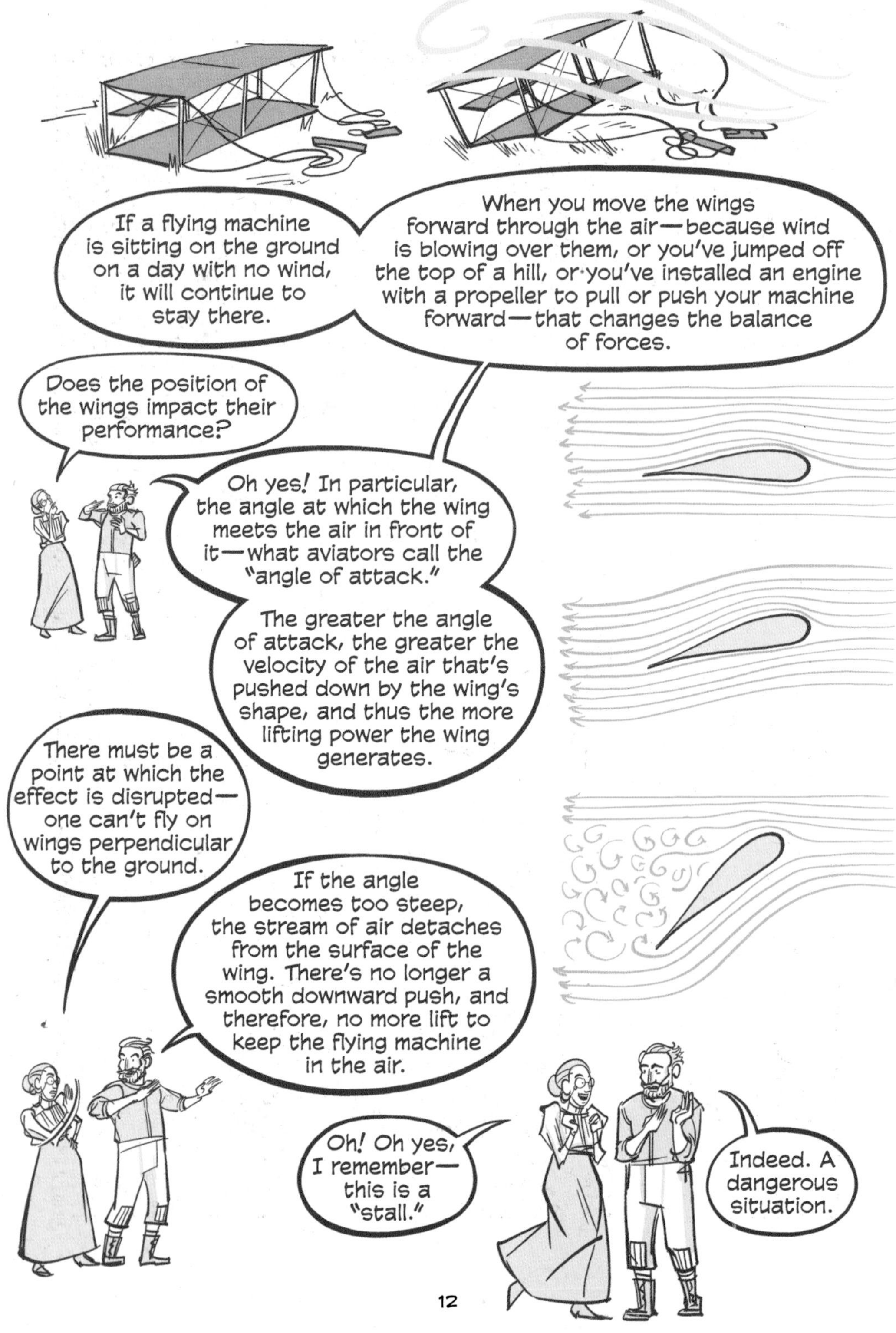
If a flying machine is sitting on the ground on a day with no wind, it will continue to stay there.
When you move the wings forward through the air—because wind is blowing over them, or you've jumped off the top of a hill, or you've installed an engine with a propeller to pull or push your machine forward—that changes the balance of forces.
Does the position of the wings impact their performance?
Oh yes! In particular, the angle at which the wing meets the air in front of it—what aviators call the "angle of attack."
The greater the angle of attack, the greater the velocity of the air that's pushed down by the wing's shape, and thus the more lifting power the wing generates.
There must be a point at which the effect is disrupted—one can't fly on wings perpendicular to the ground.
If the angle becomes too steep, the stream of air detaches from the surface of the wing. There's no longer a smooth downward push, and therefore, no more lift to keep the flying machine in the air.
Oh! Oh yes, I remember—this is a "stall."
Indeed. A dangerous situation.

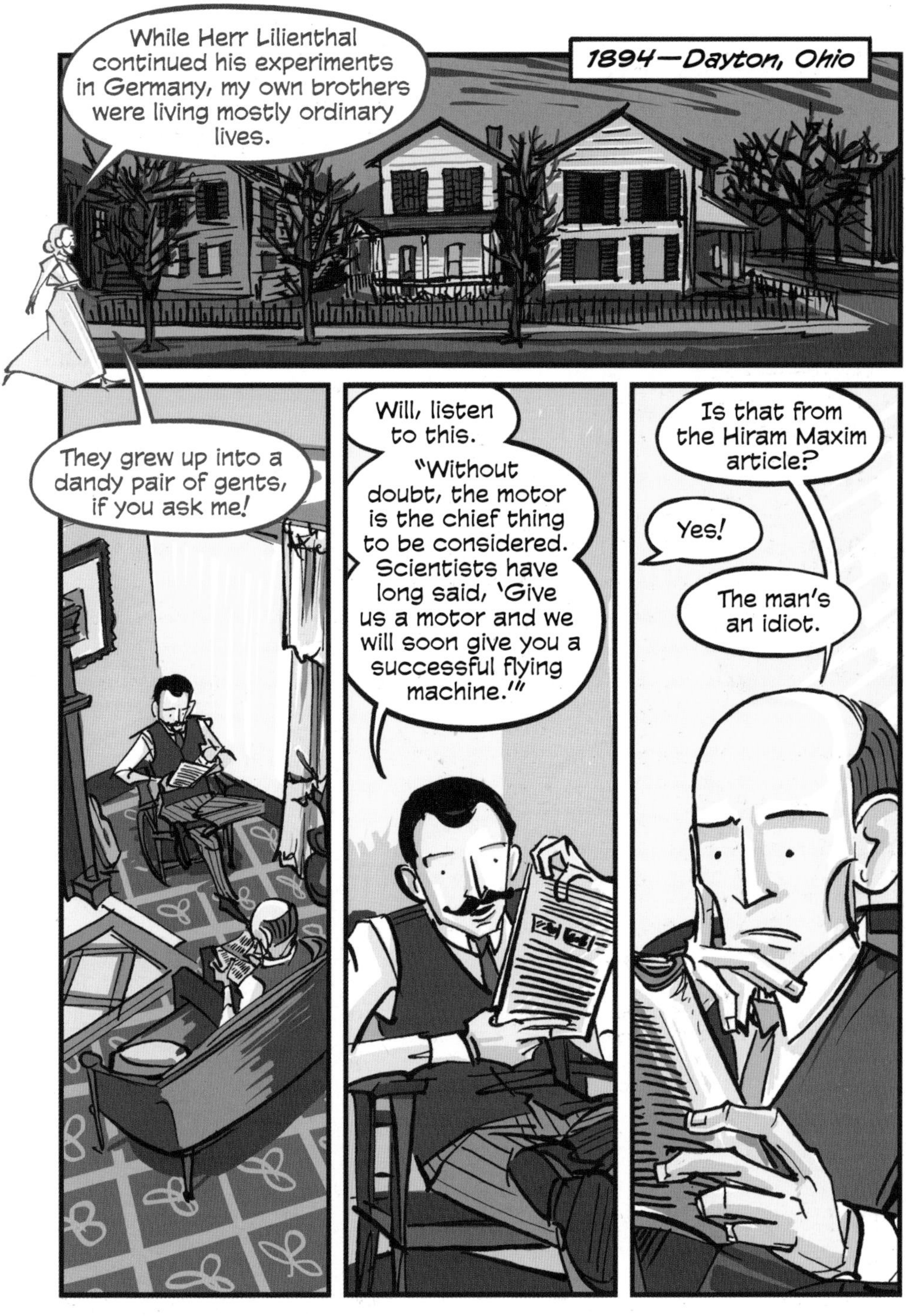
While Herr Lilienthal continued his experiments in Germany, my own brothers were living mostly ordinary lives.
1894—Dayton, Ohio
They grew up into a dandy pair of gents, if you ask me!
Will, listen to this.
"Without doubt, the motor is the chief thing to be considered. Scientists have long said, 'Give us a motor and we will soon give you a successful flying machine.'"
Is that from the Hiram Maxim article?
Yes!
The man's an idiot.

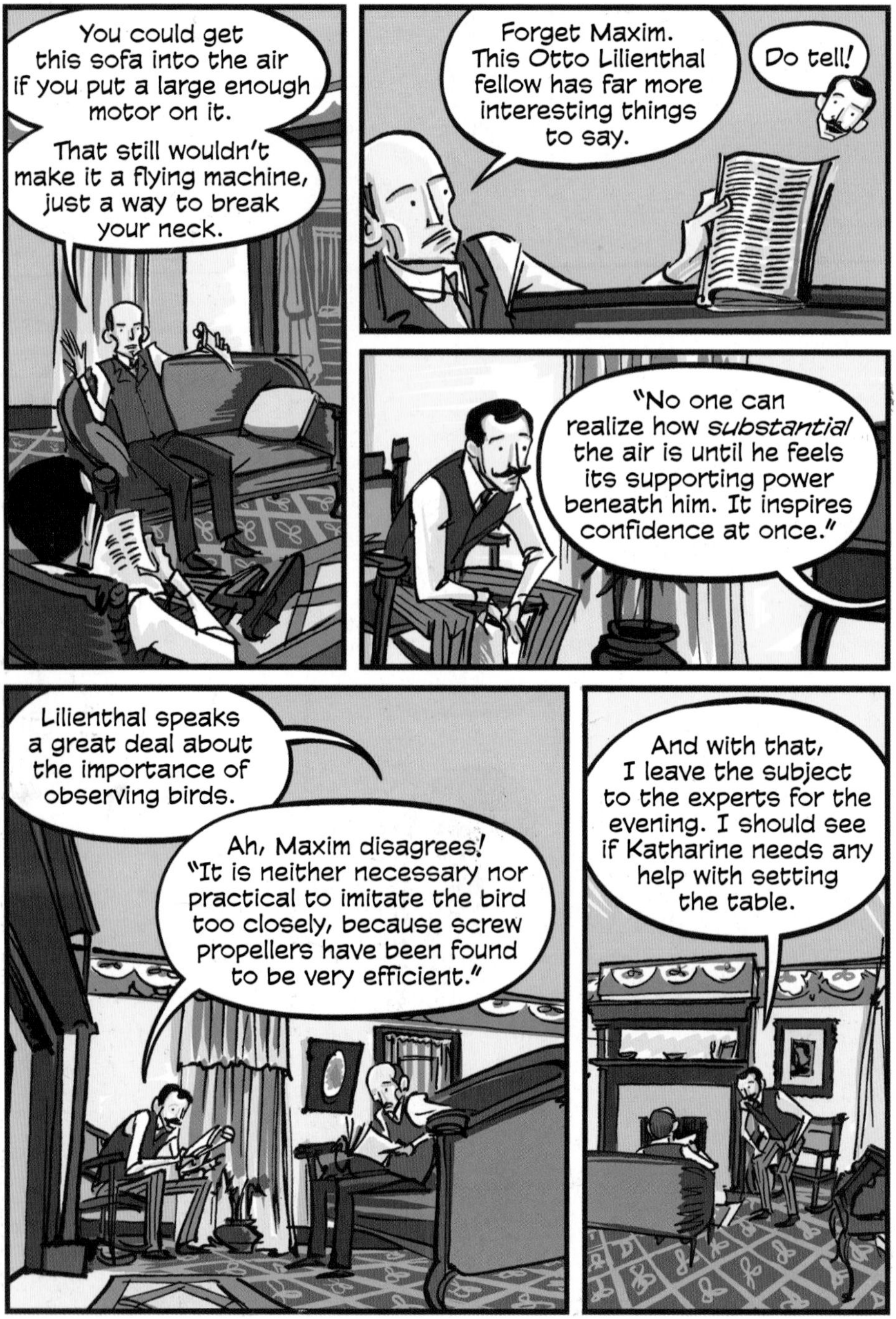
You could get this sofa into the air if you put a large enough motor on it.
That still wouldn't make it a flying machine, just a way to break your neck.
Forget Maxim. This Otto Lilienthal fellow has far more interesting things to say.
Do tell!
"No one can realize how *substantial* the air is until he feels its supporting power beneath him. It inspires confidence at once."
Lilienthal speaks a great deal about the importance of observing birds.
Ah, Maxim disagrees! "It is neither necessary nor practical to imitate the bird too closely, because screw propellers have been found to be very efficient."
And with that, I leave the subject to the experts for the evening. I should see if Katharine needs any help with setting the table.

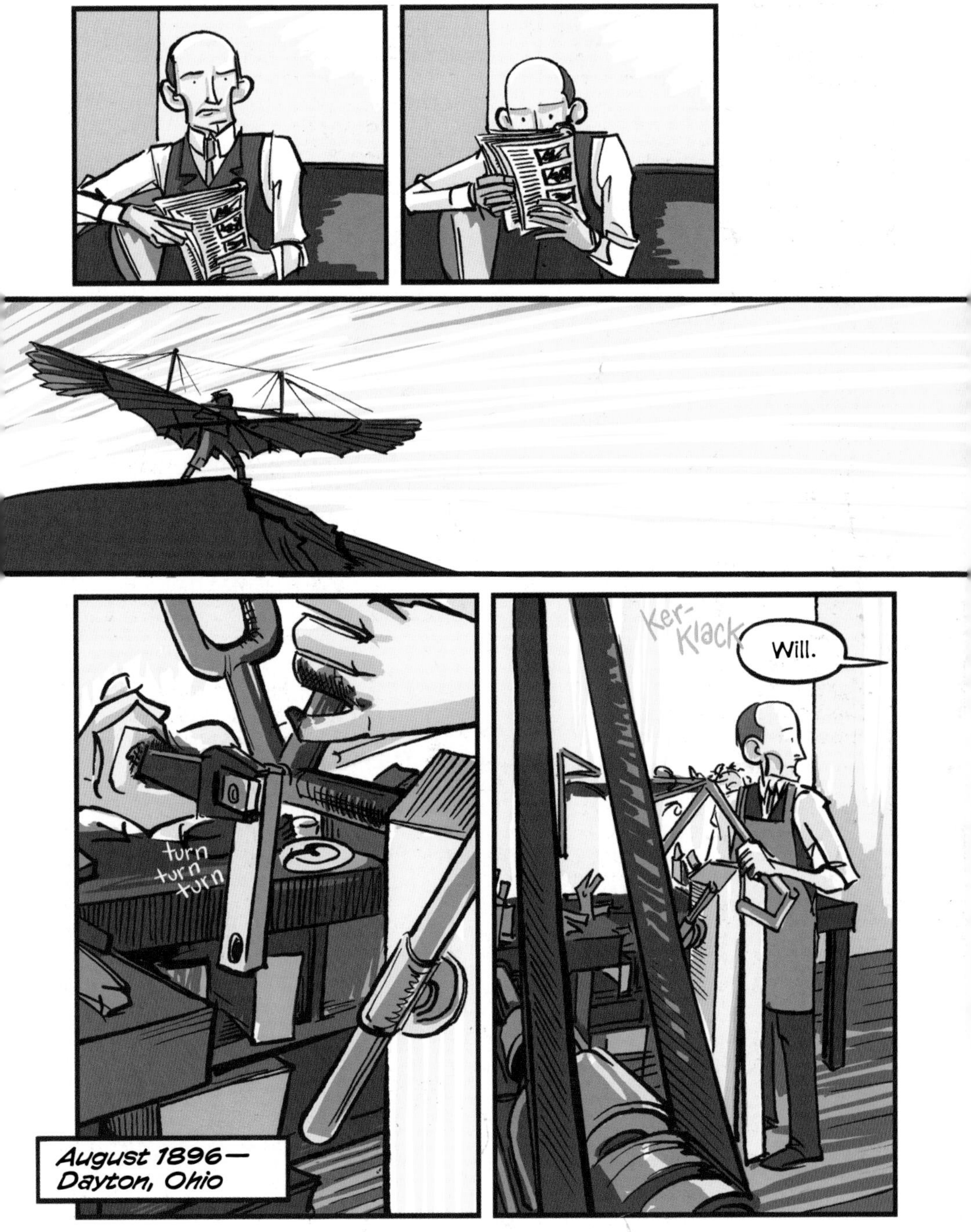
turn
turn
turn
August 1896—
Dayton, Ohio
Ker-
Klack
Will.

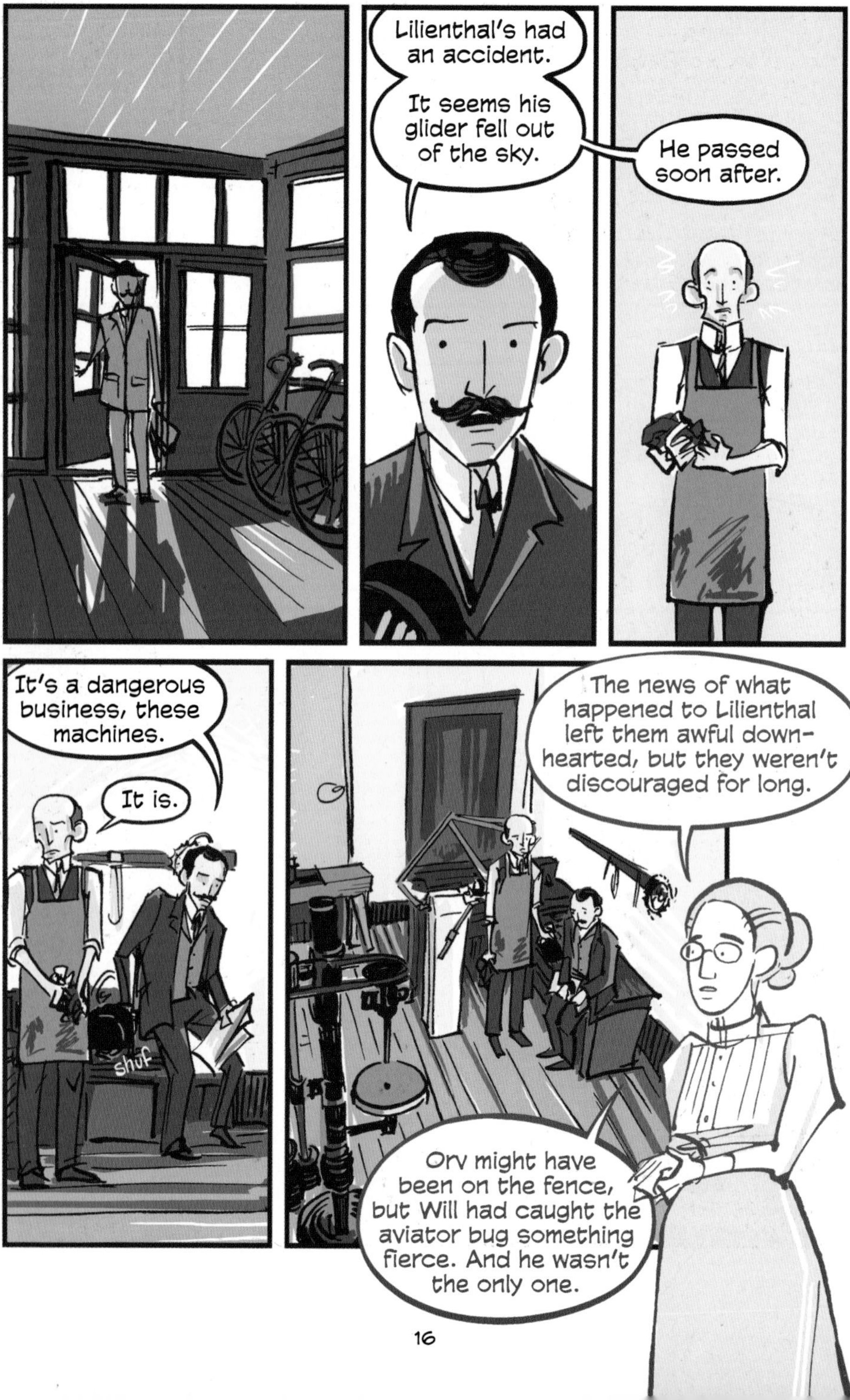
Lilienthal's had an accident.
It seems his glider fell out of the sky.
He passed soon after.
It's a dangerous business, these machines.
It is.
shuf
The news of what happened to Lilienthal left them awful down-hearted, but they weren't discouraged for long.
Orv might have been on the fence, but Will had caught the aviator bug something fierce. And he wasn't the only one.

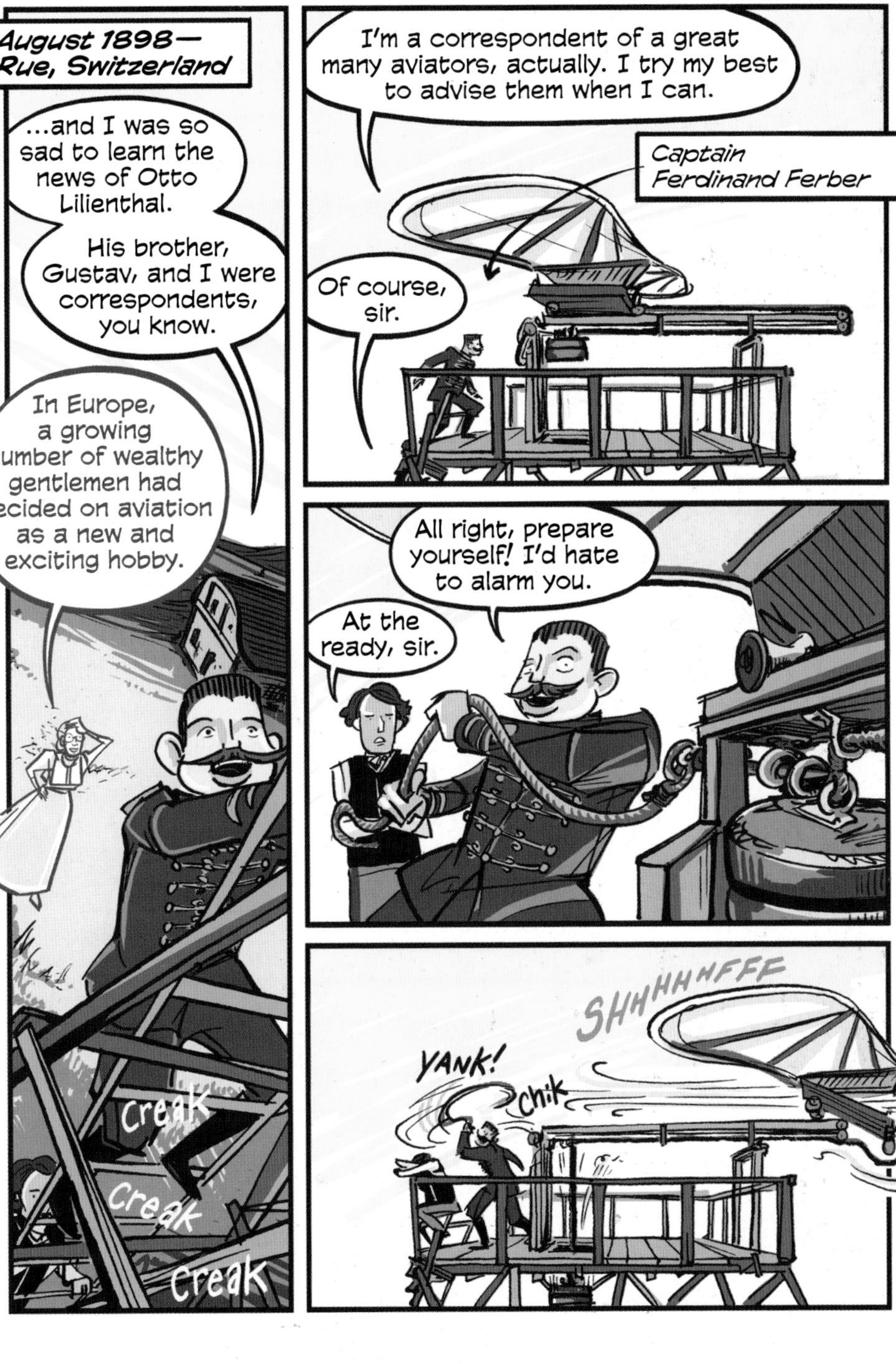

August 1898—
Rue, Switzerland
...and I was so sad to learn the news of Otto Lilienthal.
His brother, Gustav, and I were correspondents, you know.
In Europe, a growing number of wealthy gentlemen had decided on aviation as a new and exciting hobby.
Creak
Creak
Creak
I'm a correspondent of a great many aviators, actually. I try my best to advise them when I can.
Captain Ferdinand Ferber
Of course, sir.
All right, prepare yourself! I'd hate to alarm you.
At the ready, sir.
SHHHHHFFF
YANK!
Chik

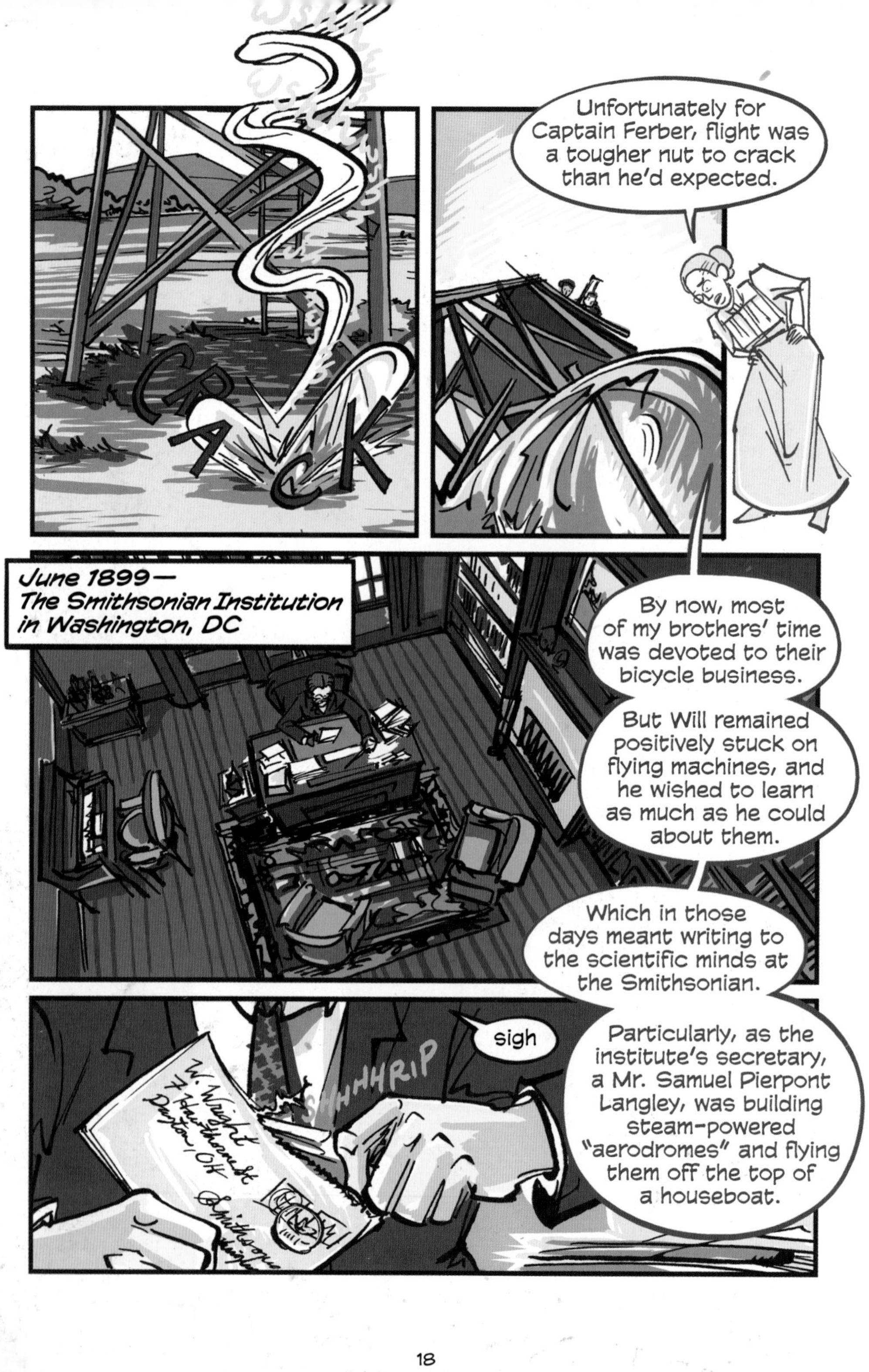
CRACK
Unfortunately for Captain Ferber, flight was a tougher nut to crack than he'd expected.
June 1899— The Smithsonian Institution in Washington, DC
By now, most of my brothers' time was devoted to their bicycle business.
But Will remained positively stuck on flying machines, and he wished to learn as much as he could about them.
Which in those days meant writing to the scientific minds at the Smithsonian.
sigh
W. Wright
7 Hawthorne St
Dayton, OH
Particularly, as the institute's secretary, a Mr. Samuel Pierpont Langley, was building steam-powered "aerodromes" and flying them off the top of a houseboat.

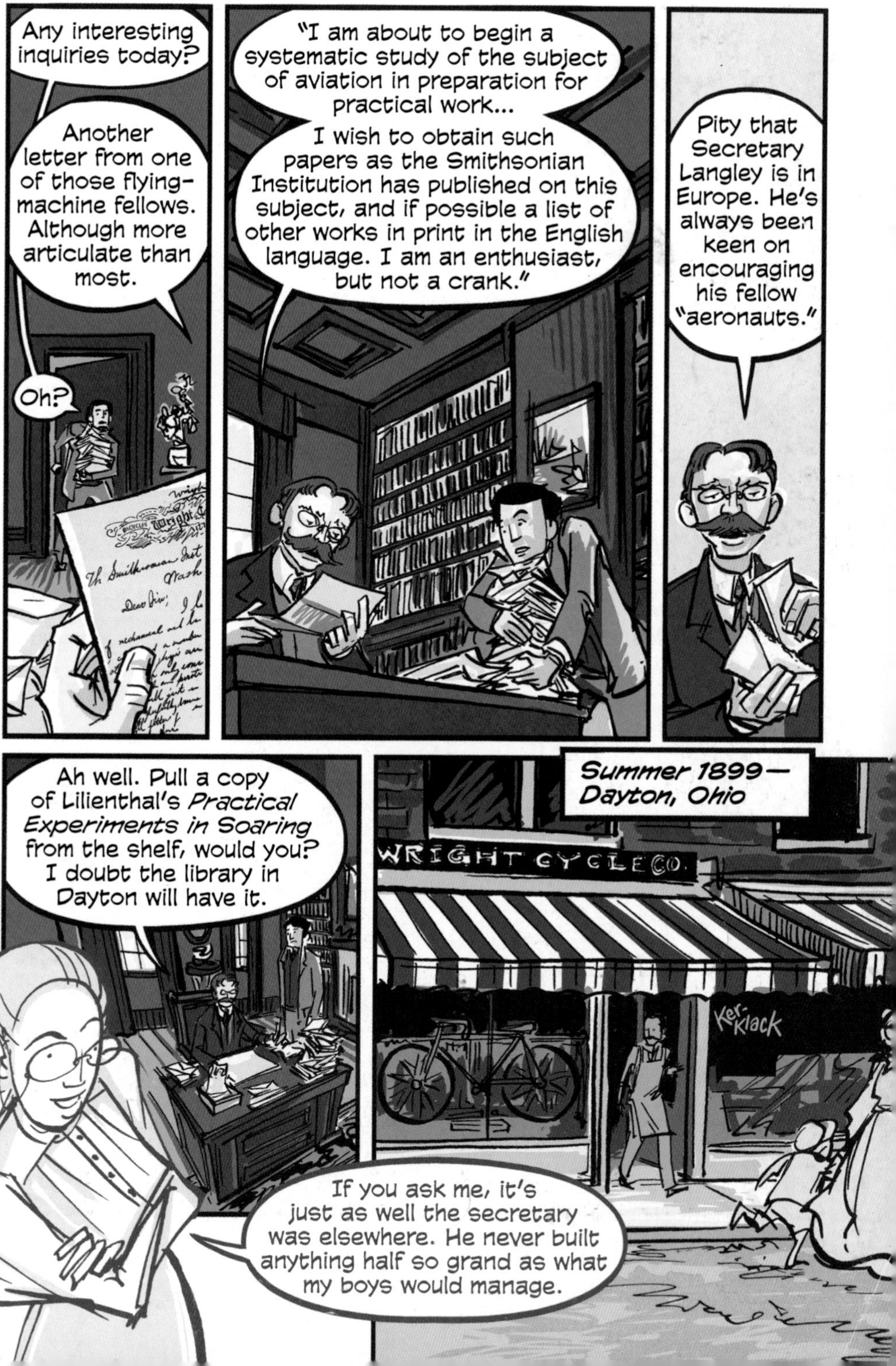
Any interesting inquiries today?
Another letter from one of those flying-machine fellows. Although more articulate than most.
Oh?
"I am about to begin a systematic study of the subject of aviation in preparation for practical work...
I wish to obtain such papers as the Smithsonian Institution has published on this subject, and if possible a list of other works in print in the English language. I am an enthusiast, but not a crank."
Pity that Secretary Langley is in Europe. He's always been keen on encouraging his fellow "aeronauts."
Ah well. Pull a copy of Lilienthal's *Practical Experiments in Soaring* from the shelf, would you? I doubt the library in Dayton will have it.
Summer 1899— Dayton, Ohio
WRIGHT CYCLE CO.
Ker-klack
If you ask me, it's just as well the secretary was elsewhere. He never built anything half so grand as what my boys would manage.

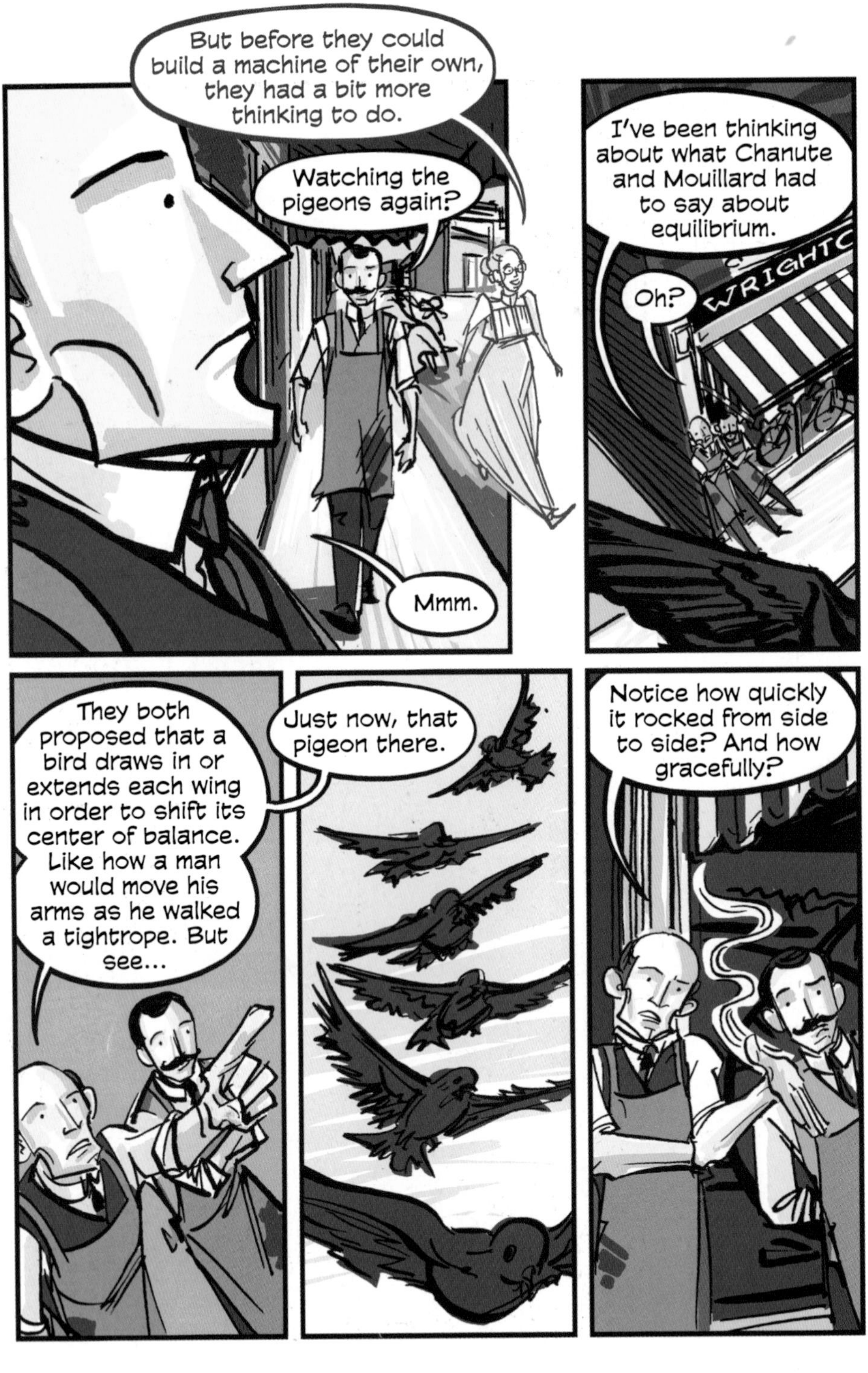
But before they could build a machine of their own, they had a bit more thinking to do.
Watching the pigeons again?
Mmm.
I've been thinking about what Chanute and Mouillard had to say about equilibrium.
Oh?
WRIGHT C
They both proposed that a bird draws in or extends each wing in order to shift its center of balance. Like how a man would move his arms as he walked a tightrope. But see...
Just now, that pigeon there.
Notice how quickly it rocked from side to side? And how gracefully?

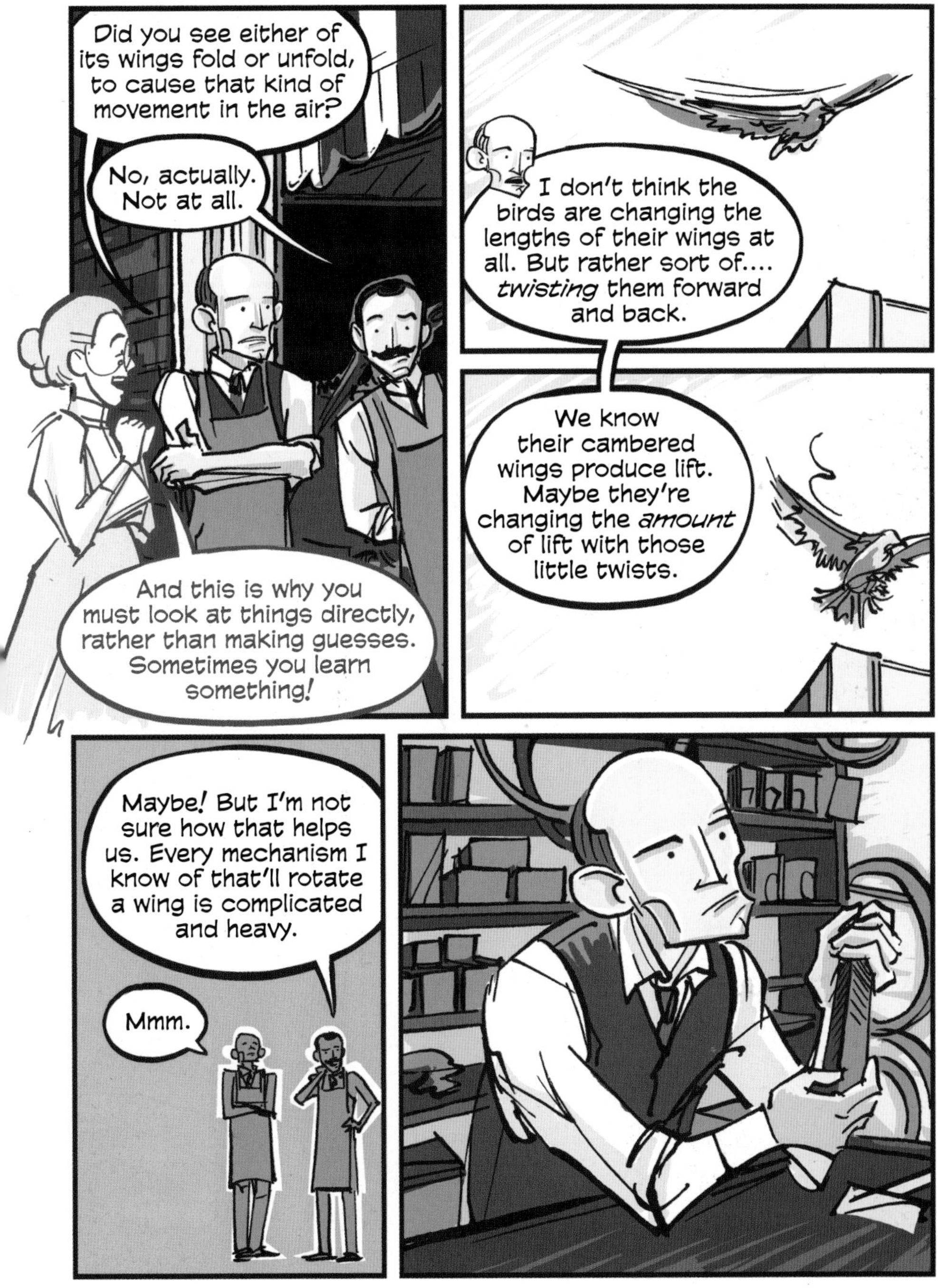
Did you see either of its wings fold or unfold, to cause that kind of movement in the air?
No, actually. Not at all.
And this is why you must look at things directly, rather than making guesses. Sometimes you learn something!
I don't think the birds are changing the lengths of their wings at all. But rather sort of.... *twisting* them forward and back.
We know their cambered wings produce lift. Maybe they're changing the *amount* of lift with those little twists.
Maybe! But I'm not sure how that helps us. Every mechanism I know of that'll rotate a wing is complicated and heavy.
Mmm.

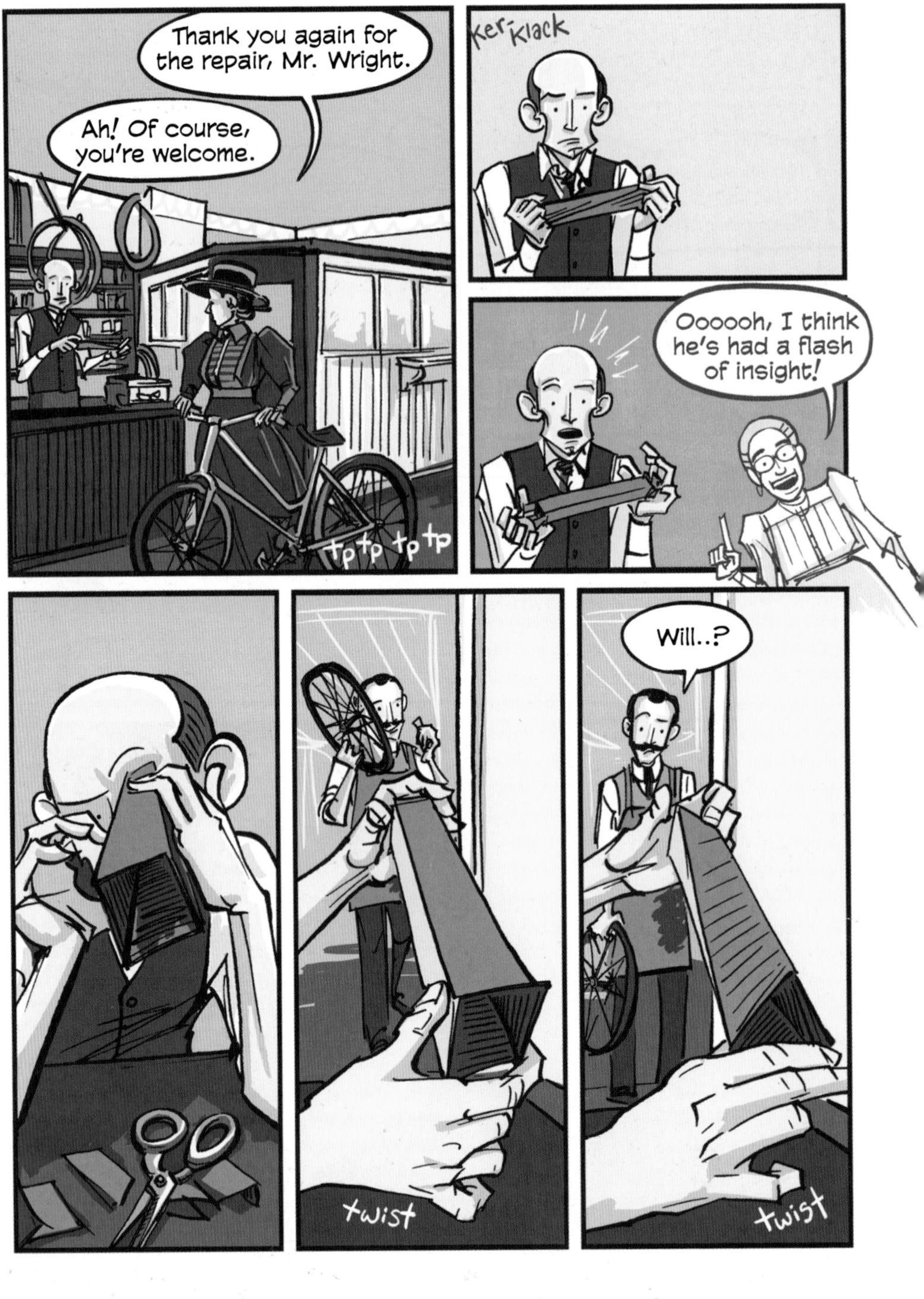
Thank you again for the repair, Mr. Wright.
Ah! Of course, you're welcome.
tp tp tp tp
Ker-Klack
Oooooh, I think he's had a flash of insight!
twist
Will..?
twist

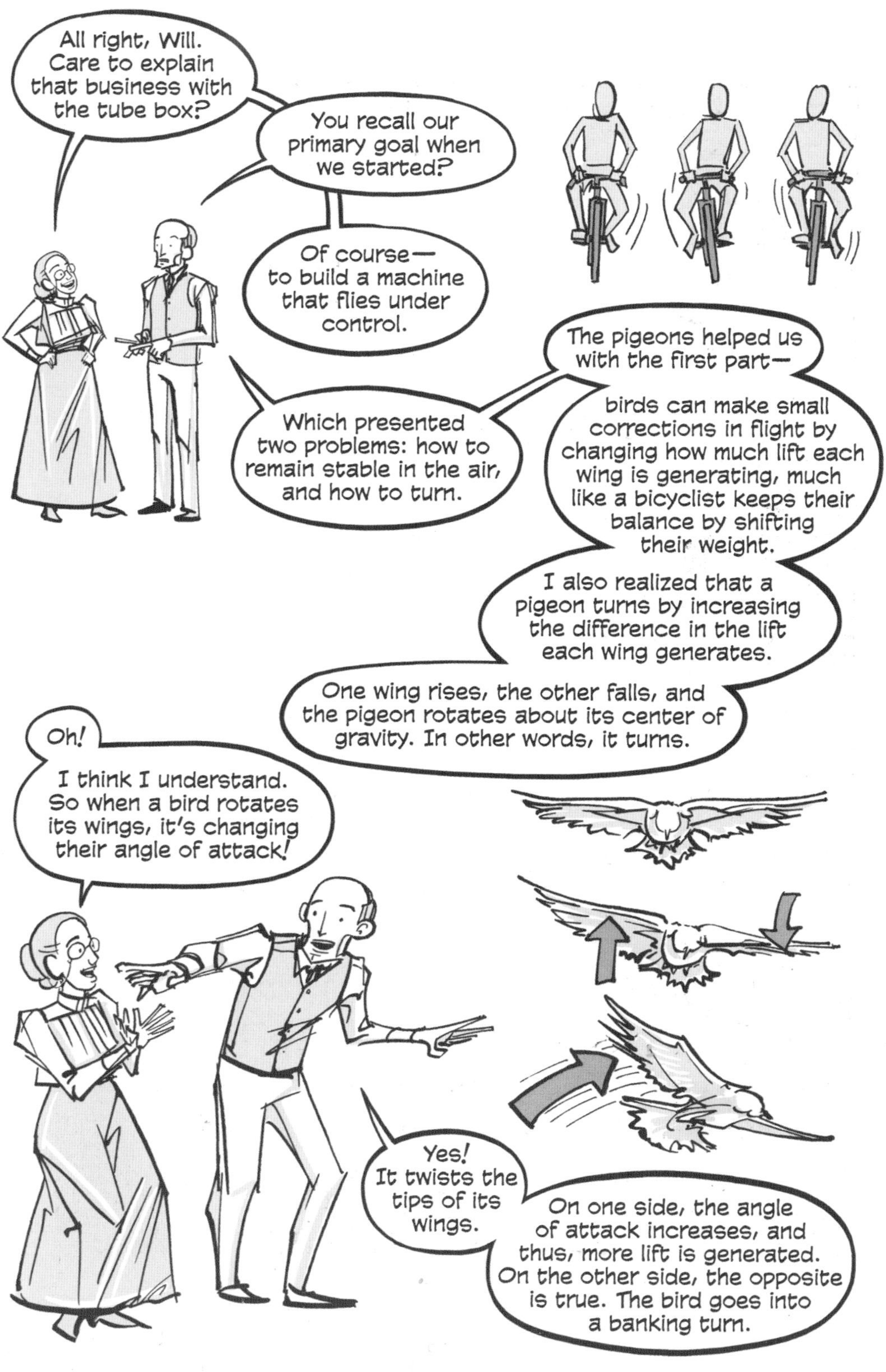
All right, Will. Care to explain that business with the tube box?
You recall our primary goal when we started?
Of course— to build a machine that flies under control.
Which presented two problems: how to remain stable in the air, and how to turn.
The pigeons helped us with the first part—
birds can make small corrections in flight by changing how much lift each wing is generating, much like a bicyclist keeps their balance by shifting their weight.
I also realized that a pigeon turns by increasing the difference in the lift each wing generates.
One wing rises, the other falls, and the pigeon rotates about its center of gravity. In other words, it turns.
Oh!
I think I understand. So when a bird rotates its wings, it's changing their angle of attack!
Yes! It twists the tips of its wings.
On one side, the angle of attack increases, and thus, more lift is generated. On the other side, the opposite is true. The bird goes into a banking turn.

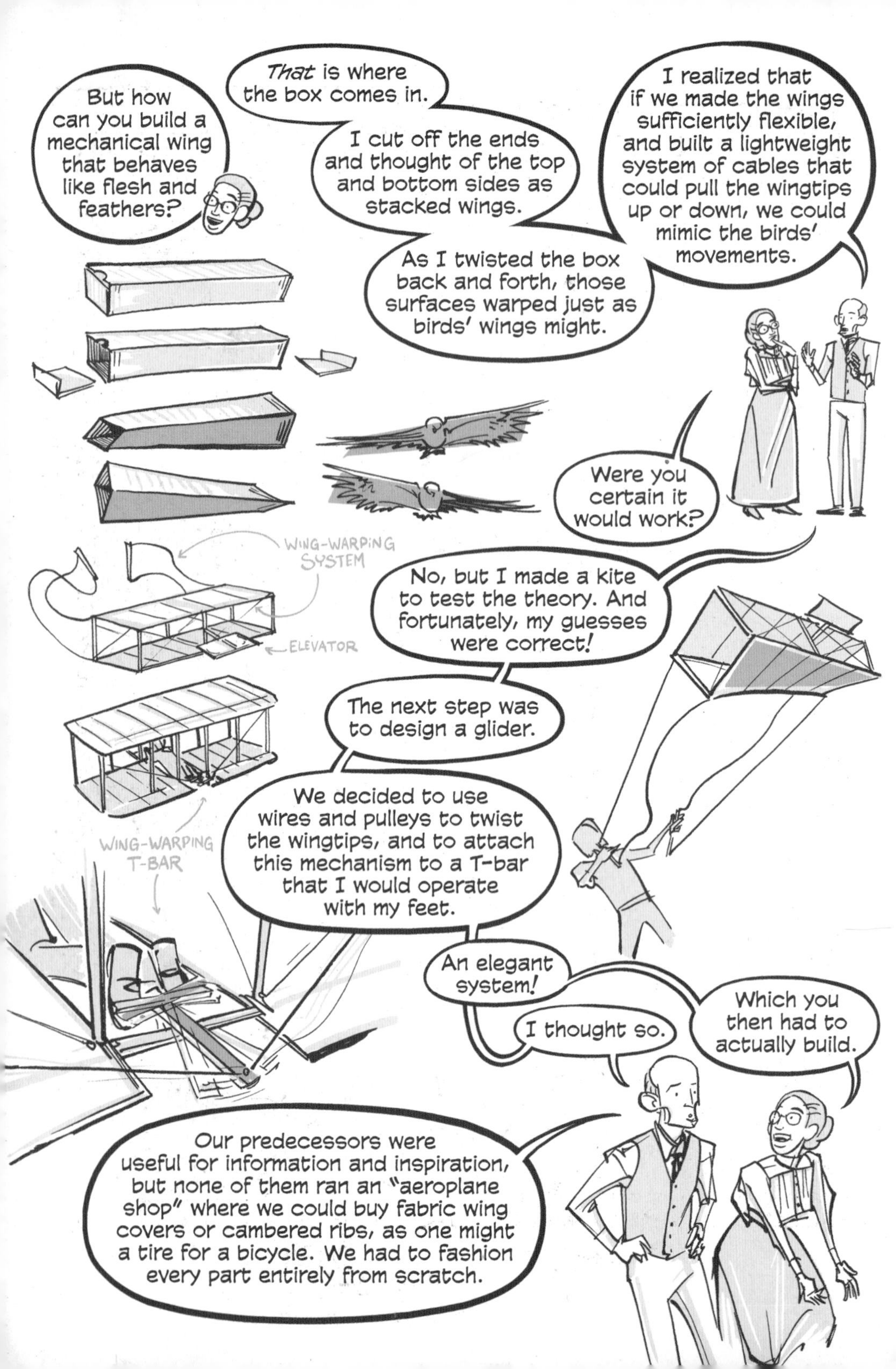
But how can you build a mechanical wing that behaves like flesh and feathers?
That is where the box comes in.
I cut off the ends and thought of the top and bottom sides as stacked wings.
As I twisted the box back and forth, those surfaces warped just as birds' wings might.
I realized that if we made the wings sufficiently flexible, and built a lightweight system of cables that could pull the wingtips up or down, we could mimic the birds' movements.
Were you certain it would work?
No, but I made a kite to test the theory. And fortunately, my guesses were correct!
WING-WARPING SYSTEM
ELEVATOR
The next step was to design a glider.
WING-WARPING T-BAR
We decided to use wires and pulleys to twist the wingtips, and to attach this mechanism to a T-bar that I would operate with my feet.
An elegant system!
I thought so.
Which you then had to actually build.
Our predecessors were useful for information and inspiration, but none of them ran an "aeroplane shop" where we could buy fabric wing covers or cambered ribs, as one might a tire for a bicycle. We had to fashion every part entirely from scratch.

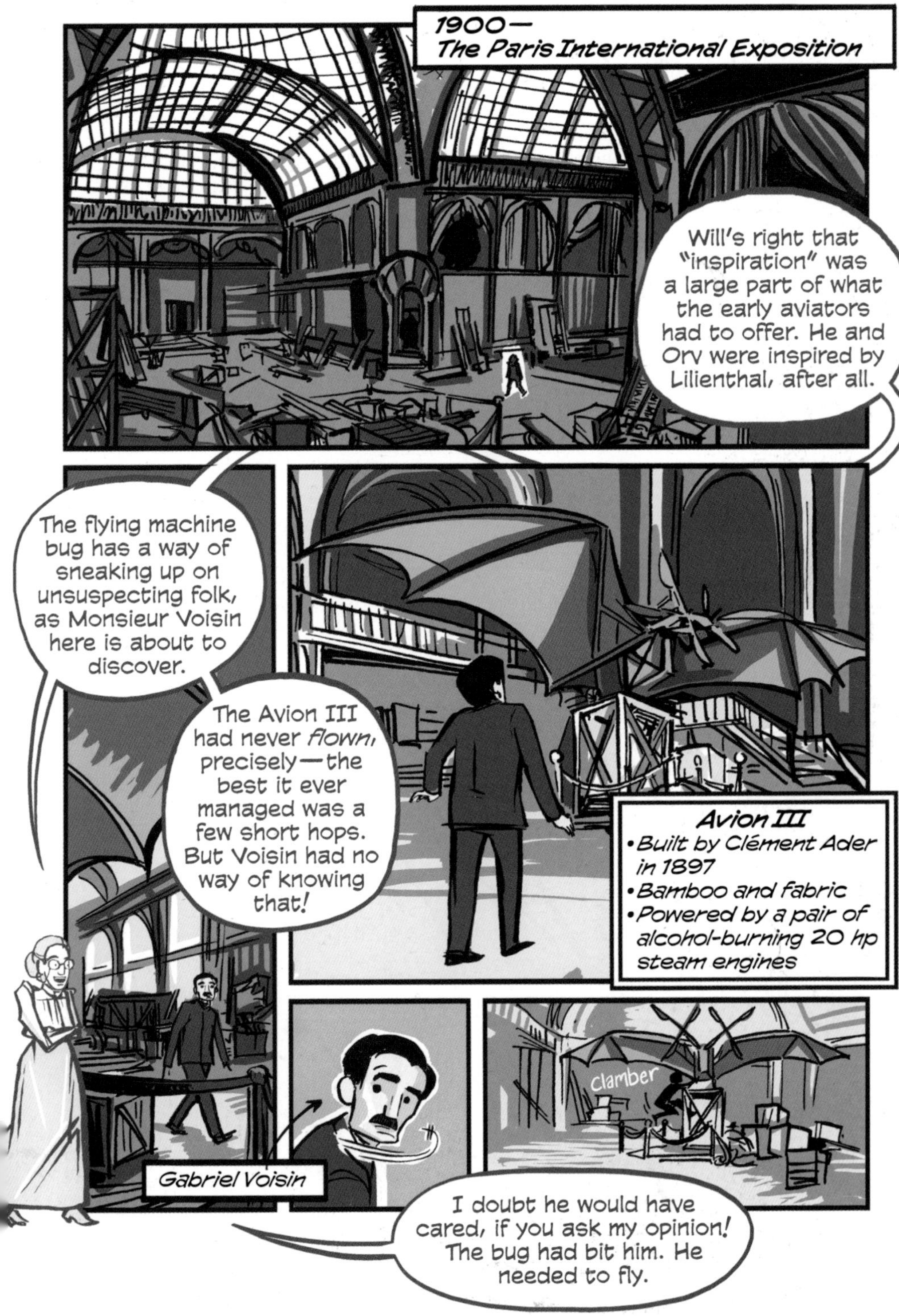

1900— The Paris International Exposition
Will's right that "inspiration" was a large part of what the early aviators had to offer. He and Orv were inspired by Lilienthal, after all.
The flying machine bug has a way of sneaking up on unsuspecting folk, as Monsieur Voisin here is about to discover.
The Avion III had never *flown*, precisely—the best it ever managed was a few short hops. But Voisin had no way of knowing that!
Avion III
•Built by Clément Ader in 1897
•Bamboo and fabric
•Powered by a pair of alcohol-burning 20 hp steam engines
Gabriel Voisin
Clamber
I doubt he would have cared, if you ask my opinion! The bug had bit him. He needed to fly.

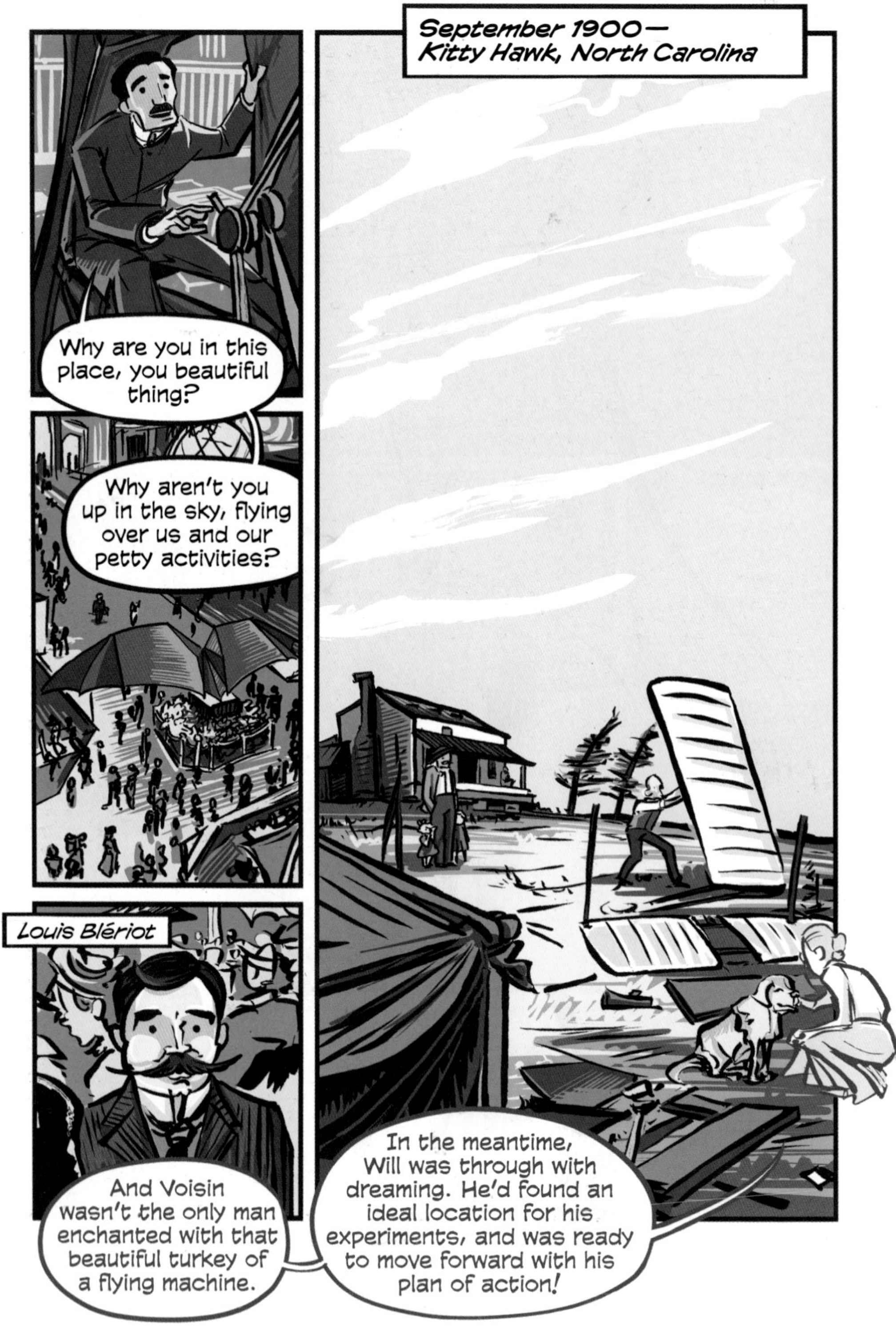
Why are you in this place, you beautiful thing?
Why aren't you up in the sky, flying over us and our petty activities?
Louis Blériot
And Voisin wasn't the only man enchanted with that beautiful turkey of a flying machine.
September 1900—
Kitty Hawk, North Carolina
In the meantime, Will was through with dreaming. He'd found an ideal location for his experiments, and was ready to move forward with his plan of action!

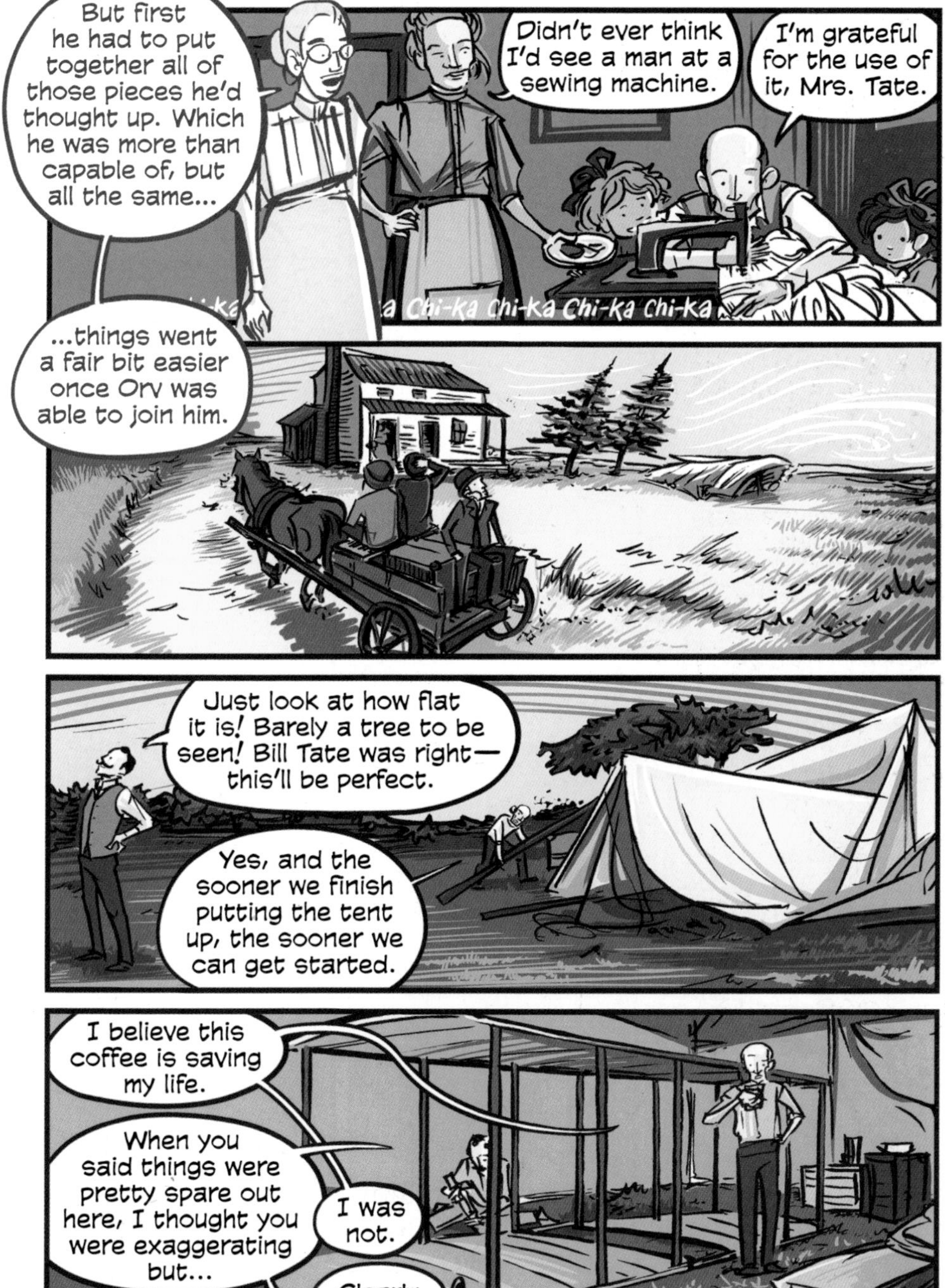
But first he had to put together all of those pieces he'd thought up. Which he was more than capable of, but all the same...
Didn't ever think I'd see a man at a sewing machine.
I'm grateful for the use of it, Mrs. Tate.
Chi-ka Chi-ka Chi-ka Chi-ka
...things went a fair bit easier once Orv was able to join him.
Just look at how flat it is! Barely a tree to be seen! Bill Tate was right— this'll be perfect.
Yes, and the sooner we finish putting the tent up, the sooner we can get started.
I believe this coffee is saving my life.
When you said things were pretty spare out here, I thought you were exaggerating but...
I was not.
Clearly.

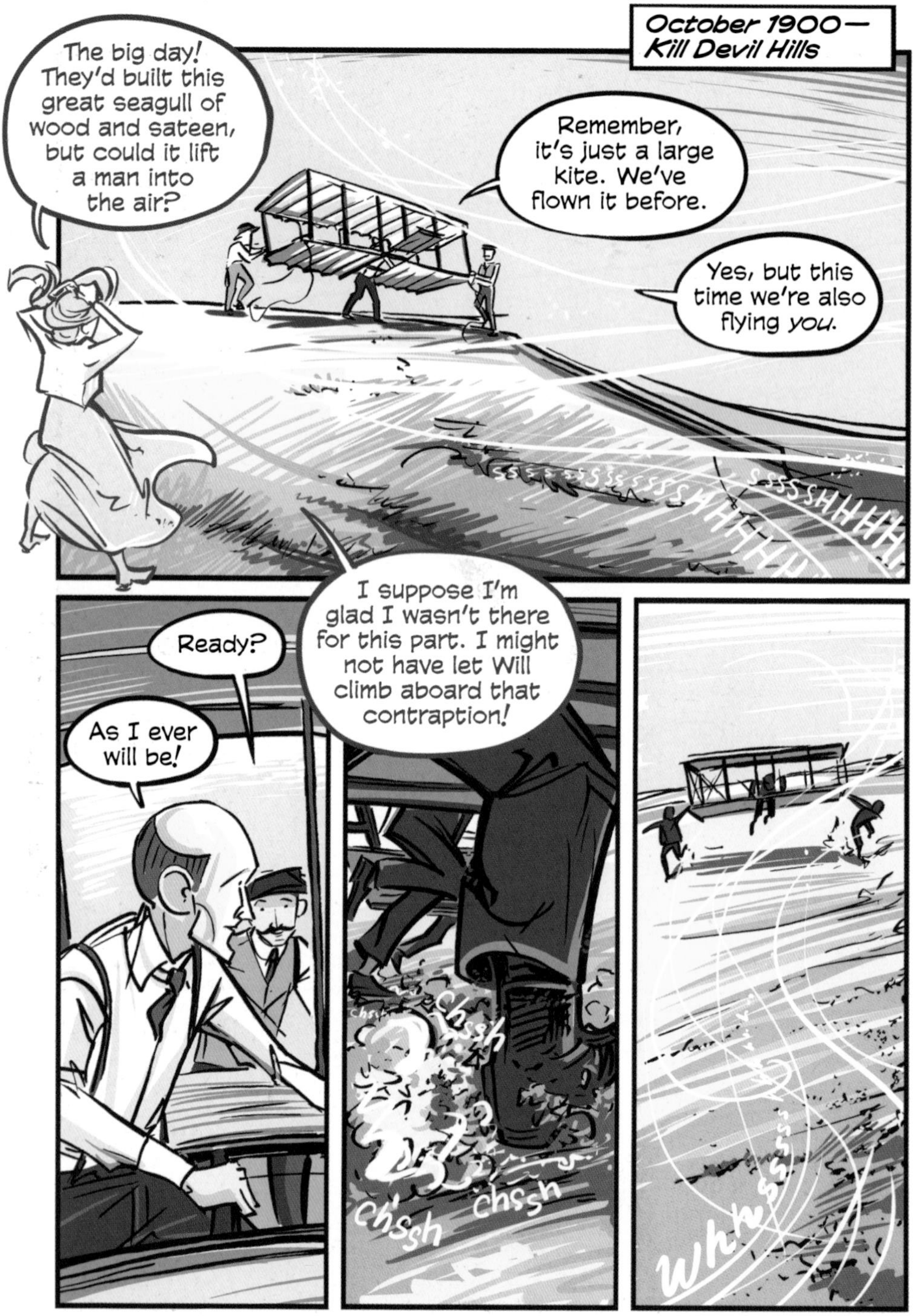
October 1900—Kill Devil Hills
The big day! They'd built this great seagull of wood and sateen, but could it lift a man into the air?
Remember, it's just a large kite. We've flown it before.
Yes, but this time we're also flying *you*.
SSSSSSSSSSSSSHHHH
SSSSSHHHHHH
I suppose I'm glad I wasn't there for this part. I might not have let Will climb aboard that contraption!
Ready?
As I ever will be!
chssh
chssh
chssh
whhsss

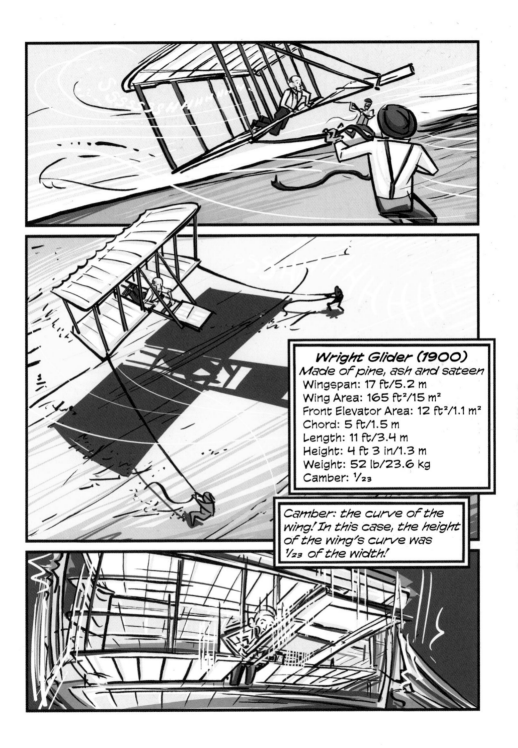

Wright Glider (1900)
Made of pine, ash and sateen
Wingspan: 17 ft/5.2 m
Wing Area: 165 ft²/15 m²
Front Elevator Area: 12 ft²/1.1 m²
Chord: 5 ft/1.5 m
Length: 11 ft/3.4 m
Height: 4 ft 3 in/1.3 m
Weight: 52 lb/23.6 kg
Camber: $\frac{1}{23}$

Camber: the curve of the wing! In this case, the height of the wing's curve was $\frac{1}{23}$ of the width!

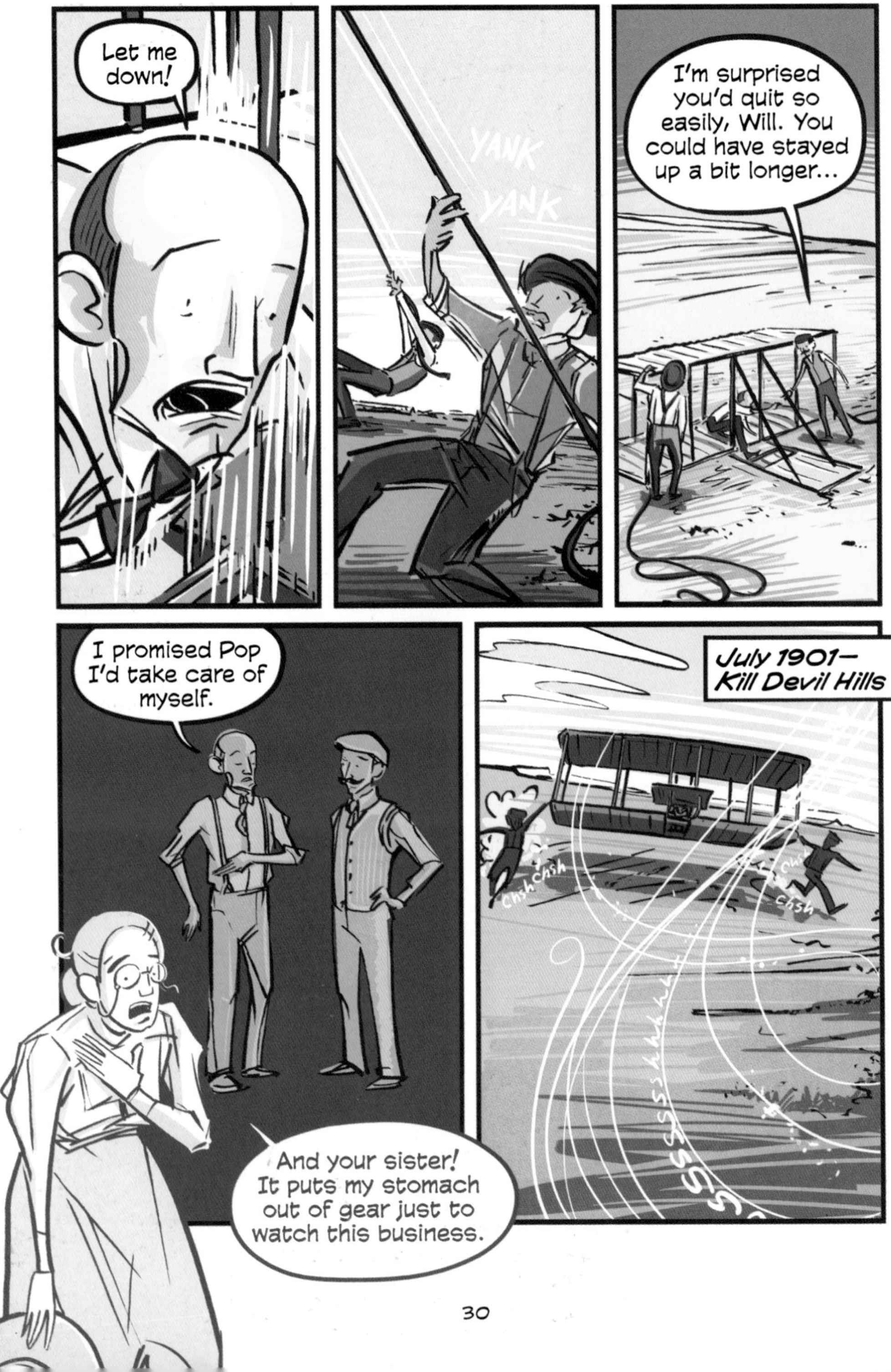
Let me down!
YANK
YANK
I'm surprised you'd quit so easily, Will. You could have stayed up a bit longer...
I promised Pop I'd take care of myself.
And your sister! It puts my stomach out of gear just to watch this business.
July 1901—Kill Devil Hills
Chsh
Chsh
Chsh
Chsh

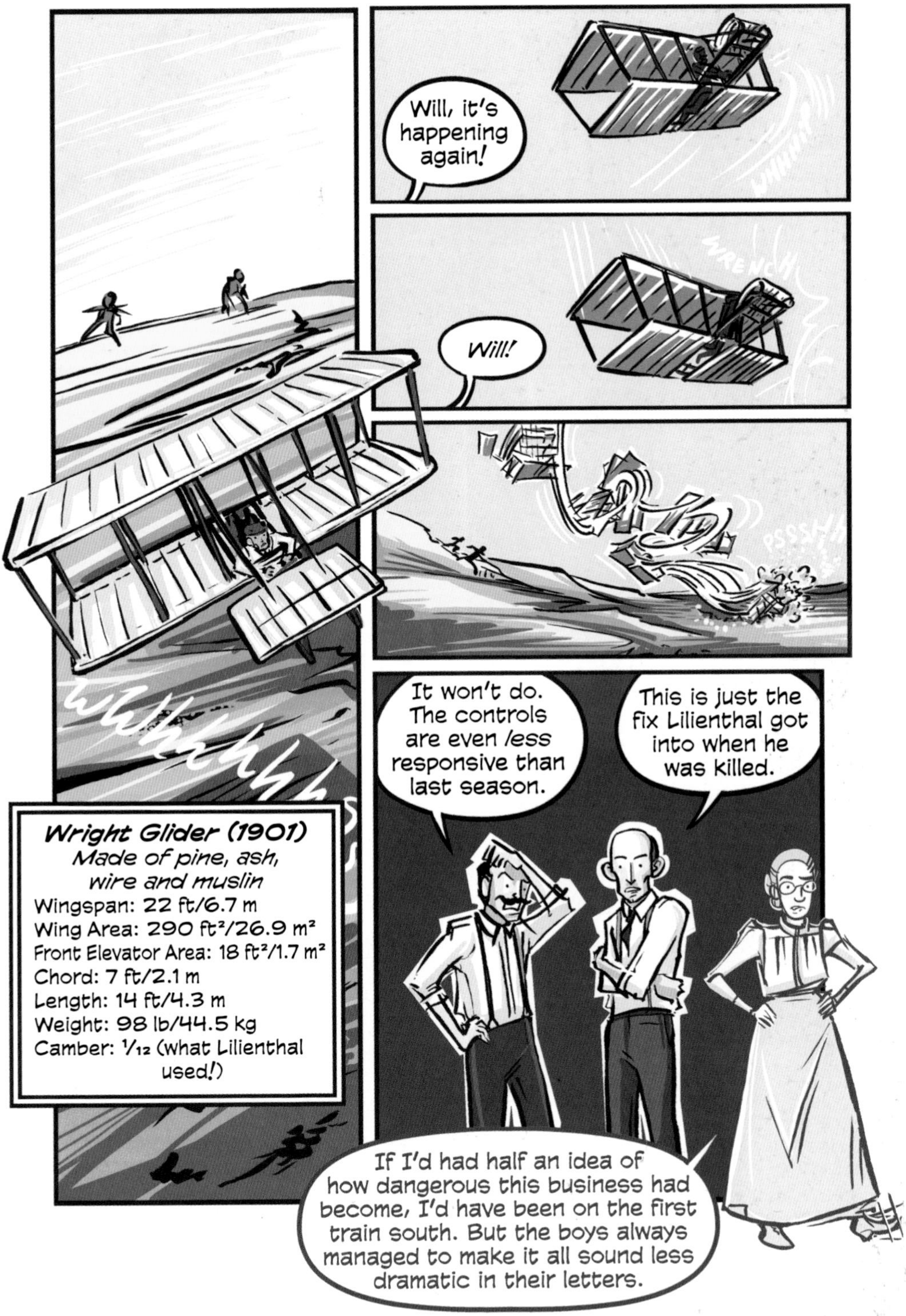
Wright Glider (1901)
Made of pine, ash, wire and muslin
Wingspan: 22 ft/6.7 m
Wing Area: 290 ft²/26.9 m²
Front Elevator Area: 18 ft²/1.7 m²
Chord: 7 ft/2.1 m
Length: 14 ft/4.3 m
Weight: 98 lb/44.5 kg
Camber: 1/12 (what Lilienthal used!)
Will, it's happening again!
Will!
WRENCH
PSSSHH
It won't do. The controls are even less responsive than last season.
This is just the fix Lilienthal got into when he was killed.
If I'd had half an idea of how dangerous this business had become, I'd have been on the first train south. But the boys always managed to make it all sound less dramatic in their letters.

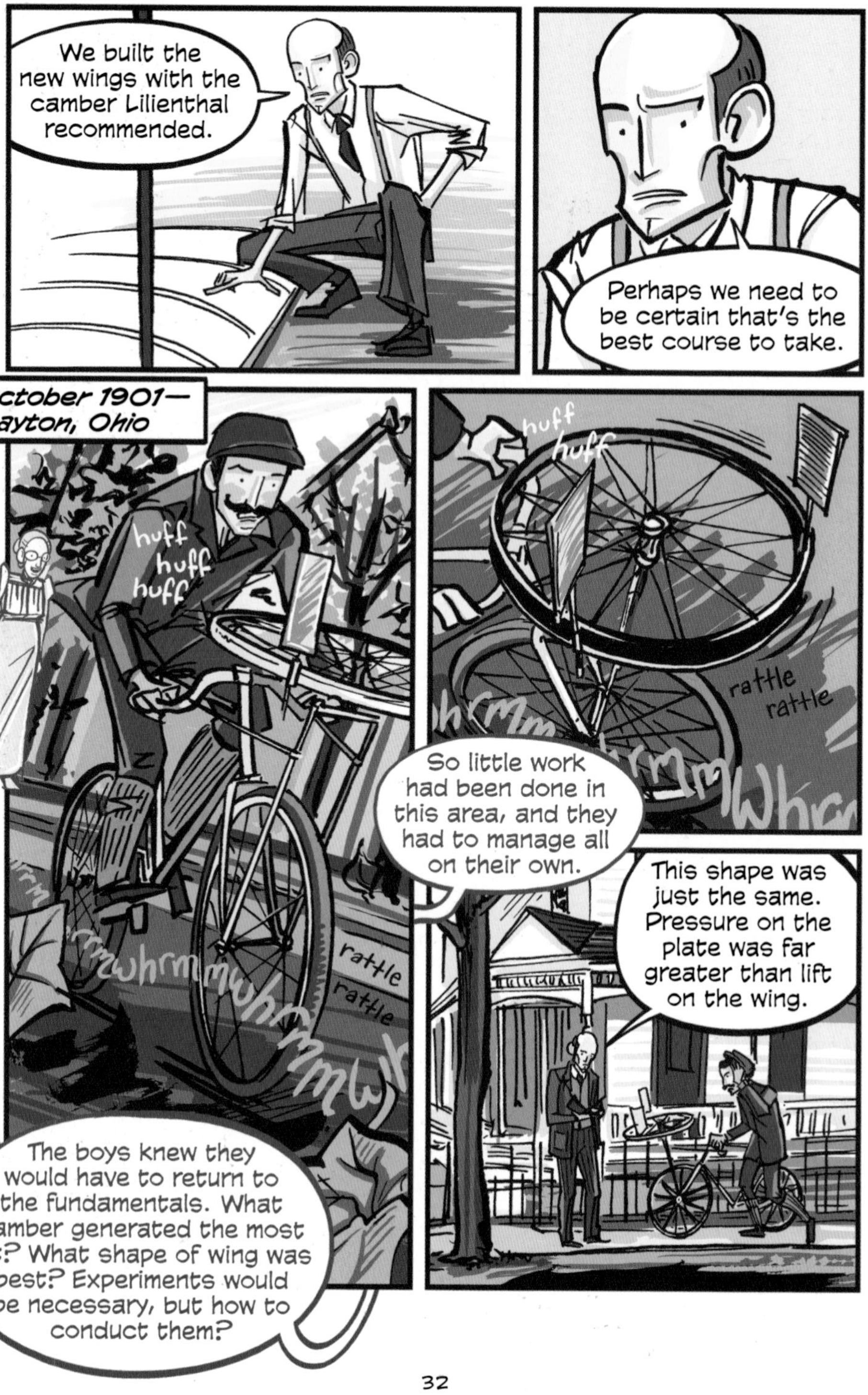
We built the new wings with the camber Lilienthal recommended.
Perhaps we need to be certain that's the best course to take.
October 1901—Dayton, Ohio
huff huff huff
huff huff
rattle rattle
whrmmwhrmmwhrmmwh
So little work had been done in this area, and they had to manage all on their own.
rattle rattle
Whrmmwhrm
This shape was just the same. Pressure on the plate was far greater than lift on the wing.
The boys knew they would have to return to the fundamentals. What camber generated the most lift? What shape of wing was best? Experiments would be necessary, but how to conduct them?

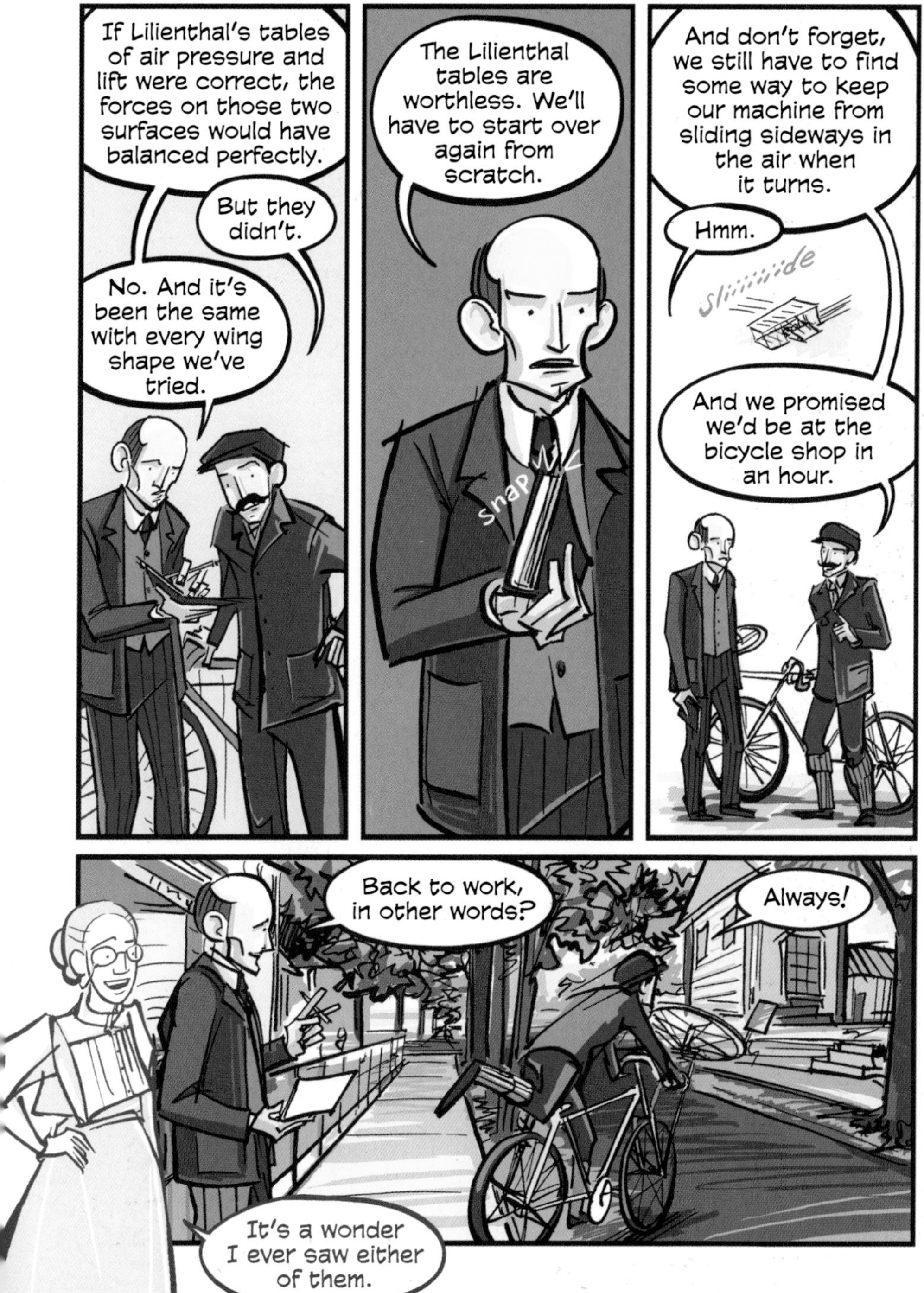
If Lilienthal's tables of air pressure and lift were correct, the forces on those two surfaces would have balanced perfectly.
But they didn't.
No. And it's been the same with every wing shape we've tried.
The Lilienthal tables are worthless. We'll have to start over again from scratch.
Snap
And don't forget, we still have to find some way to keep our machine from sliding sideways in the air when it turns.
Hmm.
Sliiiiiide
And we promised we'd be at the bicycle shop in an hour.
Back to work, in other words?
Always!
It's a wonder I ever saw either of them.

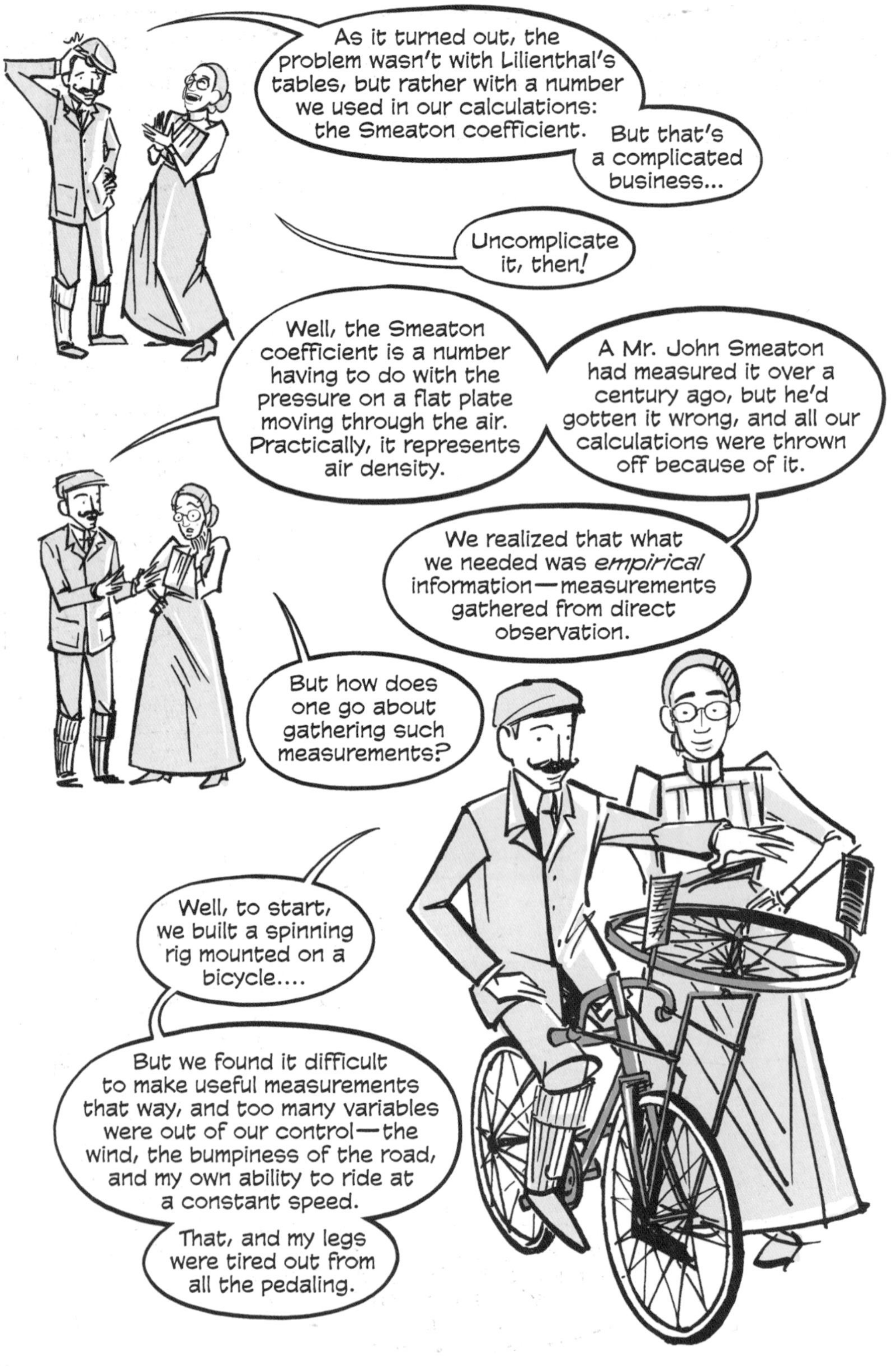
As it turned out, the problem wasn't with Lilienthal's tables, but rather with a number we used in our calculations: the Smeaton coefficient.
But that's a complicated business...
Uncomplicate it, then!
Well, the Smeaton coefficient is a number having to do with the pressure on a flat plate moving through the air. Practically, it represents air density.
A Mr. John Smeaton had measured it over a century ago, but he'd gotten it wrong, and all our calculations were thrown off because of it.
We realized that what we needed was *empirical* information—measurements gathered from direct observation.
But how does one go about gathering such measurements?
Well, to start, we built a spinning rig mounted on a bicycle....
But we found it difficult to make useful measurements that way, and too many variables were out of our control—the wind, the bumpiness of the road, and my own ability to ride at a constant speed.
That, and my legs were tired out from all the pedaling.

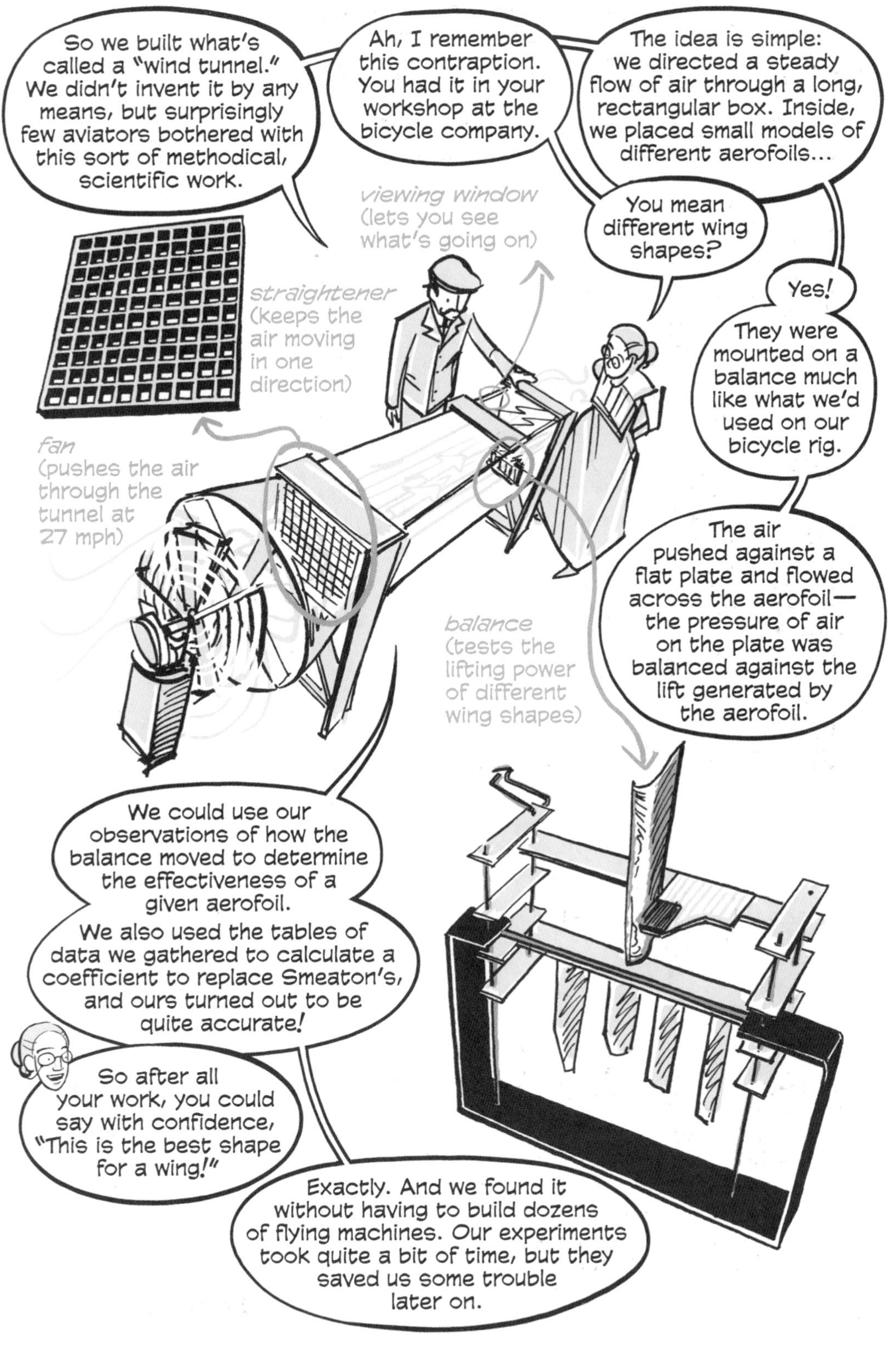
So we built what's called a "wind tunnel." We didn't invent it by any means, but surprisingly few aviators bothered with this sort of methodical, scientific work.
Ah, I remember this contraption. You had it in your workshop at the bicycle company.
The idea is simple: we directed a steady flow of air through a long, rectangular box. Inside, we placed small models of different aerofoils...
You mean different wing shapes?
Yes!
They were mounted on a balance much like what we'd used on our bicycle rig.
viewing window (lets you see what's going on)
straightener (keeps the air moving in one direction)
fan (pushes the air through the tunnel at 27 mph)
balance (tests the lifting power of different wing shapes)
The air pushed against a flat plate and flowed across the aerofoil—the pressure of air on the plate was balanced against the lift generated by the aerofoil.
We could use our observations of how the balance moved to determine the effectiveness of a given aerofoil.
We also used the tables of data we gathered to calculate a coefficient to replace Smeaton's, and ours turned out to be quite accurate!
So after all your work, you could say with confidence, "This is the best shape for a wing!"
Exactly. And we found it without having to build dozens of flying machines. Our experiments took quite a bit of time, but they saved us some trouble later on.

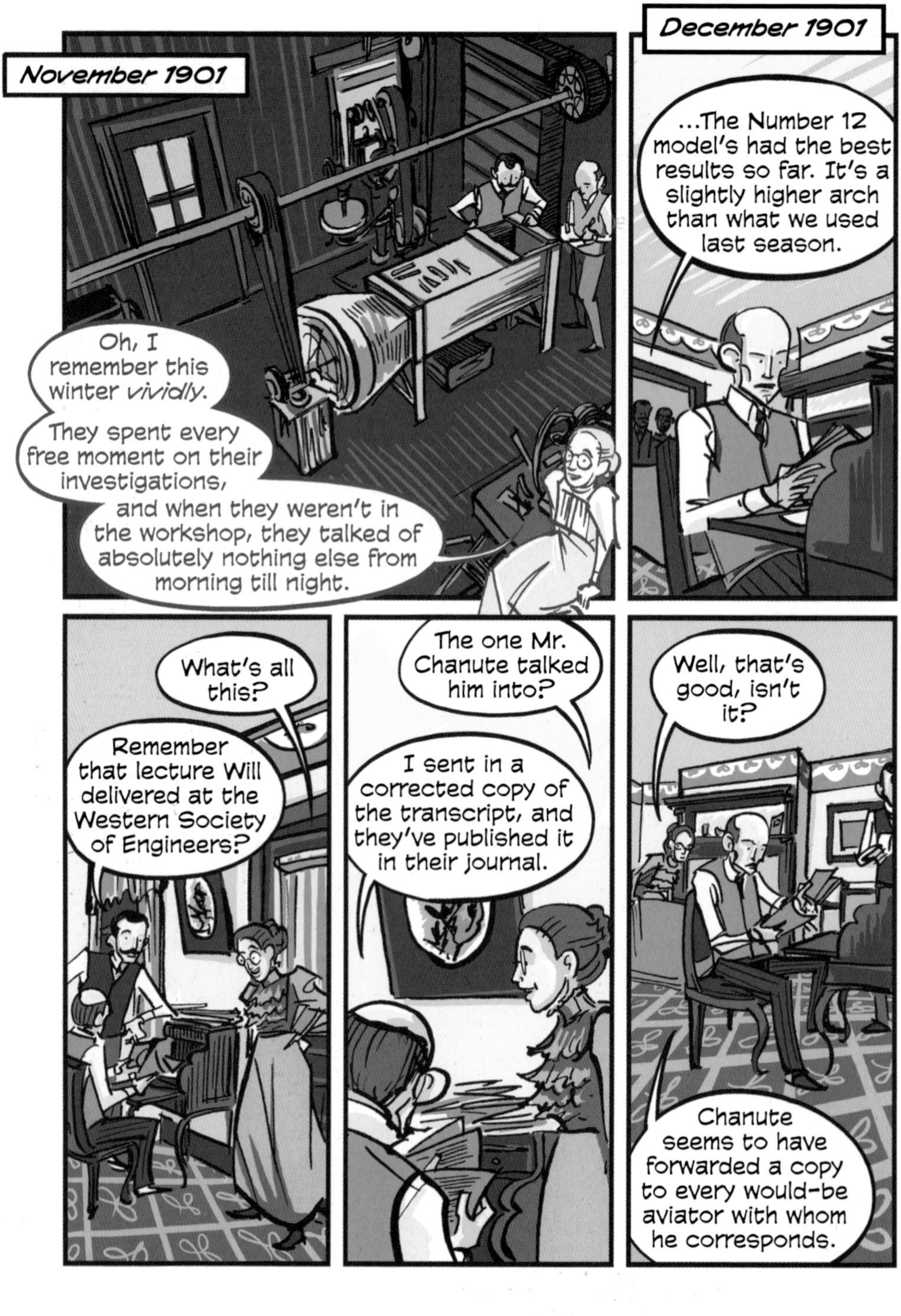
November 1901
Oh, I remember this winter *vividly*.
They spent every free moment on their investigations,
and when they weren't in the workshop, they talked of absolutely nothing else from morning till night.
December 1901
...The Number 12 model's had the best results so far. It's a slightly higher arch than what we used last season.
What's all this?
Remember that lecture Will delivered at the Western Society of Engineers?
The one Mr. Chanute talked him into?
I sent in a corrected copy of the transcript, and they've published it in their journal.
Well, that's good, isn't it?
Chanute seems to have forwarded a copy to every would-be aviator with whom he corresponds.

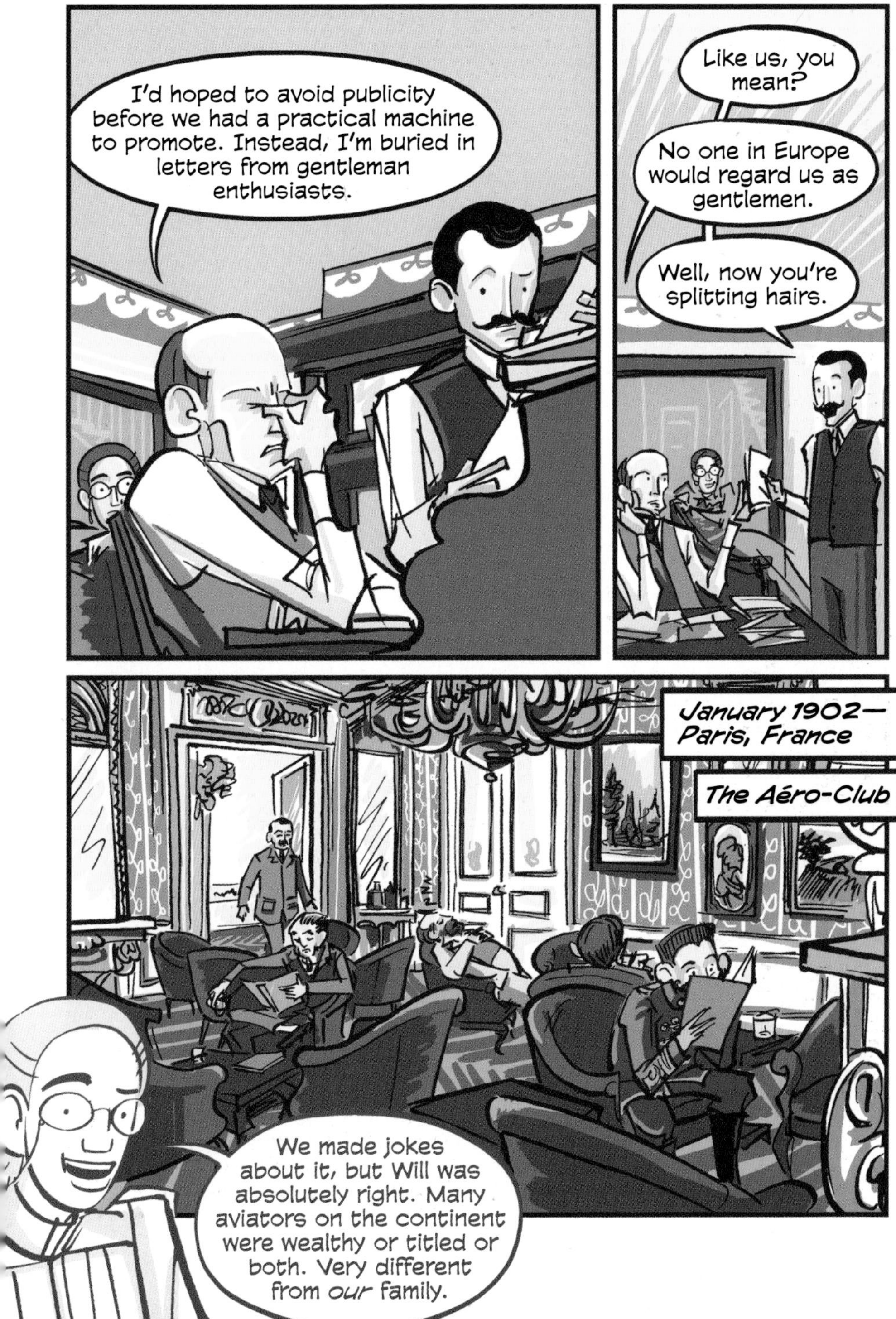
I'd hoped to avoid publicity before we had a practical machine to promote. Instead, I'm buried in letters from gentleman enthusiasts.
Like us, you mean?
No one in Europe would regard us as gentlemen.
Well, now you're splitting hairs.
January 1902— Paris, France
The Aéro-Club
We made jokes about it, but Will was absolutely right. Many aviators on the continent were wealthy or titled or both. Very different from *our* family.

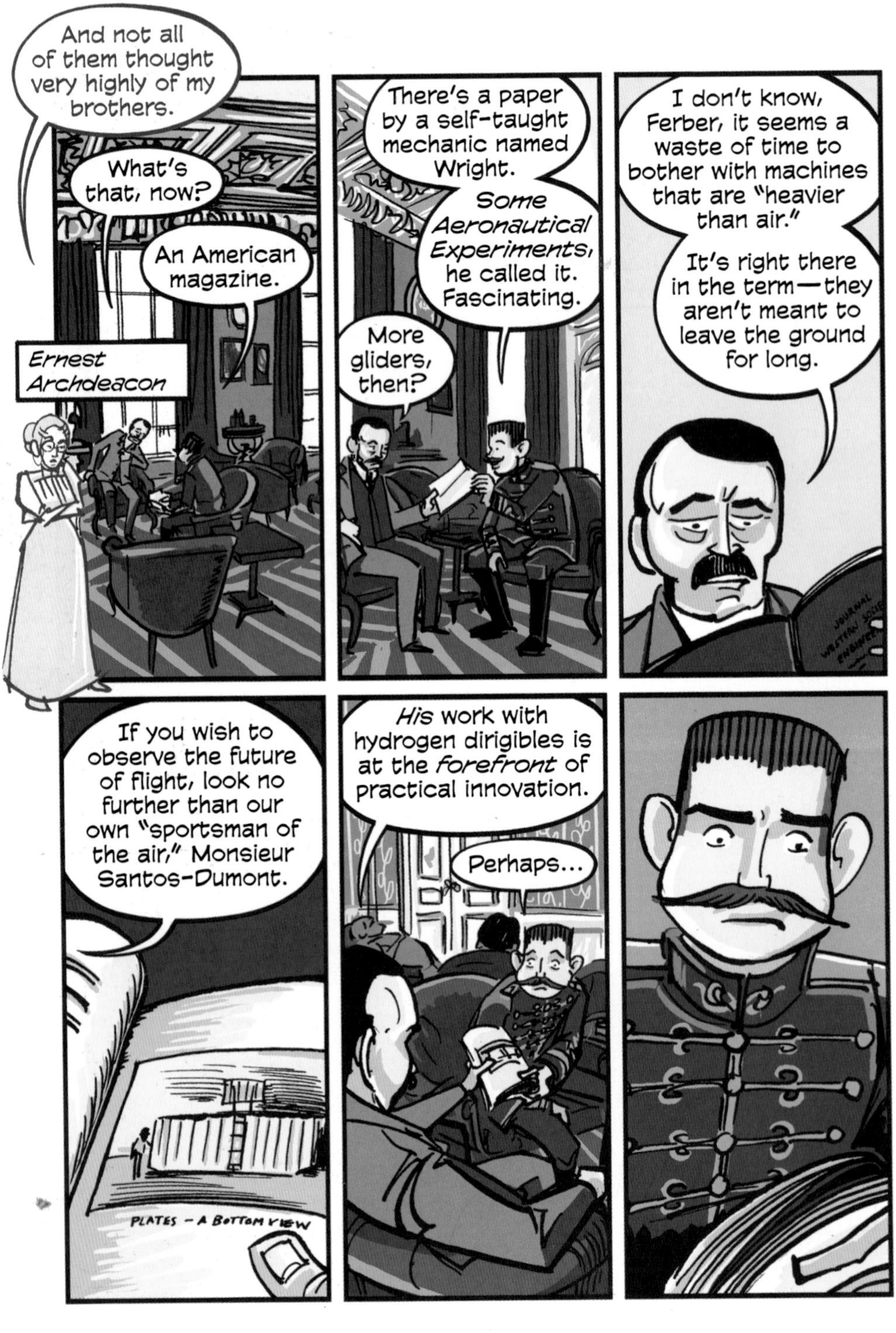
And not all of them thought very highly of my brothers.
What's that, now?
An American magazine.
Ernest Archdeacon
There's a paper by a self-taught mechanic named Wright.
Some Aeronautical Experiments, he called it. Fascinating.
More gliders, then?
I don't know, Ferber, it seems a waste of time to bother with machines that are "heavier than air."
It's right there in the term—they aren't meant to leave the ground for long.
If you wish to observe the future of flight, look no further than our own "sportsman of the air," Monsieur Santos-Dumont.
PLATES – A BOTTOM VIEW
His work with hydrogen dirigibles is at the *forefront* of practical innovation.
Perhaps...

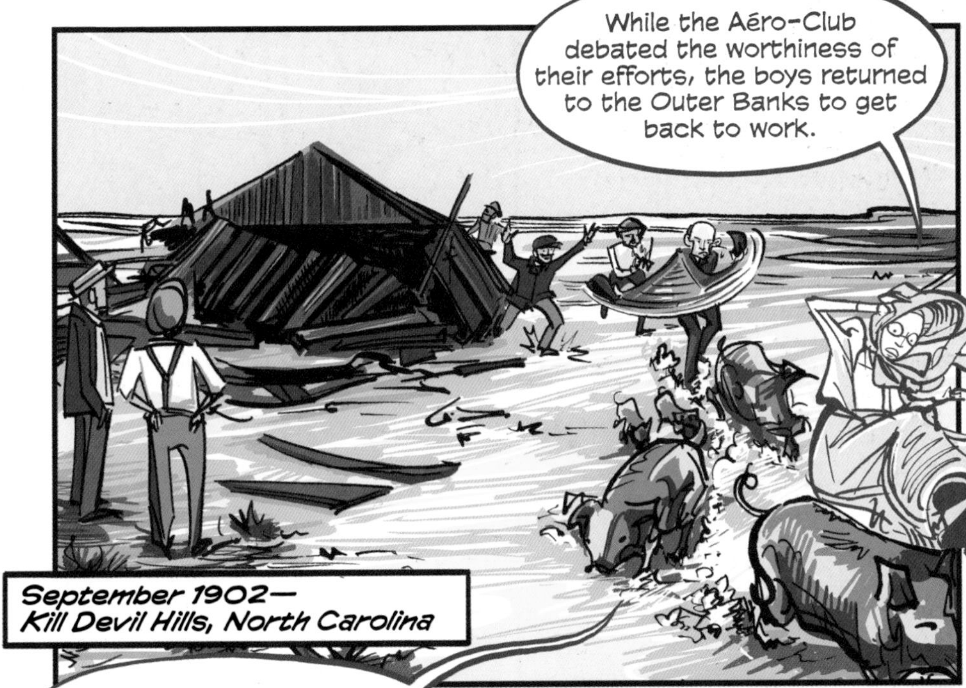
While the Aéro-Club debated the worthiness of their efforts, the boys returned to the Outer Banks to get back to work.
September 1902—
Kill Devil Hills, North Carolina

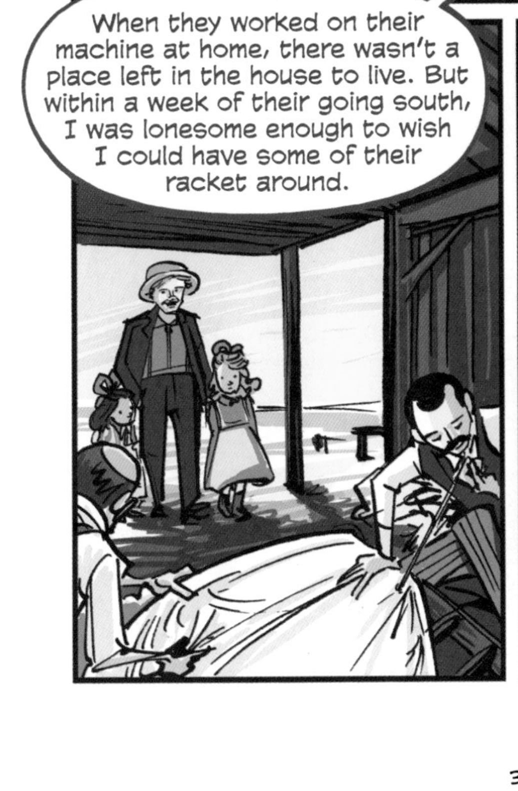
When they worked on their machine at home, there wasn't a place left in the house to live. But within a week of their going south, I was lonesome enough to wish I could have some of their racket around.

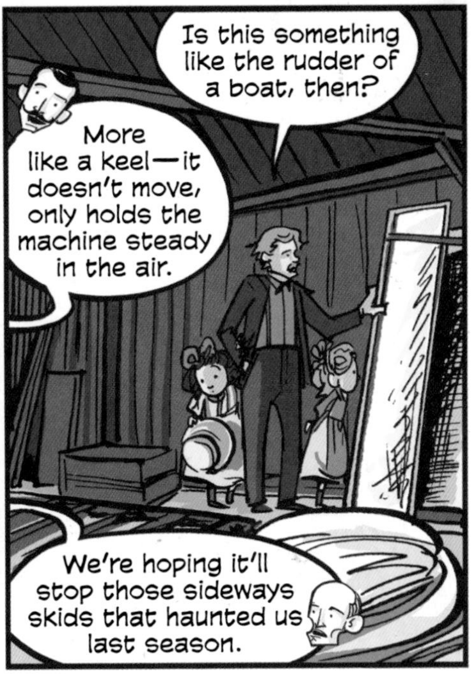
Is this something like the rudder of a boat, then?
More like a keel—it doesn't move, only holds the machine steady in the air.
We're hoping it'll stop those sideways skids that haunted us last season.

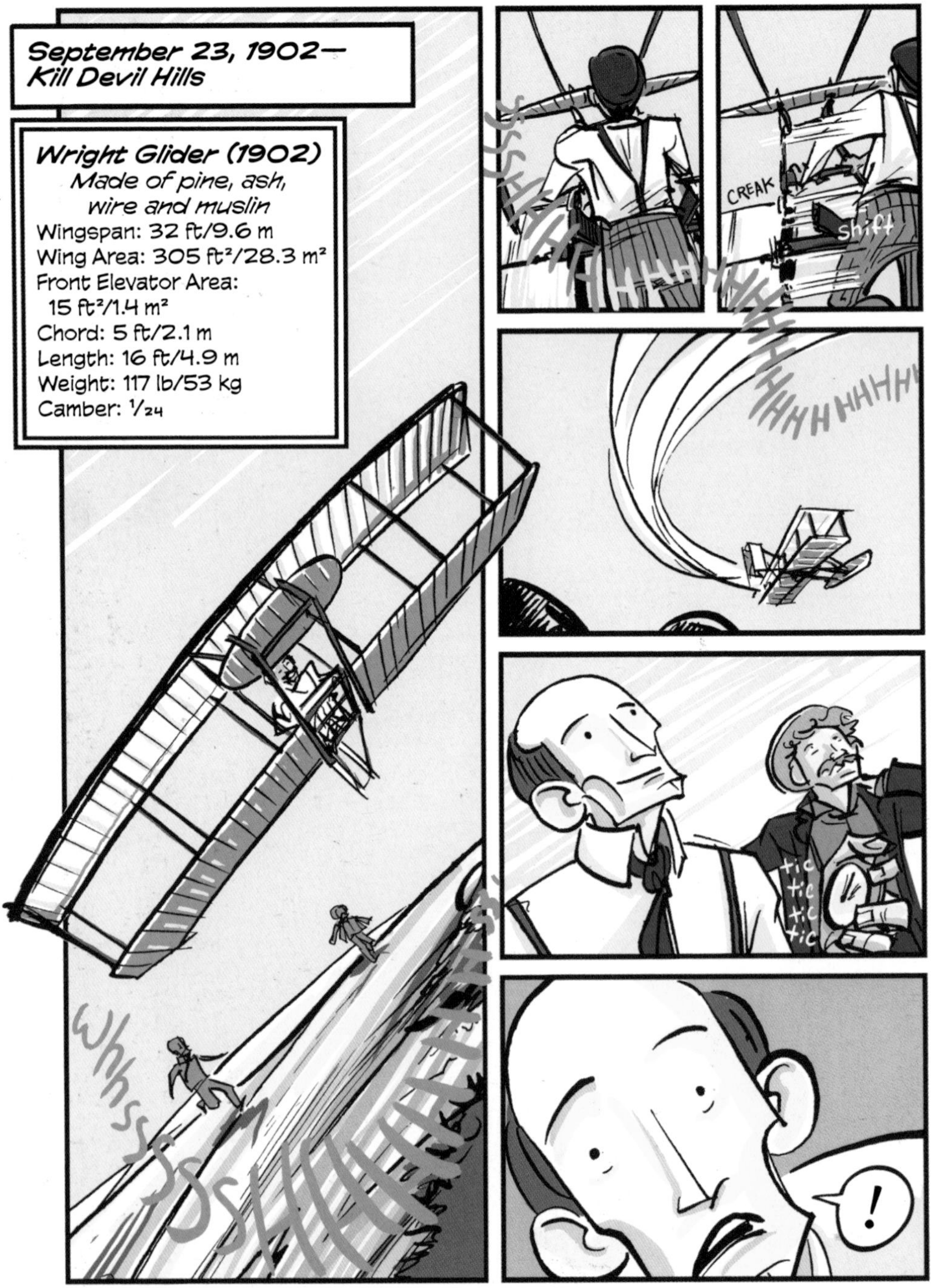

September 23, 1902—
Kill Devil Hills
Wright Glider (1902)
Made of pine, ash,
wire and muslin
Wingspan: 32 ft/9.6 m
Wing Area: 305 ft²/28.3 m²
Front Elevator Area:
15 ft²/1.4 m²
Chord: 5 ft/2.1 m
Length: 16 ft/4.9 m
Weight: 117 lb/53 kg
Camber: 1/24
whhsssSSSHHHHHHHH
CREAK
shift
tic tic tic tic
!

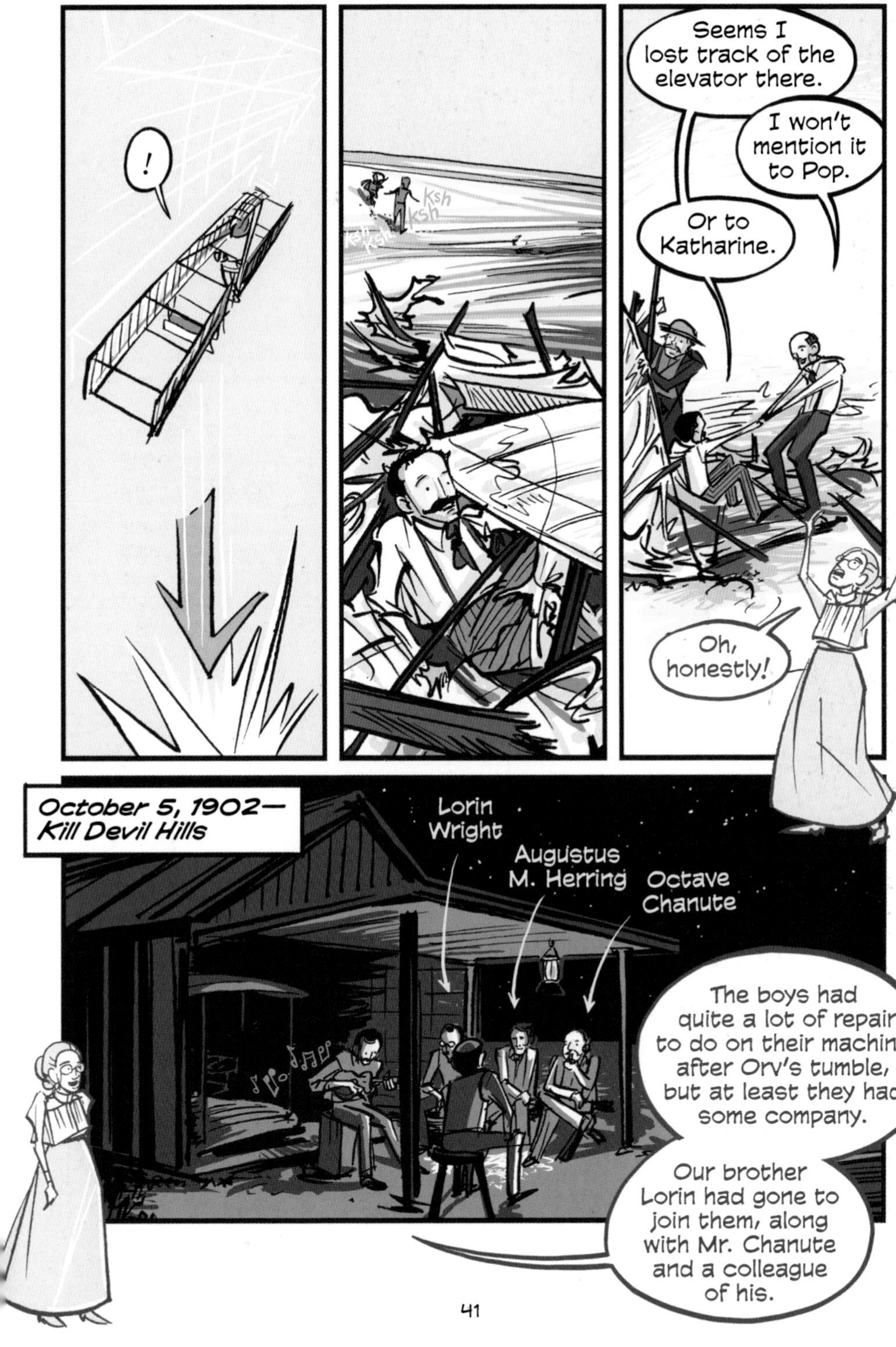
!
ksh
ksh
ksh
ksh
Seems I lost track of the elevator there.
I won't mention it to Pop.
Or to Katharine.
Oh, honestly!
October 5, 1902— Kill Devil Hills
Lorin Wright
Augustus M. Herring
Octave Chanute
The boys had quite a lot of repair to do on their machine after Orv's tumble, but at least they had some company.
Our brother Lorin had gone to join them, along with Mr. Chanute and a colleague of his.

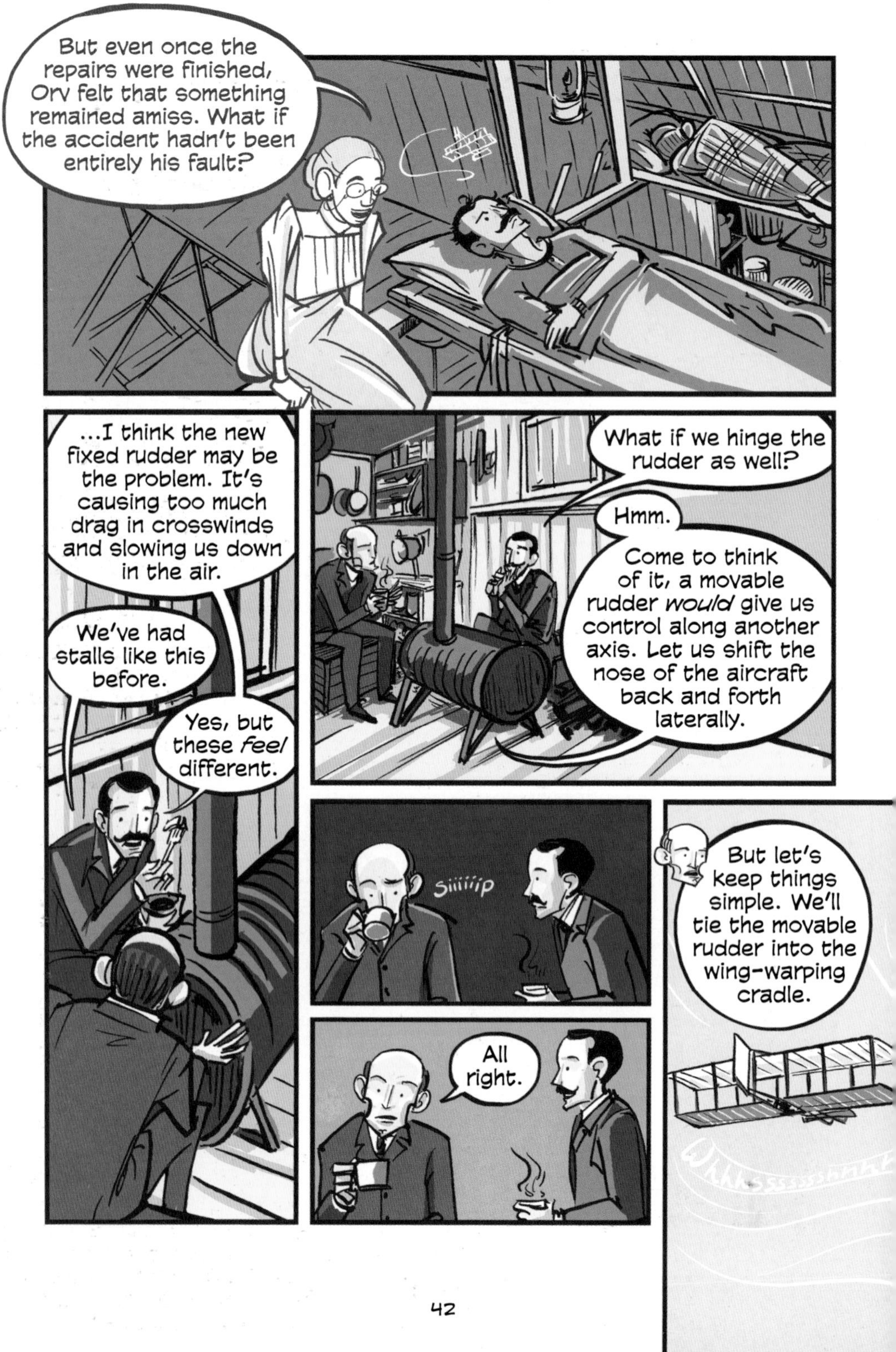

But even once the repairs were finished, Orv felt that something remained amiss. What if the accident hadn't been entirely his fault?
...I think the new fixed rudder may be the problem. It's causing too much drag in crosswinds and slowing us down in the air.
We've had stalls like this before.
Yes, but these *feel* different.
What if we hinge the rudder as well?
Hmm.
Come to think of it, a movable rudder *would* give us control along another axis. Let us shift the nose of the aircraft back and forth laterally.
Siiiiip
All right.
But let's keep things simple. We'll tie the movable rudder into the wing-warping cradle.

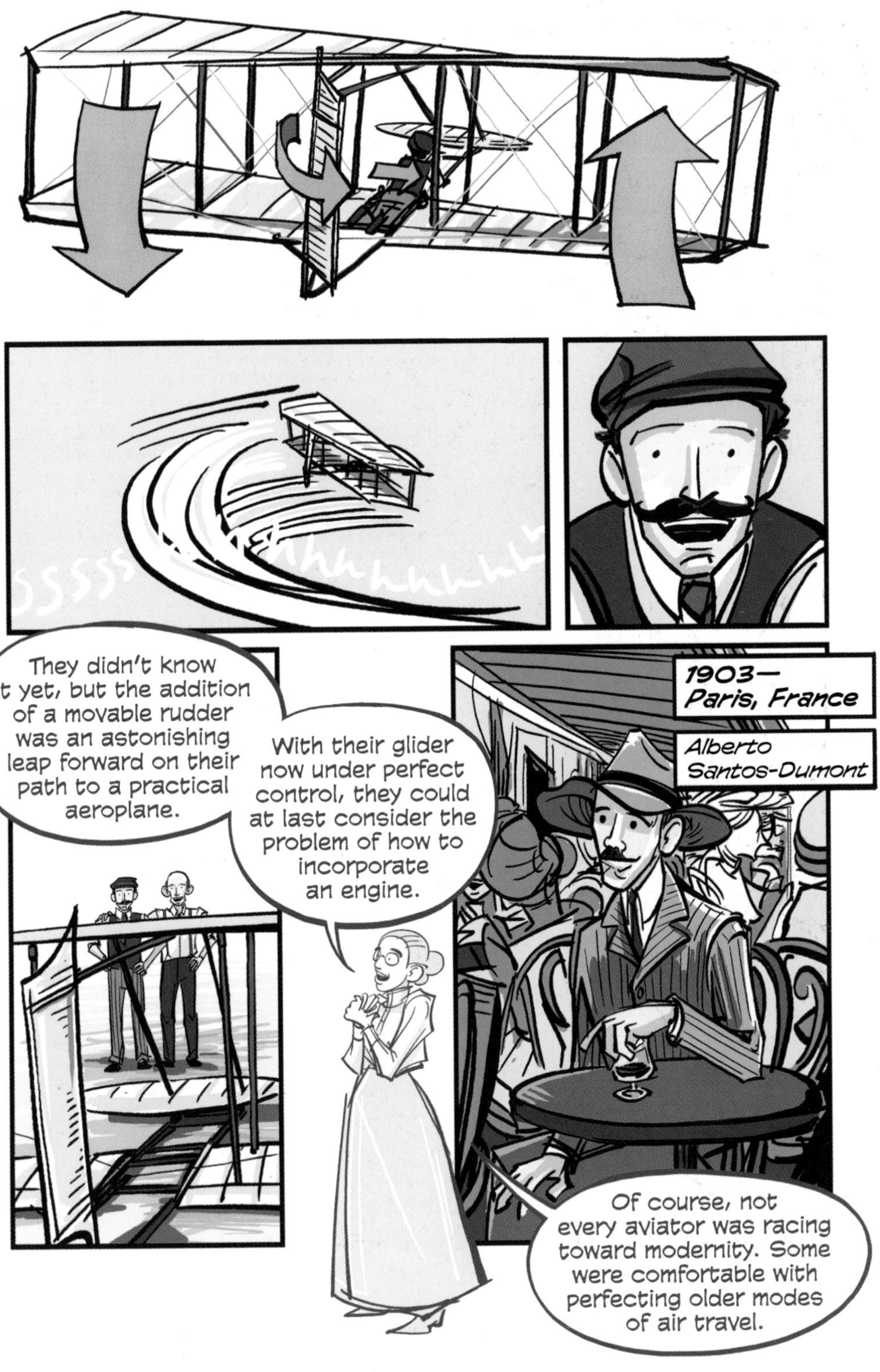

SSSSSHHHHHHHHHHHHH
They didn't know it yet, but the addition of a movable rudder was an astonishing leap forward on their path to a practical aeroplane.
With their glider now under perfect control, they could at last consider the problem of how to incorporate an engine.
1903— Paris, France
Alberto Santos-Dumont
Of course, not every aviator was racing toward modernity. Some were comfortable with perfecting older modes of air travel.

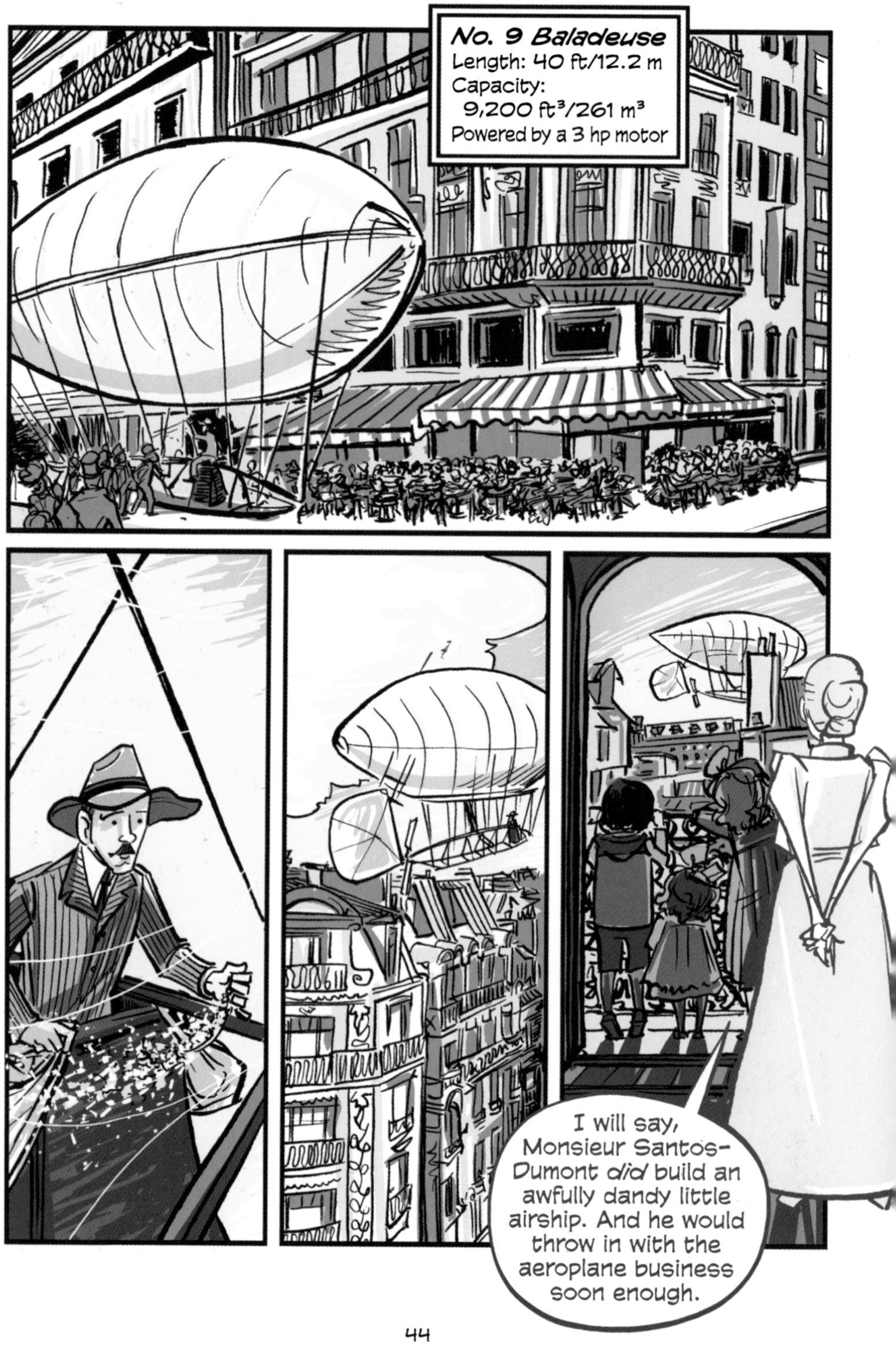
No. 9 Baladeuse
Length: 40 ft/12.2 m
Capacity:
9,200 ft³/261 m³
Powered by a 3 hp motor
I will say, Monsieur Santos-Dumont *did* build an awfully dandy little airship. And he would throw in with the aeroplane business soon enough.

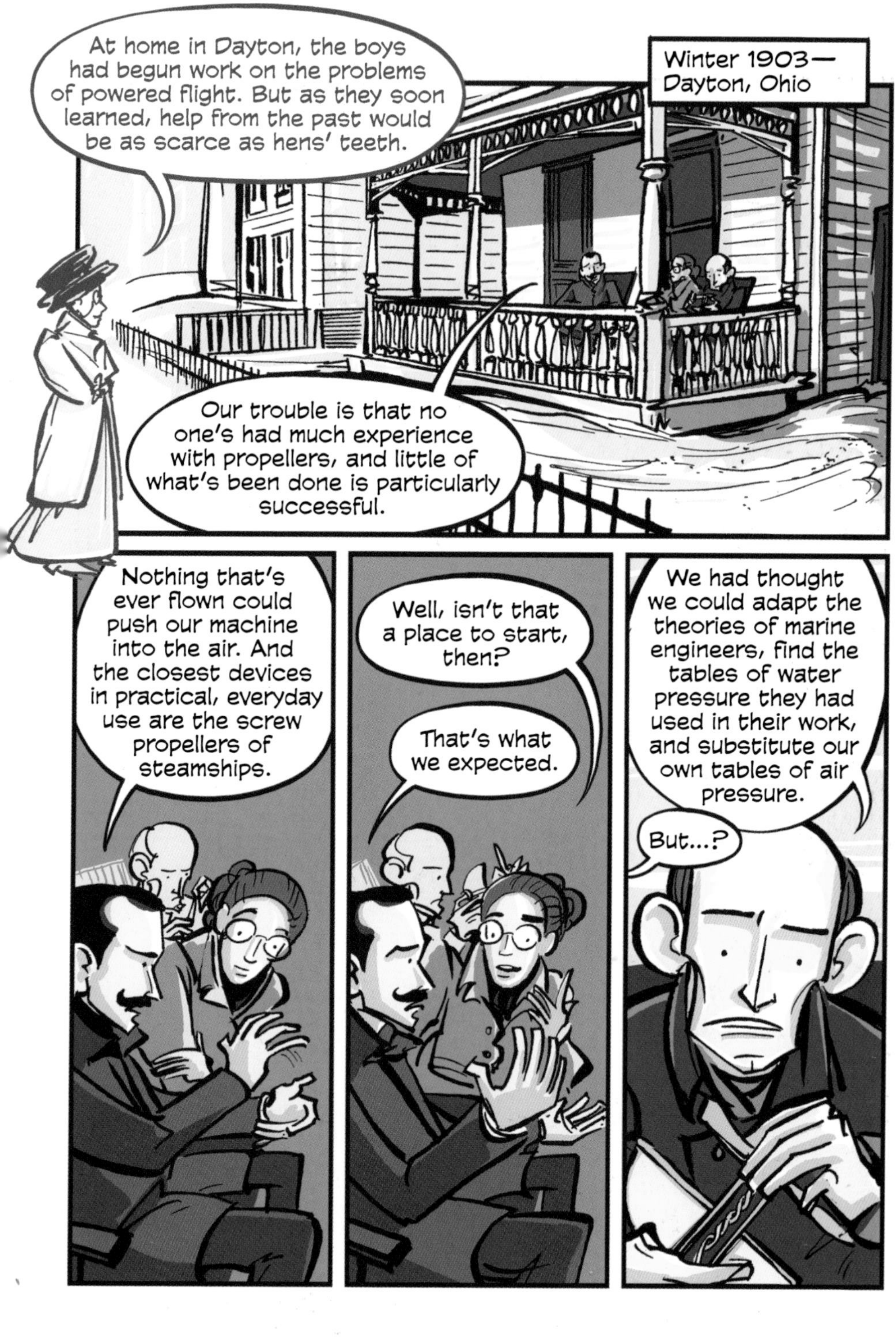
At home in Dayton, the boys had begun work on the problems of powered flight. But as they soon learned, help from the past would be as scarce as hens' teeth.
Winter 1903— Dayton, Ohio
Our trouble is that no one's had much experience with propellers, and little of what's been done is particularly successful.
Nothing that's ever flown could push our machine into the air. And the closest devices in practical, everyday use are the screw propellers of steamships.
Well, isn't that a place to start, then?
That's what we expected.
We had thought we could adapt the theories of marine engineers, find the tables of water pressure they had used in their work, and substitute our own tables of air pressure.
But...?

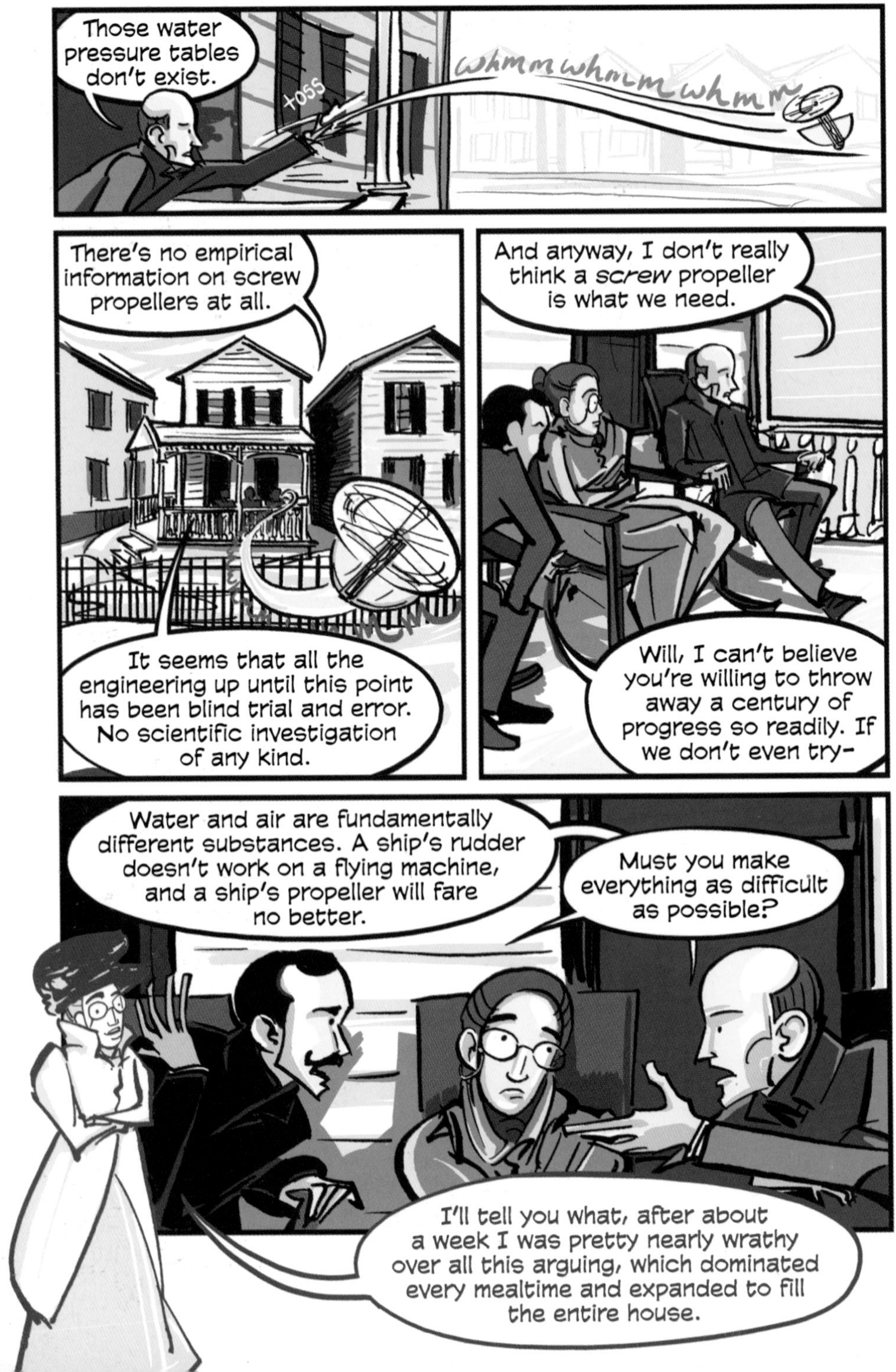
Those water pressure tables don't exist.
TOSS
whmmwhmmwhmm
There's no empirical information on screw propellers at all.
It seems that all the engineering up until this point has been blind trial and error. No scientific investigation of any kind.
And anyway, I don't really think a *screw* propeller is what we need.
Will, I can't believe you're willing to throw away a century of progress so readily. If we don't even try-
Water and air are fundamentally different substances. A ship's rudder doesn't work on a flying machine, and a ship's propeller will fare no better.
Must you make everything as difficult as possible?
I'll tell you what, after about a week I was pretty nearly wrathy over all this arguing, which dominated every mealtime and expanded to fill the entire house.

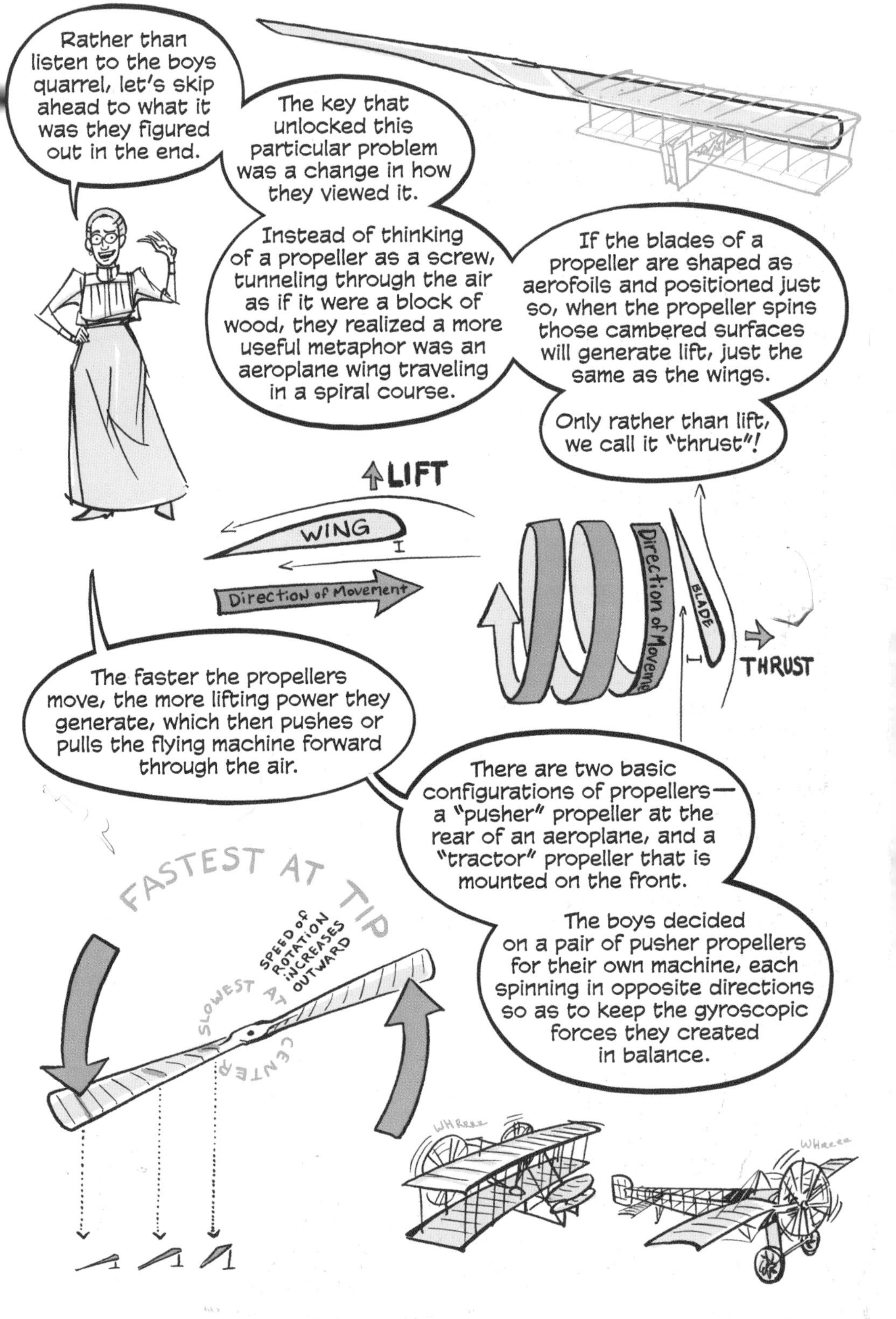

Rather than listen to the boys quarrel, let's skip ahead to what it was they figured out in the end.
The key that unlocked this particular problem was a change in how they viewed it.
Instead of thinking of a propeller as a screw, tunneling through the air as if it were a block of wood, they realized a more useful metaphor was an aeroplane wing traveling in a spiral course.
If the blades of a propeller are shaped as aerofoils and positioned just so, when the propeller spins those cambered surfaces will generate lift, just the same as the wings.
Only rather than lift, we call it "thrust"!
LIFT
WING
Direction of Movement
Direction of Moveme
BLADE
THRUST
The faster the propellers move, the more lifting power they generate, which then pushes or pulls the flying machine forward through the air.
There are two basic configurations of propellers— a "pusher" propeller at the rear of an aeroplane, and a "tractor" propeller that is mounted on the front.
The boys decided on a pair of pusher propellers for their own machine, each spinning in opposite directions so as to keep the gyroscopic forces they created in balance.
FASTEST AT TIP
SPEED OF ROTATION INCREASES OUTWARD
SLOWEST AT CENTER

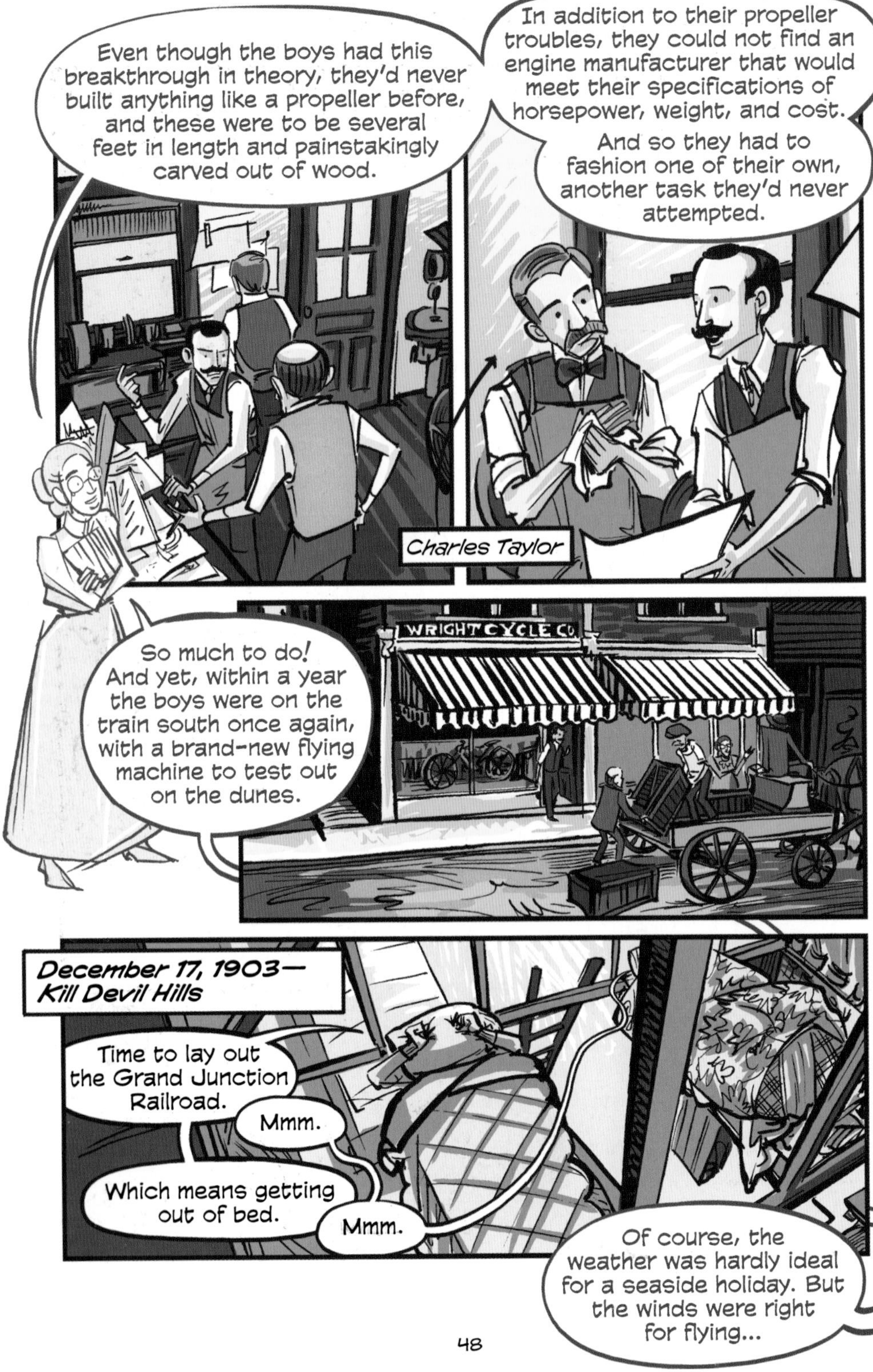
Even though the boys had this breakthrough in theory, they'd never built anything like a propeller before, and these were to be several feet in length and painstakingly carved out of wood.
In addition to their propeller troubles, they could not find an engine manufacturer that would meet their specifications of horsepower, weight, and cost.
And so they had to fashion one of their own, another task they'd never attempted.
Charles Taylor
WRIGHT CYCLE CO
So much to do! And yet, within a year the boys were on the train south once again, with a brand-new flying machine to test out on the dunes.
December 17, 1903—
Kill Devil Hills
Time to lay out the Grand Junction Railroad.
Mmm.
Which means getting out of bed.
Mmm.
Of course, the weather was hardly ideal for a seaside holiday. But the winds were right for flying...

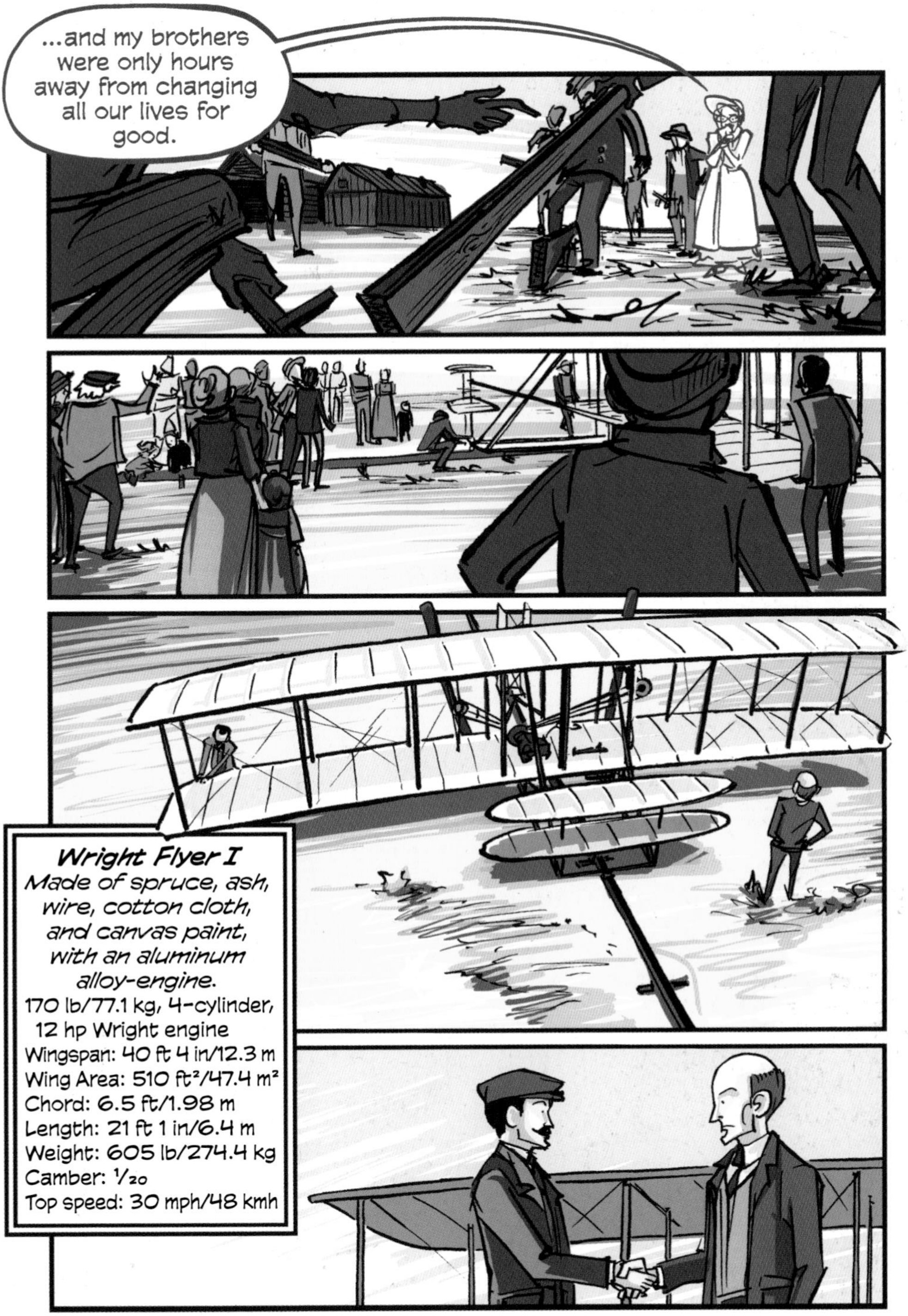
...and my brothers were only hours away from changing all our lives for good.
Wright Flyer I
Made of spruce, ash, wire, cotton cloth, and canvas paint, with an aluminum alloy-engine.
170 lb/77.1 kg, 4-cylinder, 12 hp Wright engine
Wingspan: 40 ft 4 in/12.3 m
Wing Area: 510 ft^2/47.4 m^2
Chord: 6.5 ft/1.98 m
Length: 21 ft 1 in/6.4 m
Weight: 605 lb/274.4 kg
Camber: $1/20$
Top speed: 30 mph/48 kmh

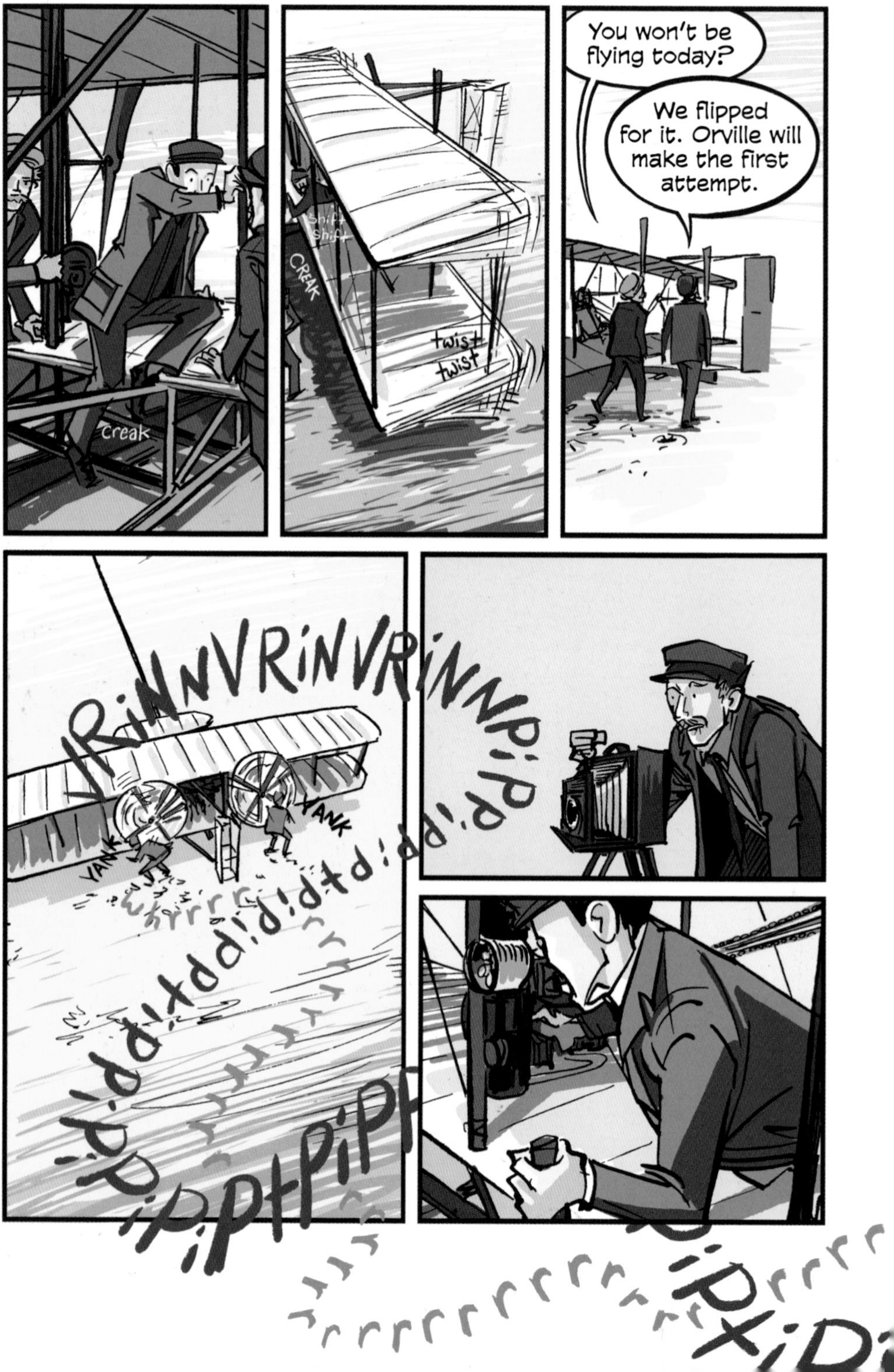
creak
shift
shift
CREAK
twist
twist
You won't be flying today?
We flipped for it. Orville will make the first attempt.
YANK
YANK

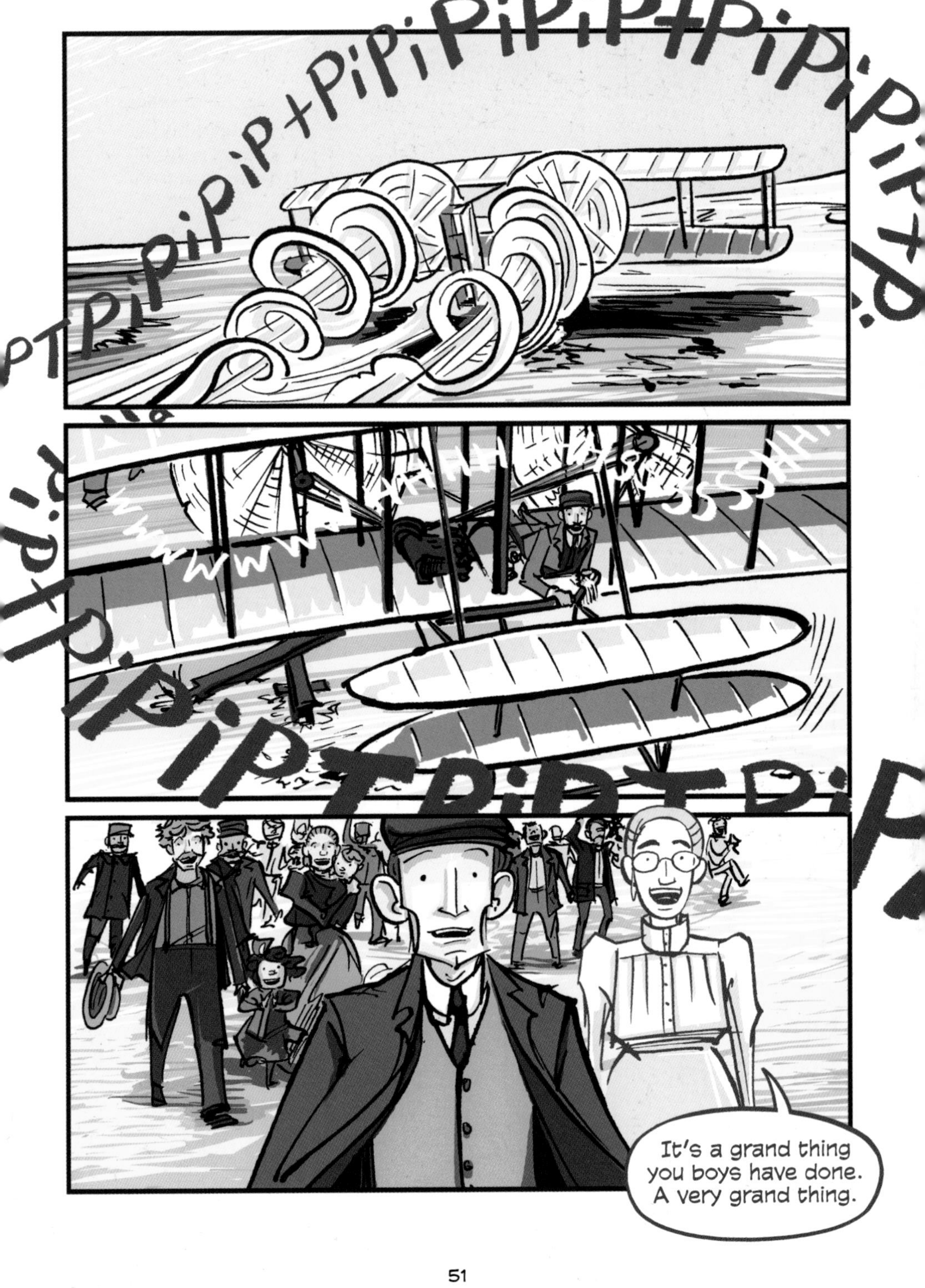
It's a grand thing you boys have done. A very grand thing.

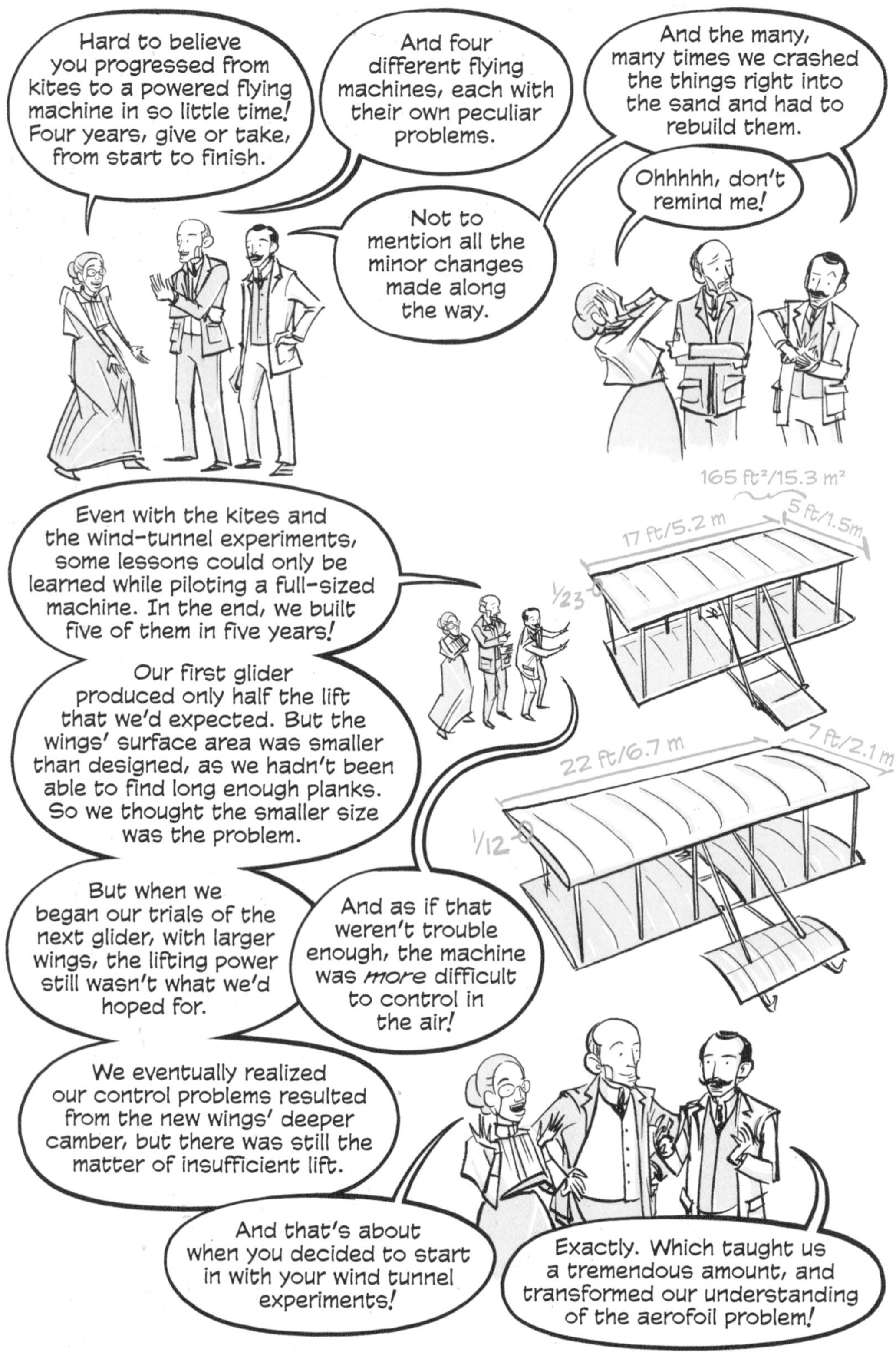
Hard to believe you progressed from kites to a powered flying machine in so little time! Four years, give or take, from start to finish.
And four different flying machines, each with their own peculiar problems.
Not to mention all the minor changes made along the way.
And the many, many times we crashed the things right into the sand and had to rebuild them.
Ohhhhh, don't remind me!
Even with the kites and the wind-tunnel experiments, some lessons could only be learned while piloting a full-sized machine. In the end, we built five of them in five years!
Our first glider produced only half the lift that we'd expected. But the wings' surface area was smaller than designed, as we hadn't been able to find long enough planks. So we thought the smaller size was the problem.
165 ft²/15.3 m²
17 ft/5.2 m
5 ft/1.5m
1/23
But when we began our trials of the next glider, with larger wings, the lifting power still wasn't what we'd hoped for.
And as if that weren't trouble enough, the machine was *more* difficult to control in the air!
22 ft/6.7 m
7 ft/2.1 m
1/12
We eventually realized our control problems resulted from the new wings' deeper camber, but there was still the matter of insufficient lift.
And that's about when you decided to start in with your wind tunnel experiments!
Exactly. Which taught us a tremendous amount, and transformed our understanding of the aerofoil problem!

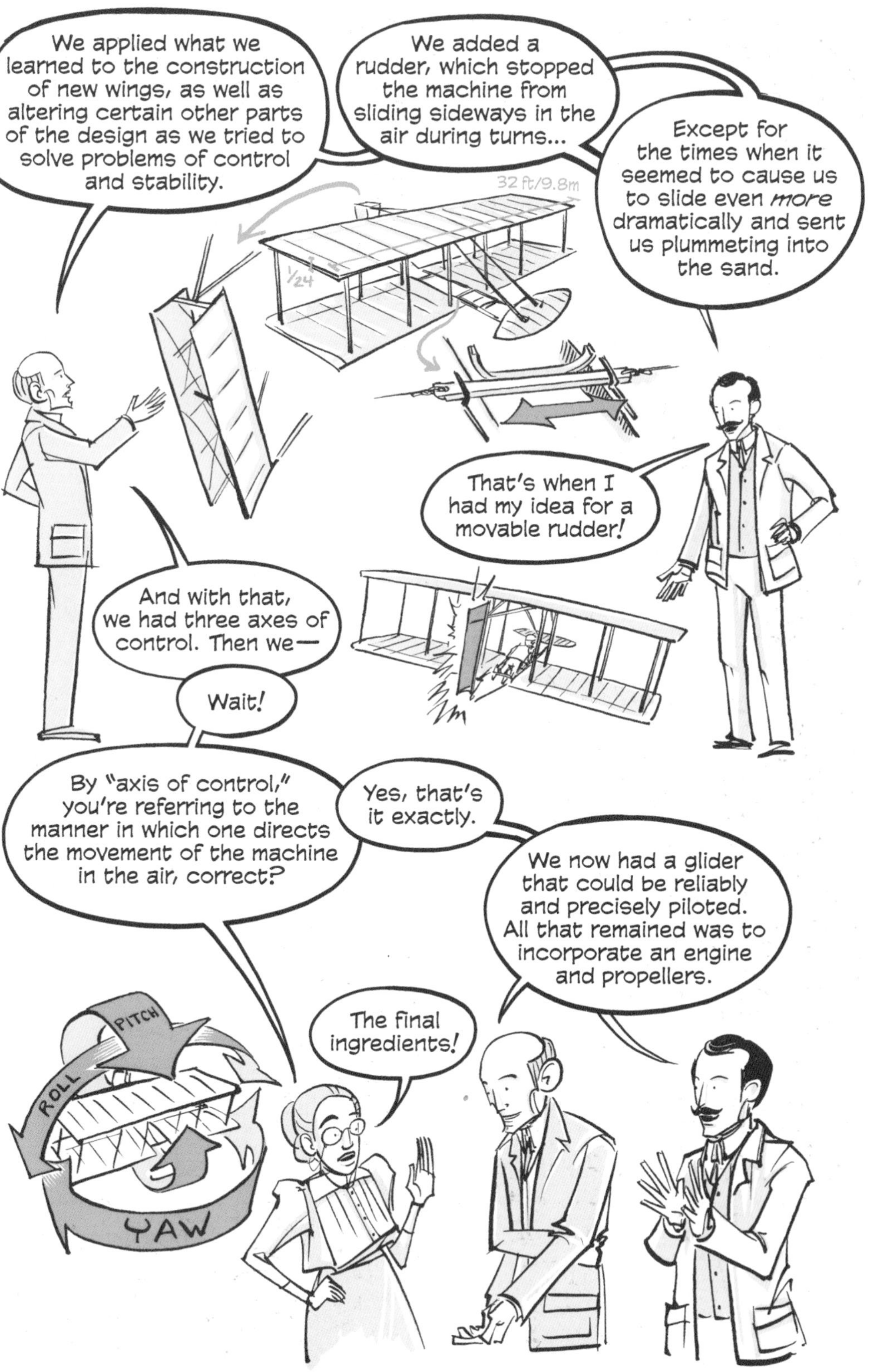

We applied what we learned to the construction of new wings, as well as altering certain other parts of the design as we tried to solve problems of control and stability.
We added a rudder, which stopped the machine from sliding sideways in the air during turns...
Except for the times when it seemed to cause us to slide even *more* dramatically and sent us plummeting into the sand.
32 ft/9.8m
1/24
That's when I had my idea for a movable rudder!
And with that, we had three axes of control. Then we—
Wait!
By "axis of control," you're referring to the manner in which one directs the movement of the machine in the air, correct?
Yes, that's it exactly.
We now had a glider that could be reliably and precisely piloted. All that remained was to incorporate an engine and propellers.
The final ingredients!
PITCH
ROLL
YAW

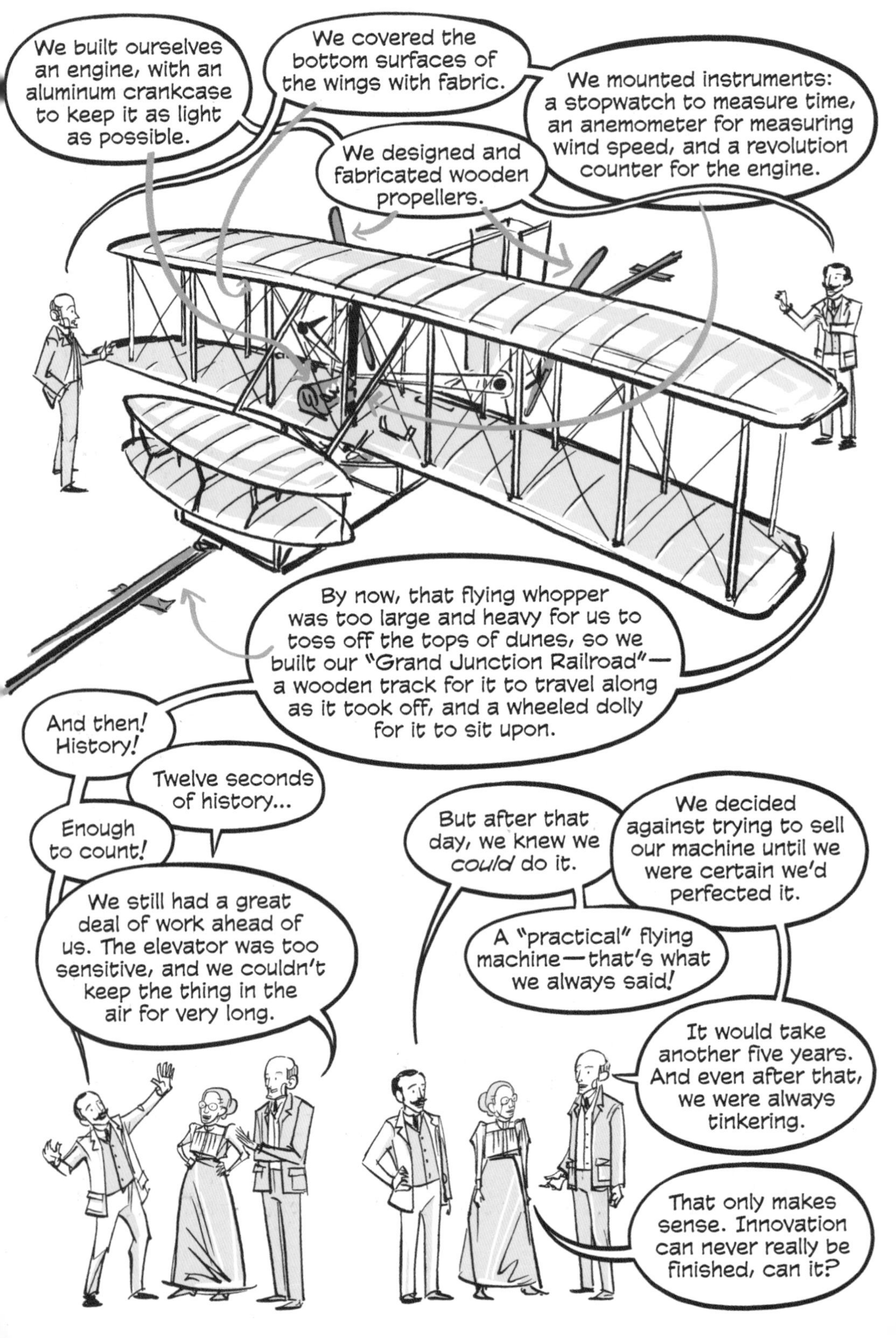
We built ourselves an engine, with an aluminum crankcase to keep it as light as possible.
We covered the bottom surfaces of the wings with fabric.
We designed and fabricated wooden propellers.
We mounted instruments: a stopwatch to measure time, an anemometer for measuring wind speed, and a revolution counter for the engine.
By now, that flying whopper was too large and heavy for us to toss off the tops of dunes, so we built our "Grand Junction Railroad"—a wooden track for it to travel along as it took off, and a wheeled dolly for it to sit upon.
And then! History!
Twelve seconds of history...
Enough to count!
We still had a great deal of work ahead of us. The elevator was too sensitive, and we couldn't keep the thing in the air for very long.
But after that day, we knew we *could* do it.
We decided against trying to sell our machine until we were certain we'd perfected it.
A "practical" flying machine—that's what we always said!
It would take another five years. And even after that, we were always tinkering.
That only makes sense. Innovation can never really be finished, can it?

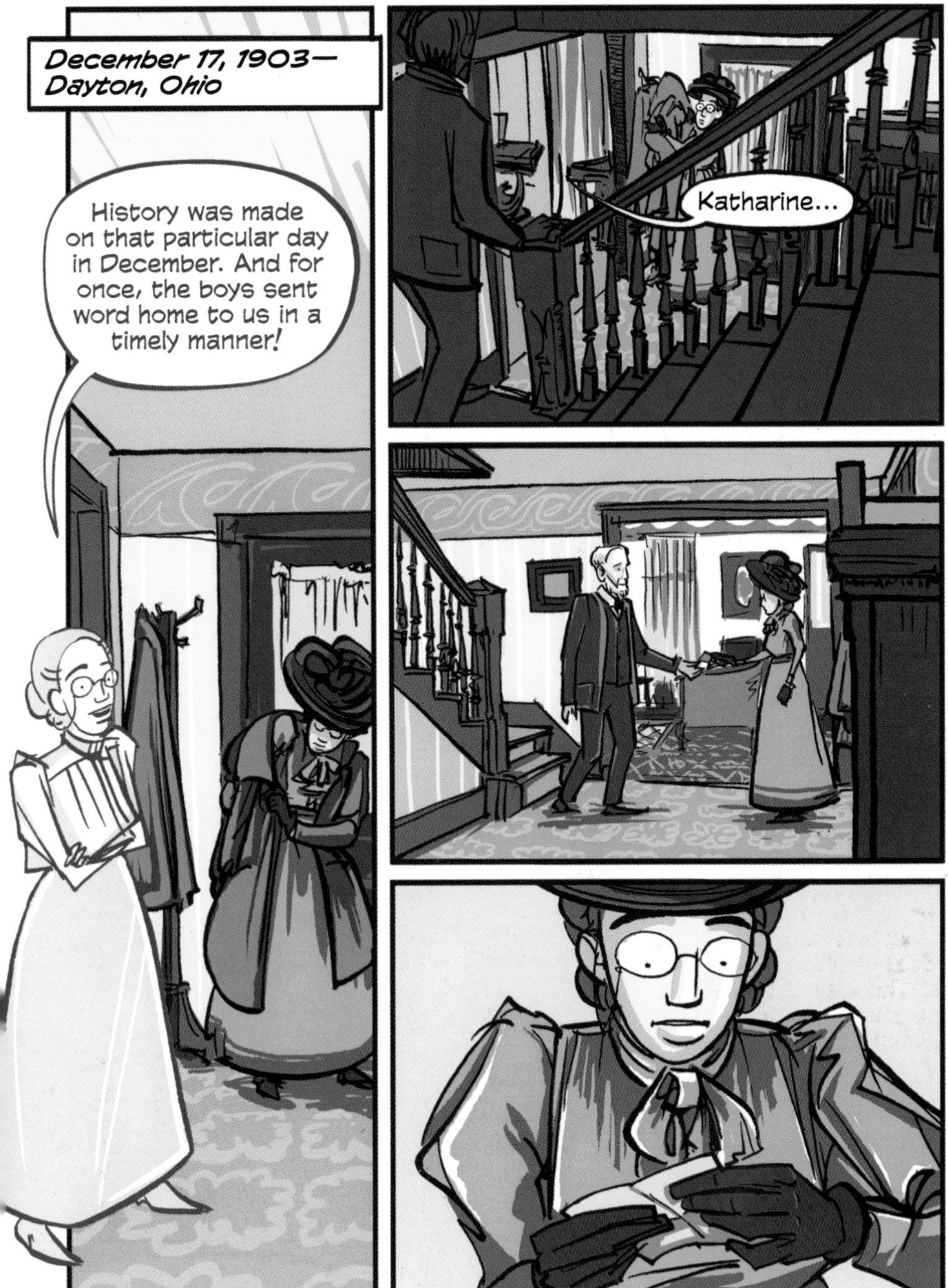
December 17, 1903—
Dayton, Ohio
History was made on that particular day in December. And for once, the boys sent word home to us in a timely manner!
Katharine...

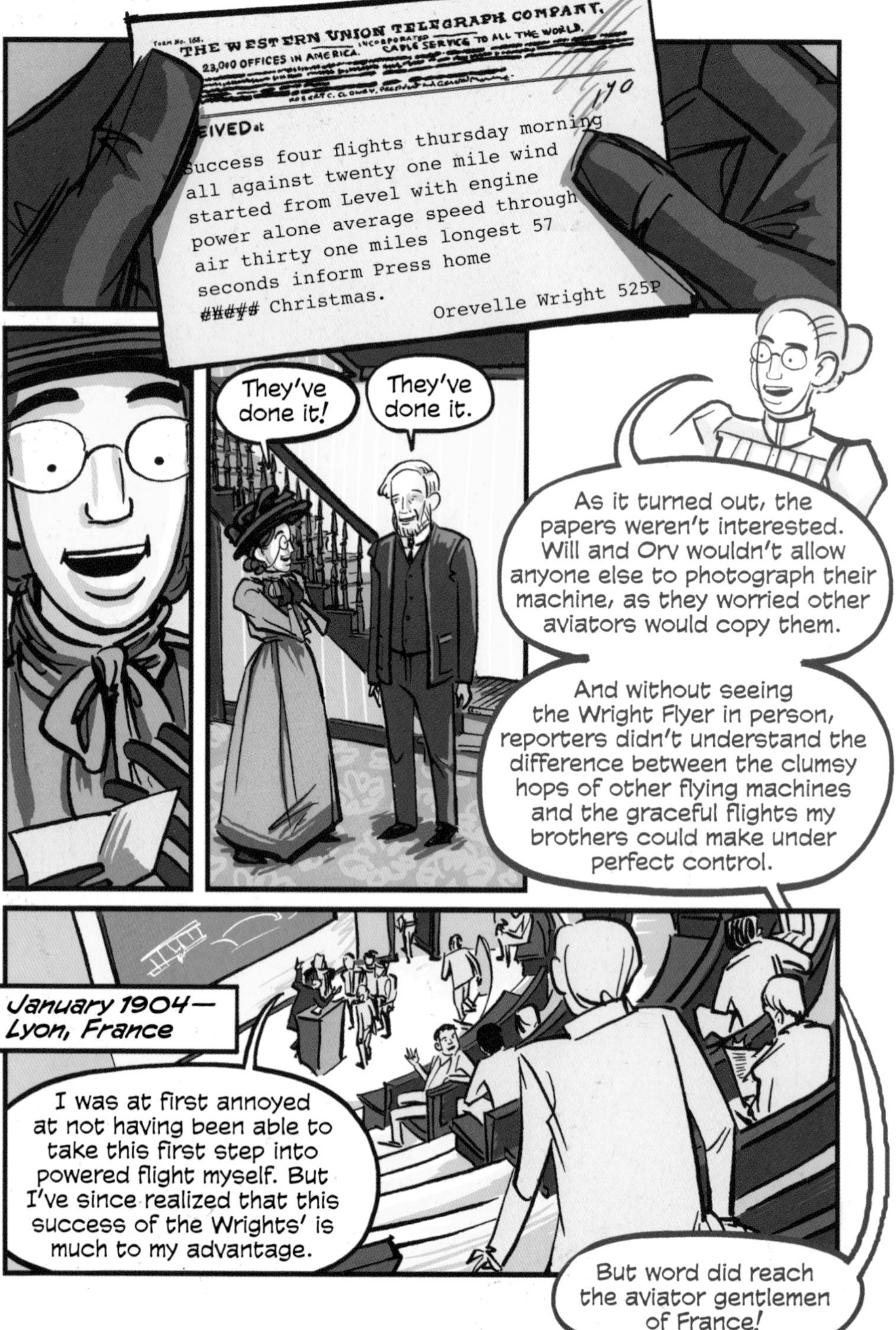
THE WESTERN UNION TELEGRAPH COMPANY.
23,000 OFFICES IN AMERICA. INCORPORATED CABLE SERVICE TO ALL THE WORLD.
170
EIVED at
Success four flights thursday morning all against twenty one mile wind started from Level with engine power alone average speed through air thirty one miles longest 57 seconds inform Press home #¥¢y# Christmas.
Orevelle Wright 525P
They've done it!
They've done it.
As it turned out, the papers weren't interested. Will and Orv wouldn't allow anyone else to photograph their machine, as they worried other aviators would copy them.
And without seeing the Wright Flyer in person, reporters didn't understand the difference between the clumsy hops of other flying machines and the graceful flights my brothers could make under perfect control.
January 1904—Lyon, France
I was at first annoyed at not having been able to take this first step into powered flight myself. But I've since realized that this success of the Wrights' is much to my advantage.
But word did reach the aviator gentlemen of France!

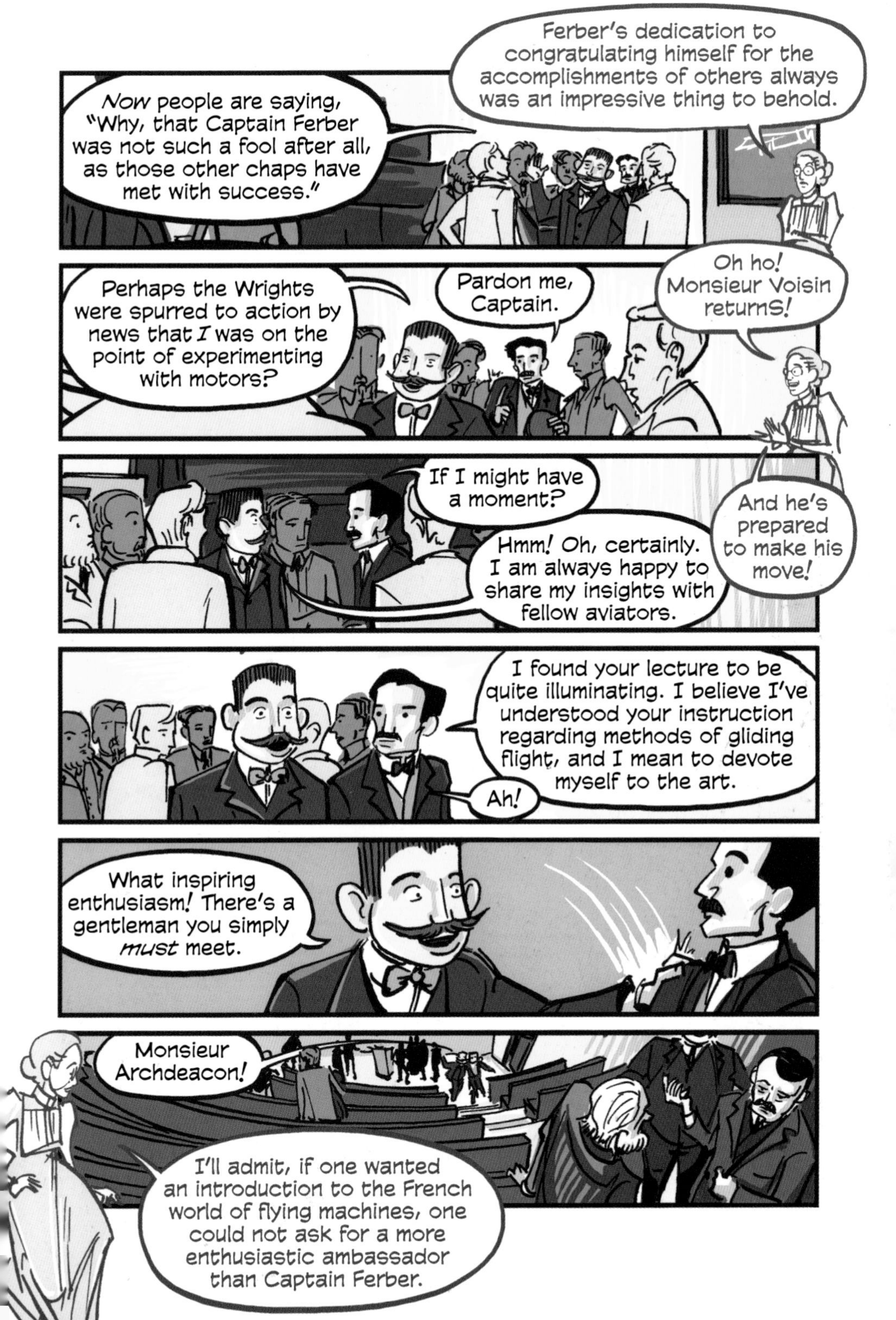
Now people are saying, "Why, that Captain Ferber was not such a fool after all, as those other chaps have met with success."
Ferber's dedication to congratulating himself for the accomplishments of others always was an impressive thing to behold.
Perhaps the Wrights were spurred to action by news that *I* was on the point of experimenting with motors?
Pardon me, Captain.
Oh ho! Monsieur Voisin returns!
If I might have a moment?
Hmm! Oh, certainly. I am always happy to share my insights with fellow aviators.
And he's prepared to make his move!
I found your lecture to be quite illuminating. I believe I've understood your instruction regarding methods of gliding flight, and I mean to devote myself to the art.
Ah!
What inspiring enthusiasm! There's a gentleman you simply *must* meet.
Monsieur Archdeacon!
I'll admit, if one wanted an introduction to the French world of flying machines, one could not ask for a more enthusiastic ambassador than Captain Ferber.

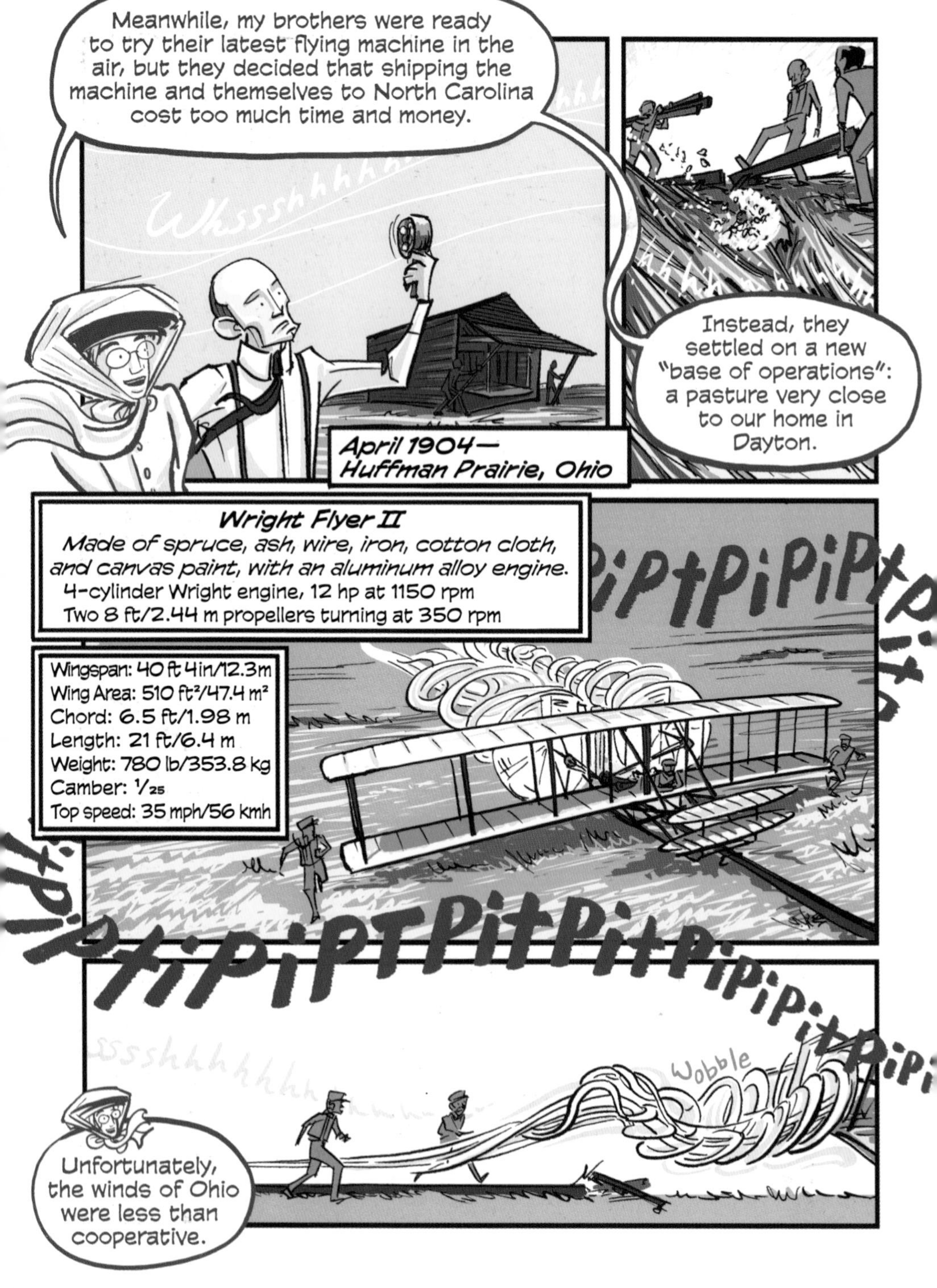

Meanwhile, my brothers were ready to try their latest flying machine in the air, but they decided that shipping the machine and themselves to North Carolina cost too much time and money.
Whksssshhhhhh
April 1904— Huffman Prairie, Ohio
Instead, they settled on a new "base of operations": a pasture very close to our home in Dayton.
Wright Flyer II
Made of spruce, ash, wire, iron, cotton cloth, and canvas paint, with an aluminum alloy engine.
4-cylinder Wright engine, 12 hp at 1150 rpm
Two 8 ft/2.44 m propellers turning at 350 rpm
Wingspan: 40 ft 4in/12.3m
Wing Area: 510 ft²/47.4 m²
Chord: 6.5 ft/1.98 m
Length: 21 ft/6.4 m
Weight: 780 lb/353.8 kg
Camber: 1/25
Top speed: 35 mph/56 kmh
PiPtPiPiPt
PiPiPtPitPitPiPiPiPitPiPi
sssshhhhhh
Wobble
Unfortunately, the winds of Ohio were less than cooperative.

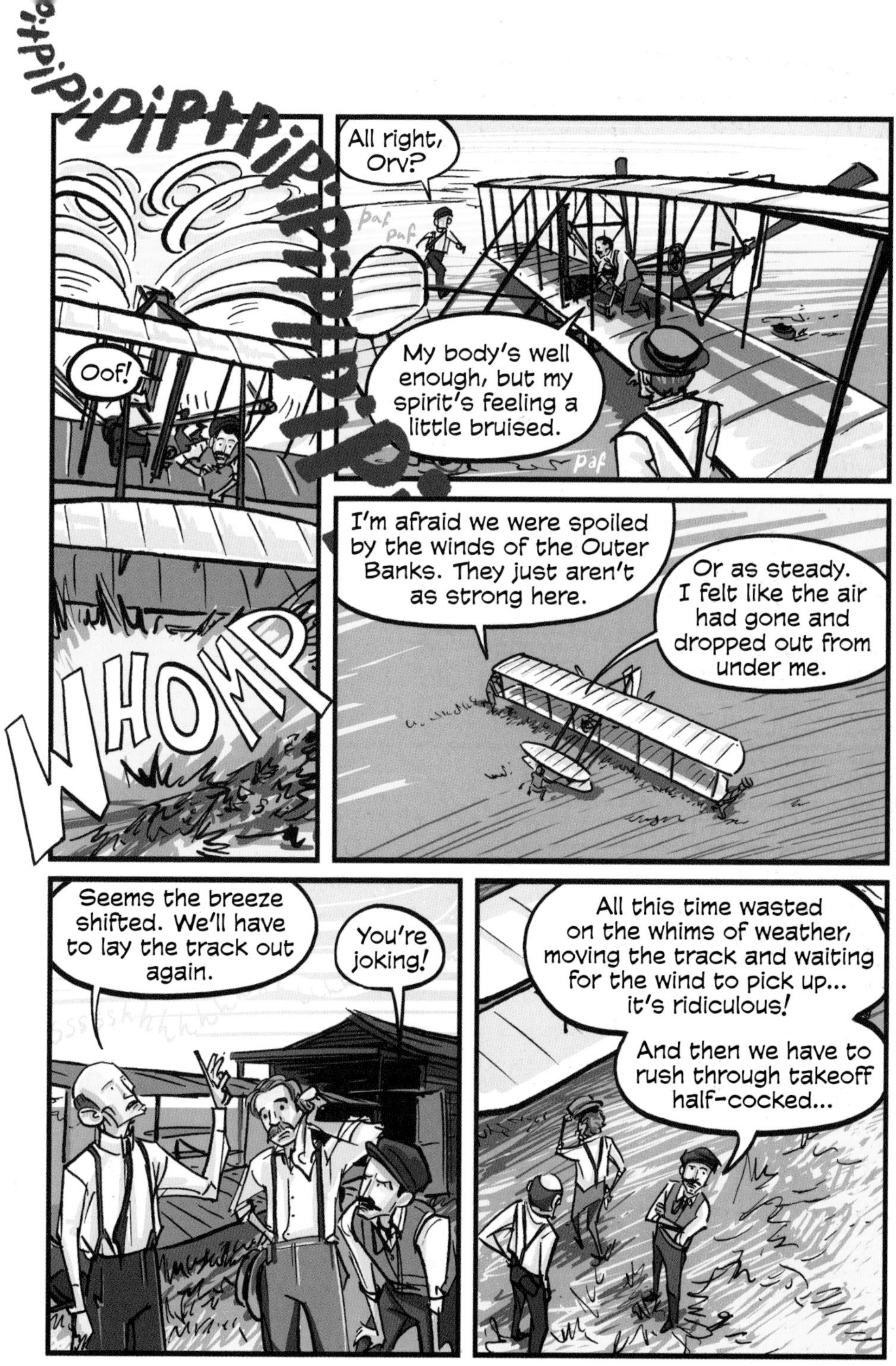
pipipipipipipipipipipipi
Oof!
WHOMP
All right, Orv?
paf paf
My body's well enough, but my spirit's feeling a little bruised.
paf
I'm afraid we were spoiled by the winds of the Outer Banks. They just aren't as strong here.
Or as steady. I felt like the air had gone and dropped out from under me.
Seems the breeze shifted. We'll have to lay the track out again.
You're joking!
All this time wasted on the whims of weather, moving the track and waiting for the wind to pick up... it's ridiculous!
And then we have to rush through takeoff half-cocked...

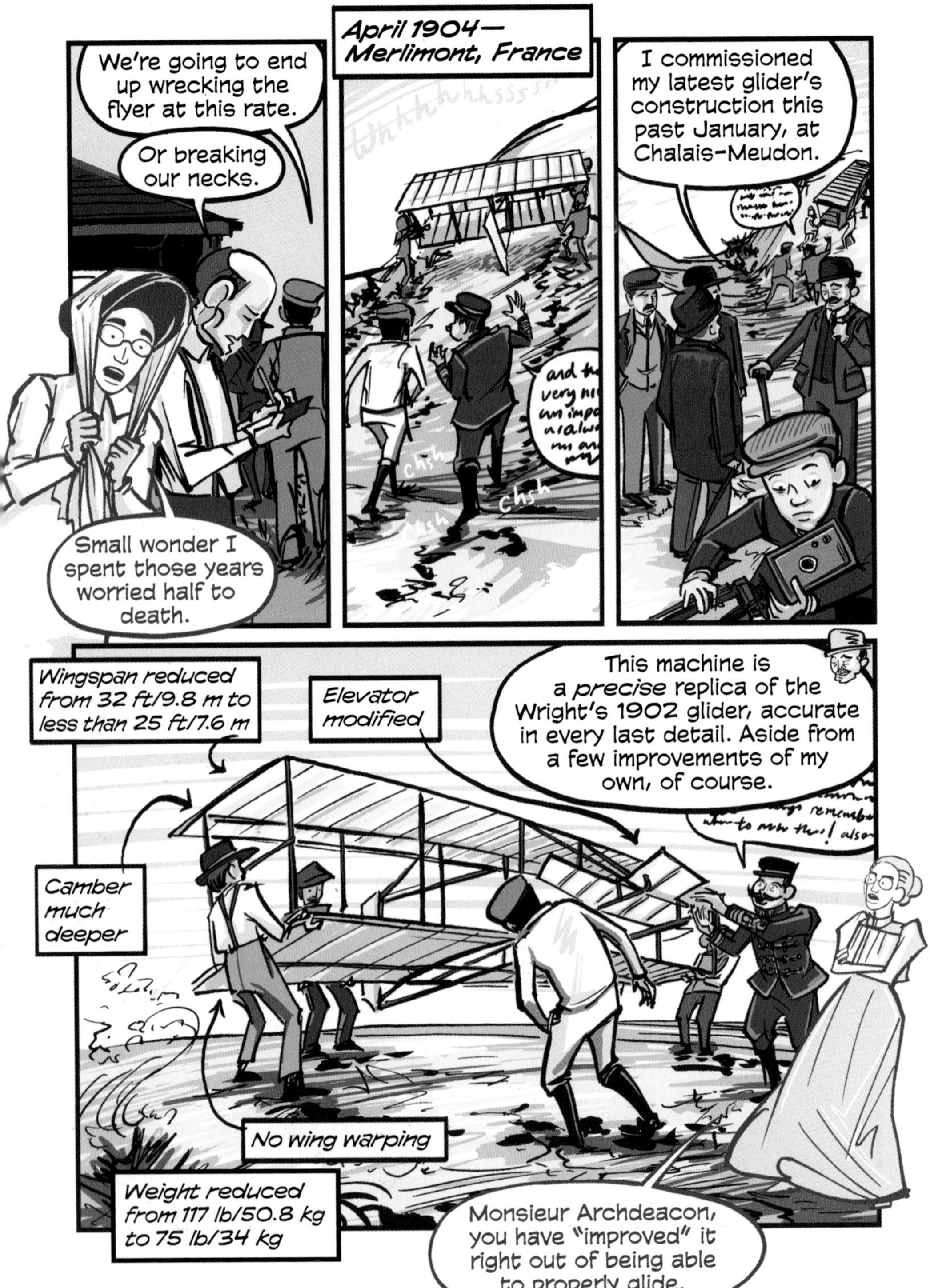
April 1904—
Merlimont, France
We're going to end up wrecking the flyer at this rate.
Or breaking our necks.
Small wonder I spent those years worried half to death.
Whhhhhhhsssss
Chsh
Chsh
I commissioned my latest glider's construction this past January, at Chalais-Meudon.
Wingspan reduced from 32 ft/9.8 m to less than 25 ft/7.6 m
Elevator modified
This machine is a *precise* replica of the Wright's 1902 glider, accurate in every last detail. Aside from a few improvements of my own, of course.
Camber much deeper
No wing warping
Weight reduced from 117 lb/50.8 kg to 75 lb/34 kg
Monsieur Archdeacon, you have "improved" it right out of being able to properly glide.

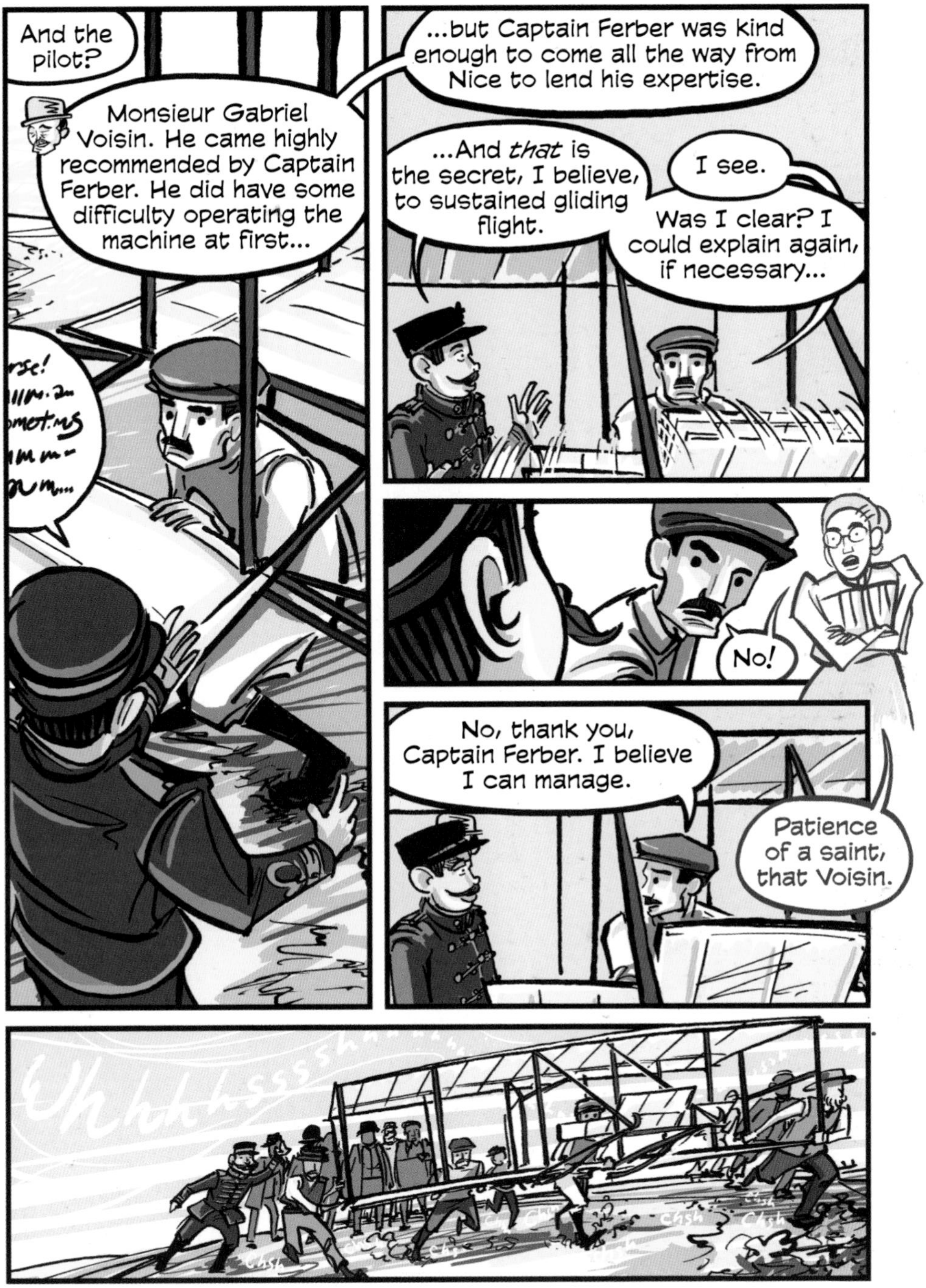
And the pilot?
Monsieur Gabriel Voisin. He came highly recommended by Captain Ferber. He did have some difficulty operating the machine at first...
...but Captain Ferber was kind enough to come all the way from Nice to lend his expertise.
...And *that* is the secret, I believe, to sustained gliding flight.
I see.
Was I clear? I could explain again, if necessary...
No!
No, thank you, Captain Ferber. I believe I can manage.
Patience of a saint, that Voisin.
Vhhhhsssssh

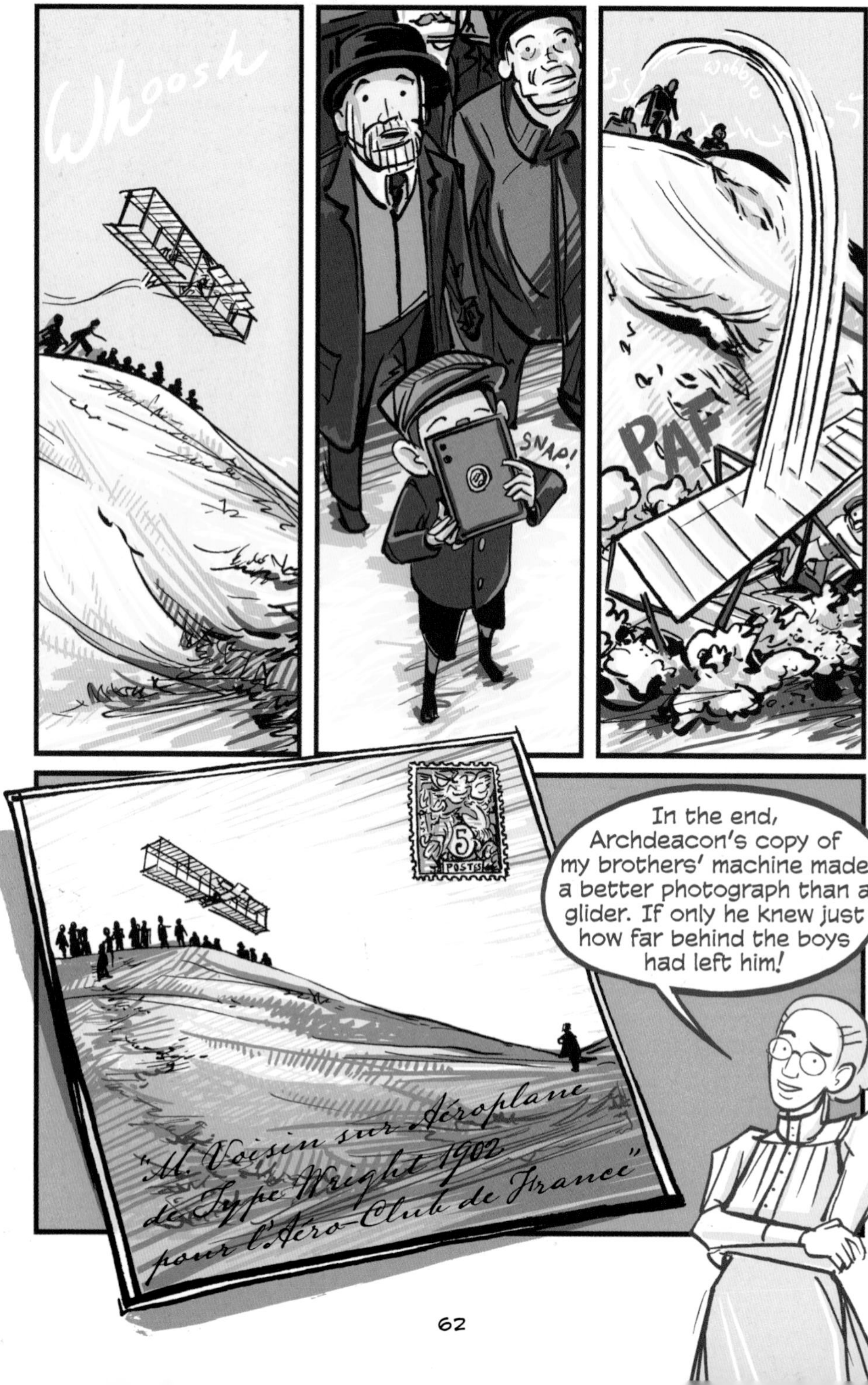
Whoosh
SNAP!
wobble
PAF
POSTES
5
In the end, Archdeacon's copy of my brothers' machine made a better photograph than a glider. If only he knew just how far behind the boys had left him!
"M. Voisin sur Aéroplane de Type Wright 1902 pour l'Aéro-Club de France"

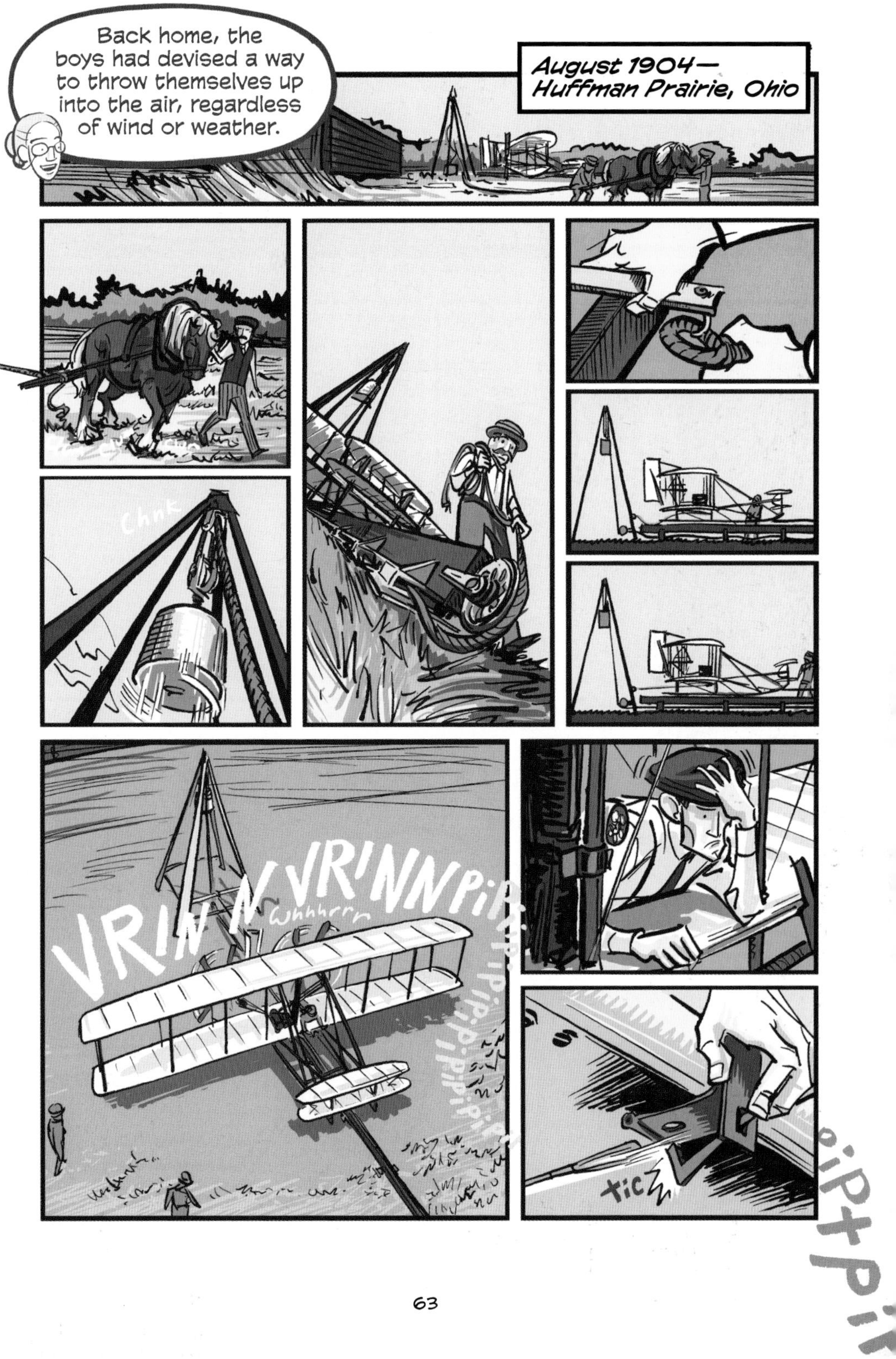
Back home, the boys had devised a way to throw themselves up into the air, regardless of wind or weather.
August 1904— Huffman Prairie, Ohio
Chnk
VRIN N VRINNN
whhhrrr
tic

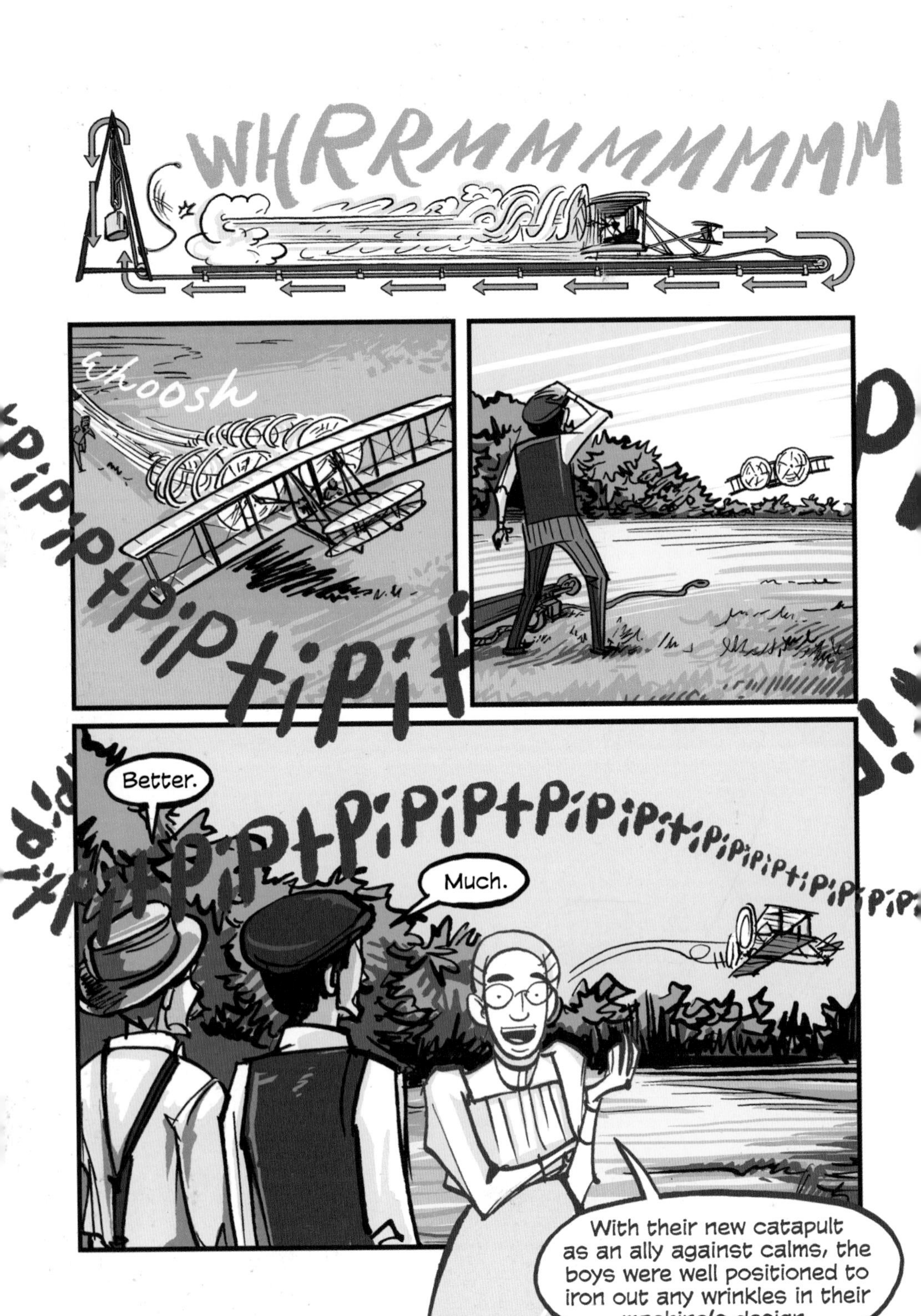
WHRRMMMMMMMMMM
whoosh
Better.
Much.
With their new catapult as an ally against calms, the boys were well positioned to iron out any wrinkles in their machine's design.

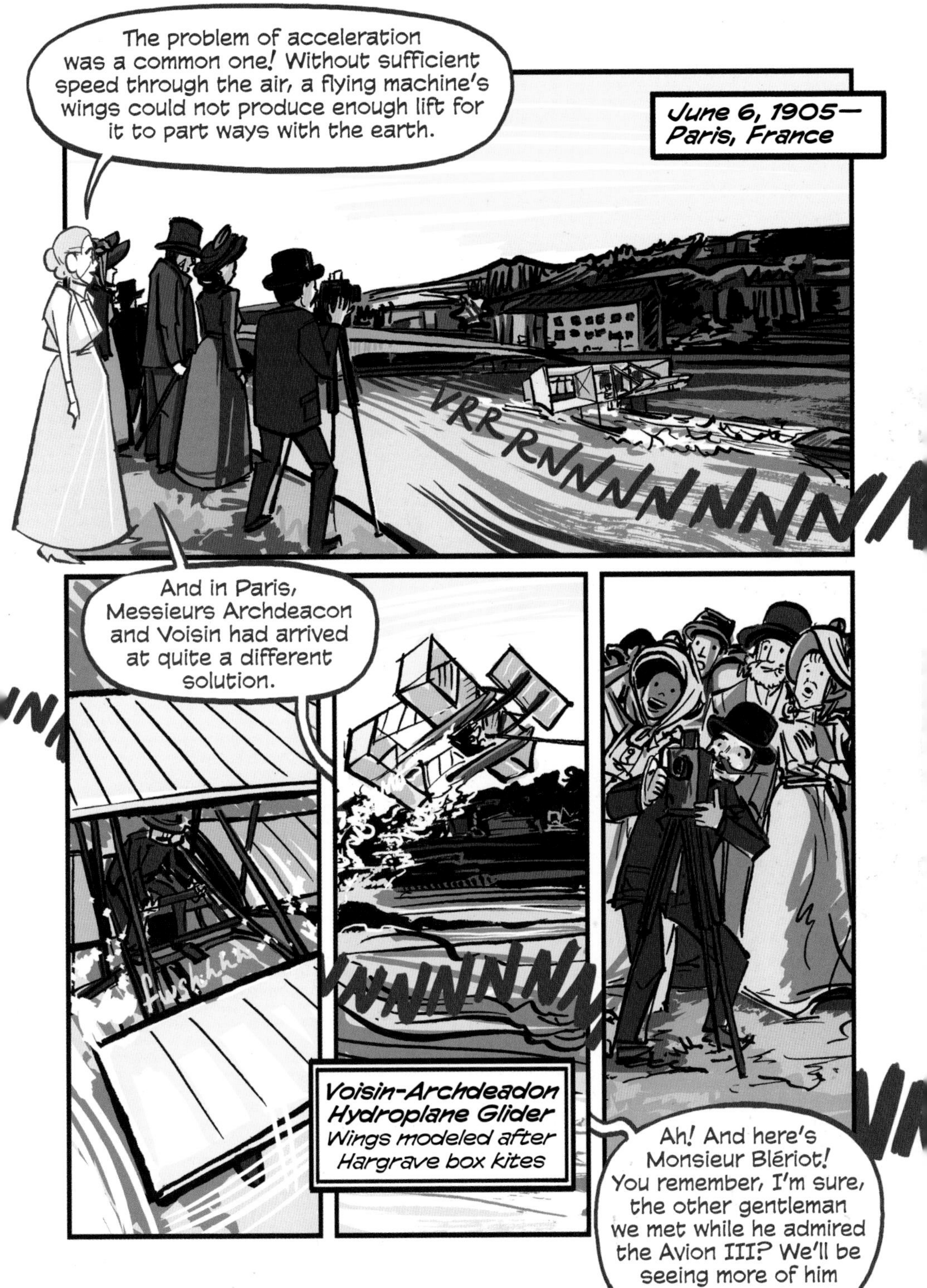

The problem of acceleration was a common one! Without sufficient speed through the air, a flying machine's wings could not produce enough lift for it to part ways with the earth.
June 6, 1905— Paris, France
VRRRRNNNNNNNNNN
And in Paris, Messieurs Archdeacon and Voisin had arrived at quite a different solution.
fwshhhh
NNNNNNN
Voisin-Archdeadon Hydroplane Glider
Wings modeled after Hargrave box kites
Ah! And here's Monsieur Blériot! You remember, I'm sure, the other gentleman we met while he admired the Avion III? We'll be seeing more of him soon enough....

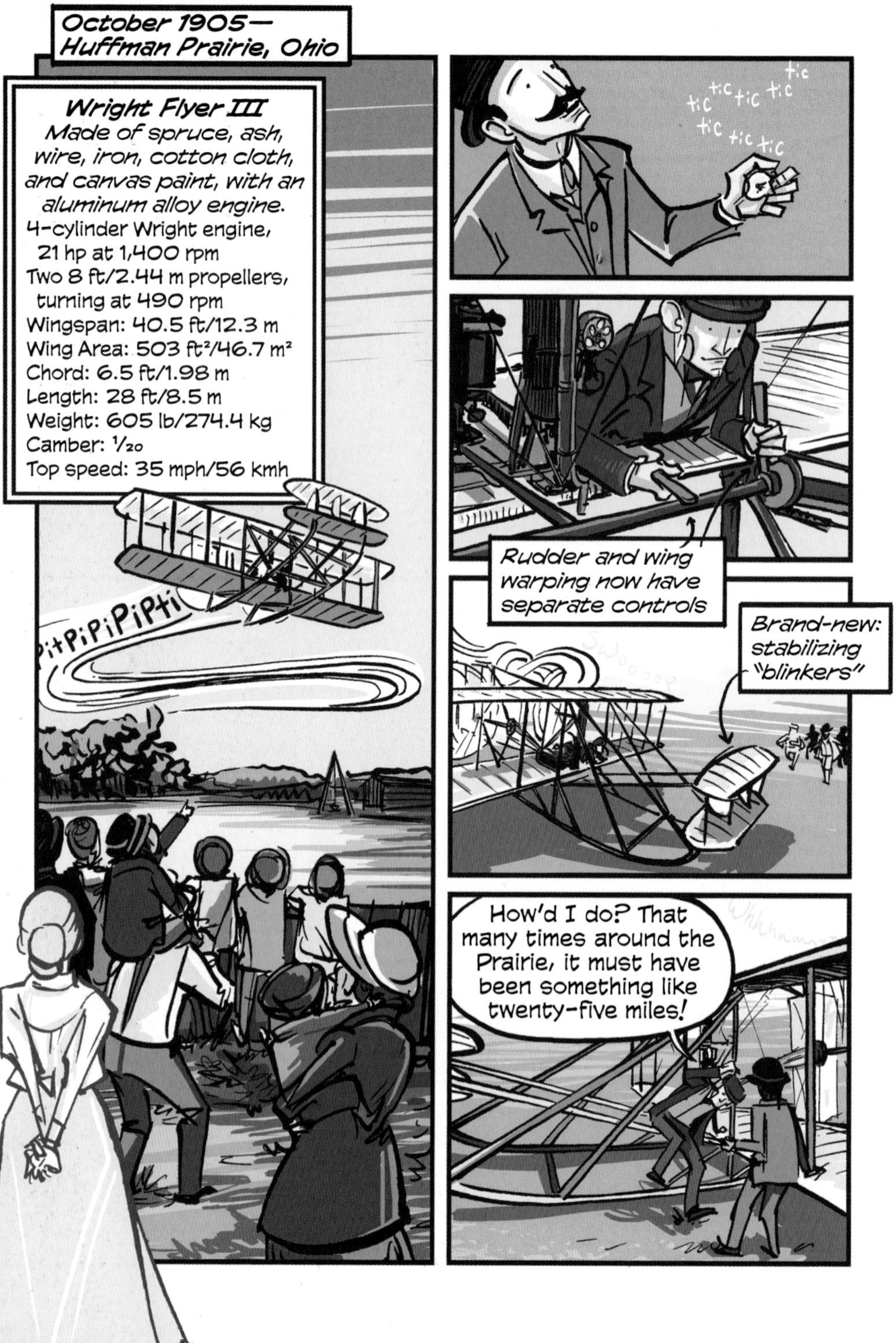

October 1905—
Huffman Prairie, Ohio
Wright Flyer III
Made of spruce, ash, wire, iron, cotton cloth, and canvas paint, with an aluminum alloy engine.
4-cylinder Wright engine, 21 hp at 1,400 rpm
Two 8 ft/2.44 m propellers, turning at 490 rpm
Wingspan: 40.5 ft/12.3 m
Wing Area: 503 ft²/46.7 m²
Chord: 6.5 ft/1.98 m
Length: 28 ft/8.5 m
Weight: 605 lb/274.4 kg
Camber: 1/20
Top speed: 35 mph/56 kmh
PitPiPiPiPti
tic tic tic tic tic tic tic tic
Rudder and wing warping now have separate controls
Brand-new: stabilizing "blinkers"
How'd I do? That many times around the Prairie, it must have been something like twenty-five miles!

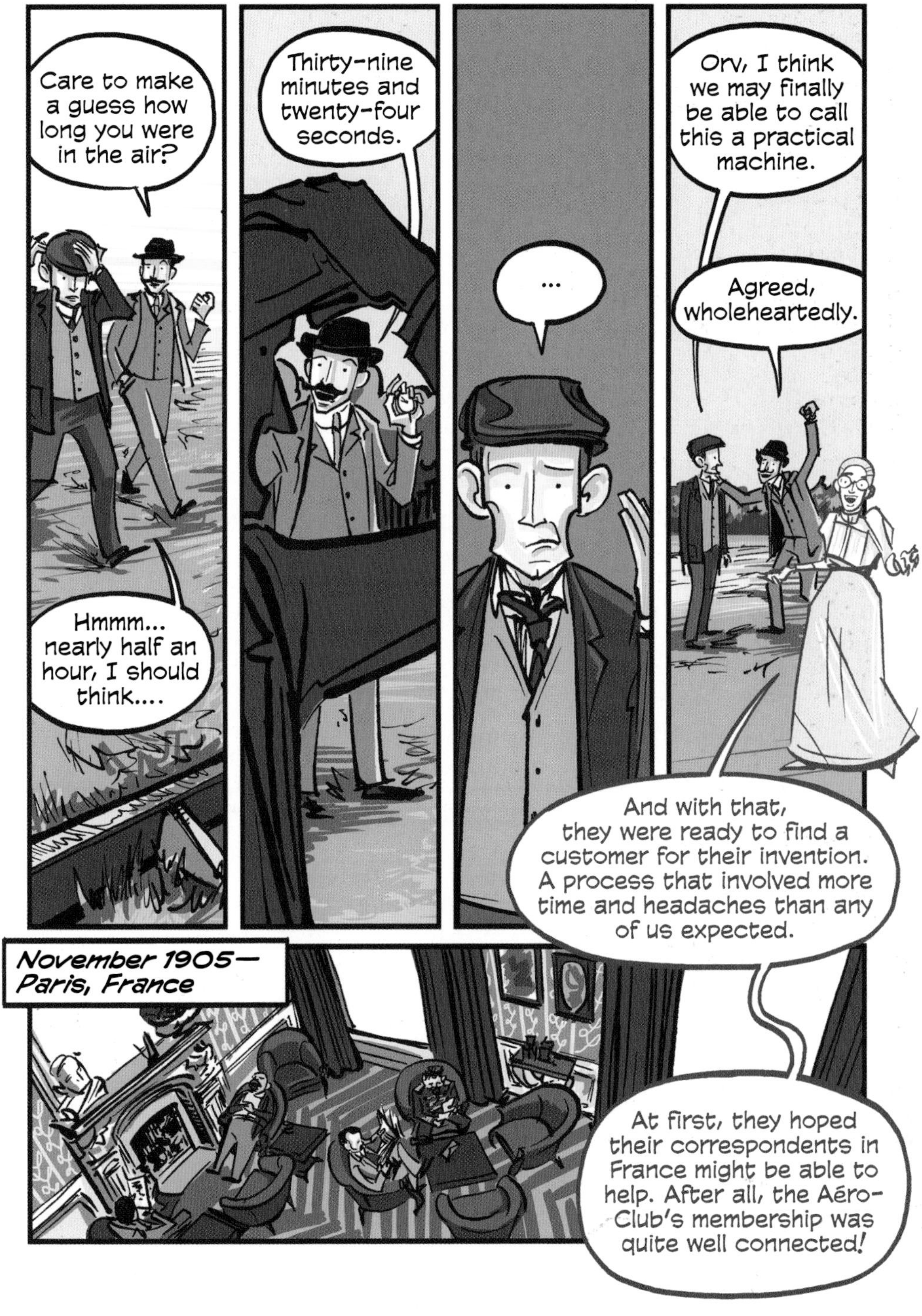
Care to make a guess how long you were in the air?
Hmmm... nearly half an hour, I should think....
Thirty-nine minutes and twenty-four seconds.
...
Orv, I think we may finally be able to call this a practical machine.
Agreed, wholeheartedly.
And with that, they were ready to find a customer for their invention. A process that involved more time and headaches than any of us expected.
November 1905—Paris, France
At first, they hoped their correspondents in France might be able to help. After all, the Aéro-Club's membership was quite well connected!

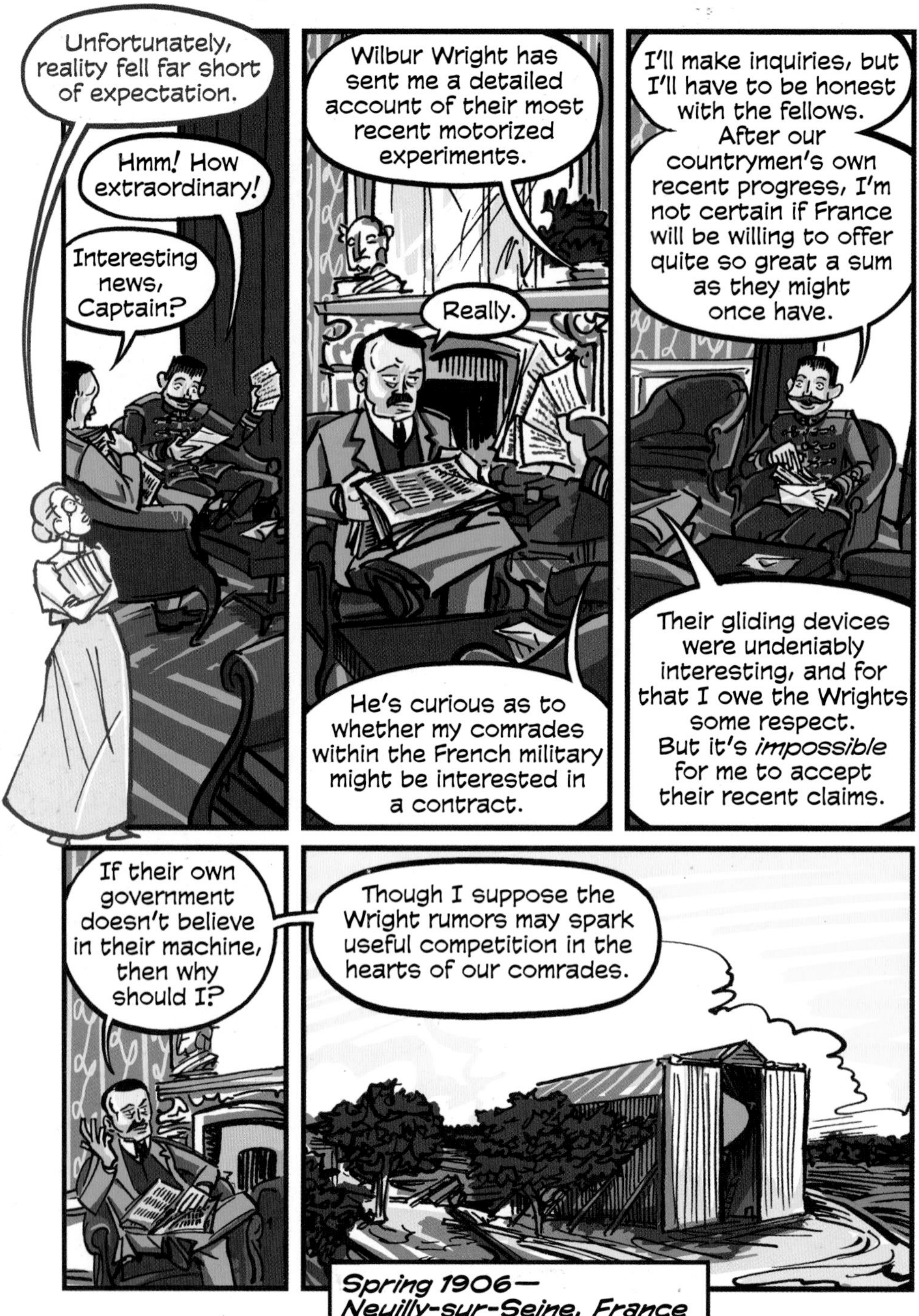
Unfortunately, reality fell far short of expectation.
Hmm! How extraordinary!
Interesting news, Captain?
Wilbur Wright has sent me a detailed account of their most recent motorized experiments.
Really.
He's curious as to whether my comrades within the French military might be interested in a contract.
I'll make inquiries, but I'll have to be honest with the fellows. After our countrymen's own recent progress, I'm not certain if France will be willing to offer quite so great a sum as they might once have.
Their gliding devices were undeniably interesting, and for that I owe the Wrights some respect. But it's *impossible* for me to accept their recent claims.
If their own government doesn't believe in their machine, then why should I?
Though I suppose the Wright rumors may spark useful competition in the hearts of our comrades.
Spring 1906—
Neuilly-sur-Seine, France

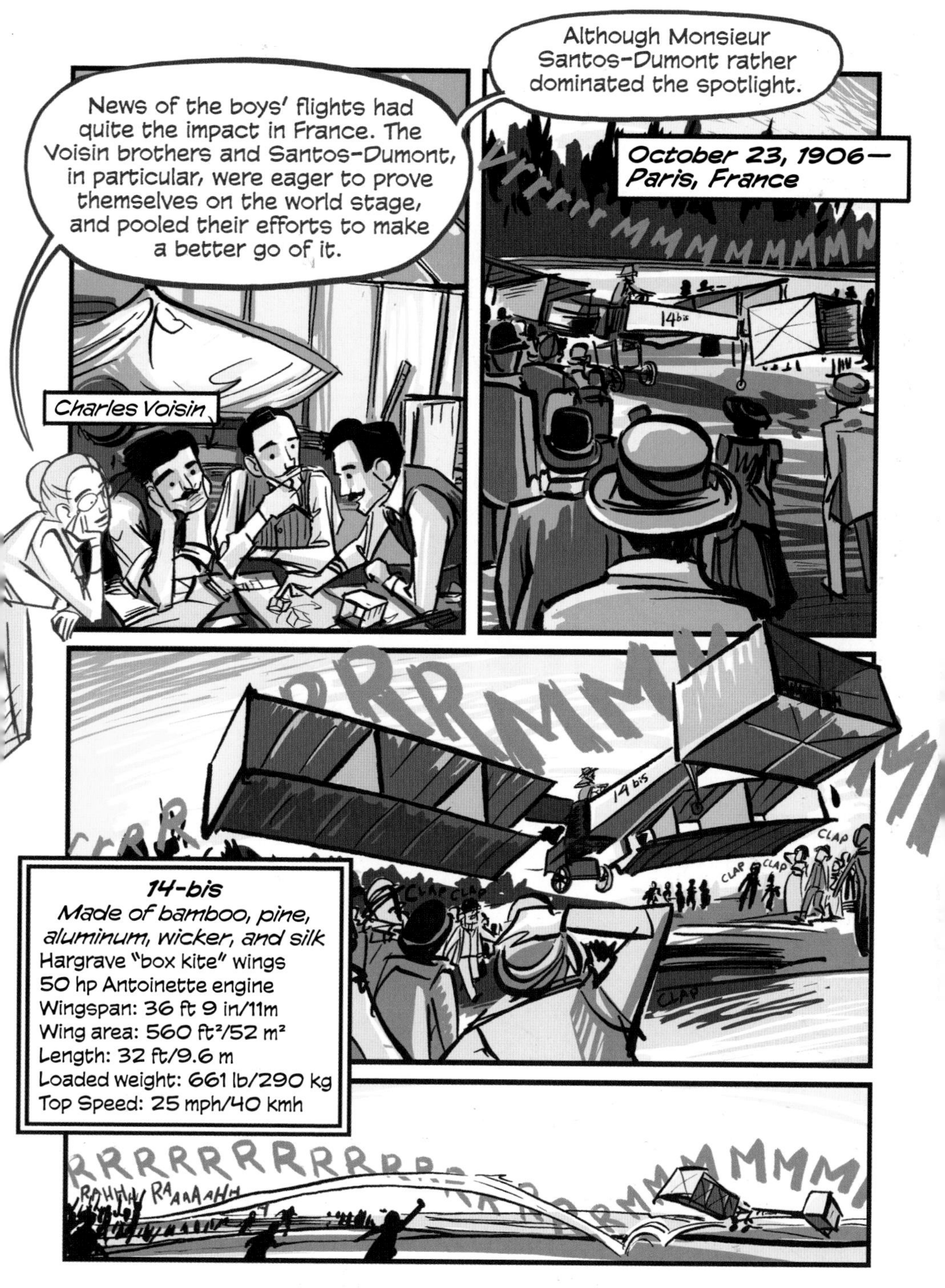
News of the boys' flights had quite the impact in France. The Voisin brothers and Santos-Dumont, in particular, were eager to prove themselves on the world stage, and pooled their efforts to make a better go of it.
Charles Voisin
Although Monsieur Santos-Dumont rather dominated the spotlight.
October 23, 1906—Paris, France
VRRRRRMMMMMMMMMN
14 bis
RRRMMMMM
CRRR
14 bis
CLAP CLAP
CLAP
CLAP
CLAP
CLAP
14-bis
Made of bamboo, pine, aluminum, wicker, and silk
Hargrave "box kite" wings
50 hp Antoinette engine
Wingspan: 36 ft 9 in/11m
Wing area: 560 ft²/52 m²
Length: 32 ft/9.6 m
Loaded weight: 661 lb/290 kg
Top Speed: 25 mph/40 kmh
RRRRRRRRRRRRRRRRRRMMMMMMM
RAHHH RAAAAAHH

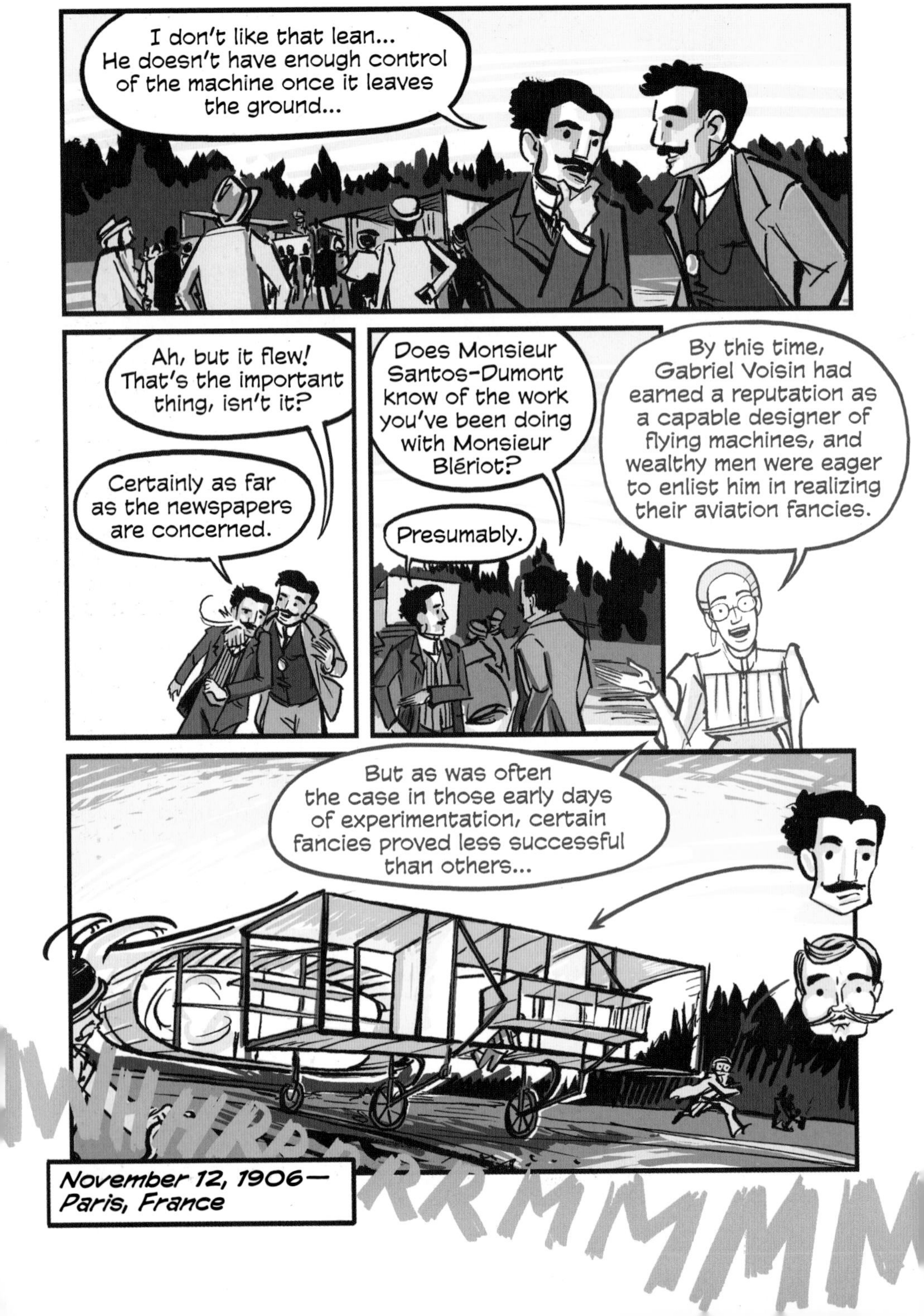
I don't like that lean... He doesn't have enough control of the machine once it leaves the ground...
Ah, but it flew! That's the important thing, isn't it?
Certainly as far as the newspapers are concerned.
Does Monsieur Santos-Dumont know of the work you've been doing with Monsieur Blériot?
Presumably.
By this time, Gabriel Voisin had earned a reputation as a capable designer of flying machines, and wealthy men were eager to enlist him in realizing their aviation fancies.
But as was often the case in those early days of experimentation, certain fancies proved less successful than others...
November 12, 1906— Paris, France

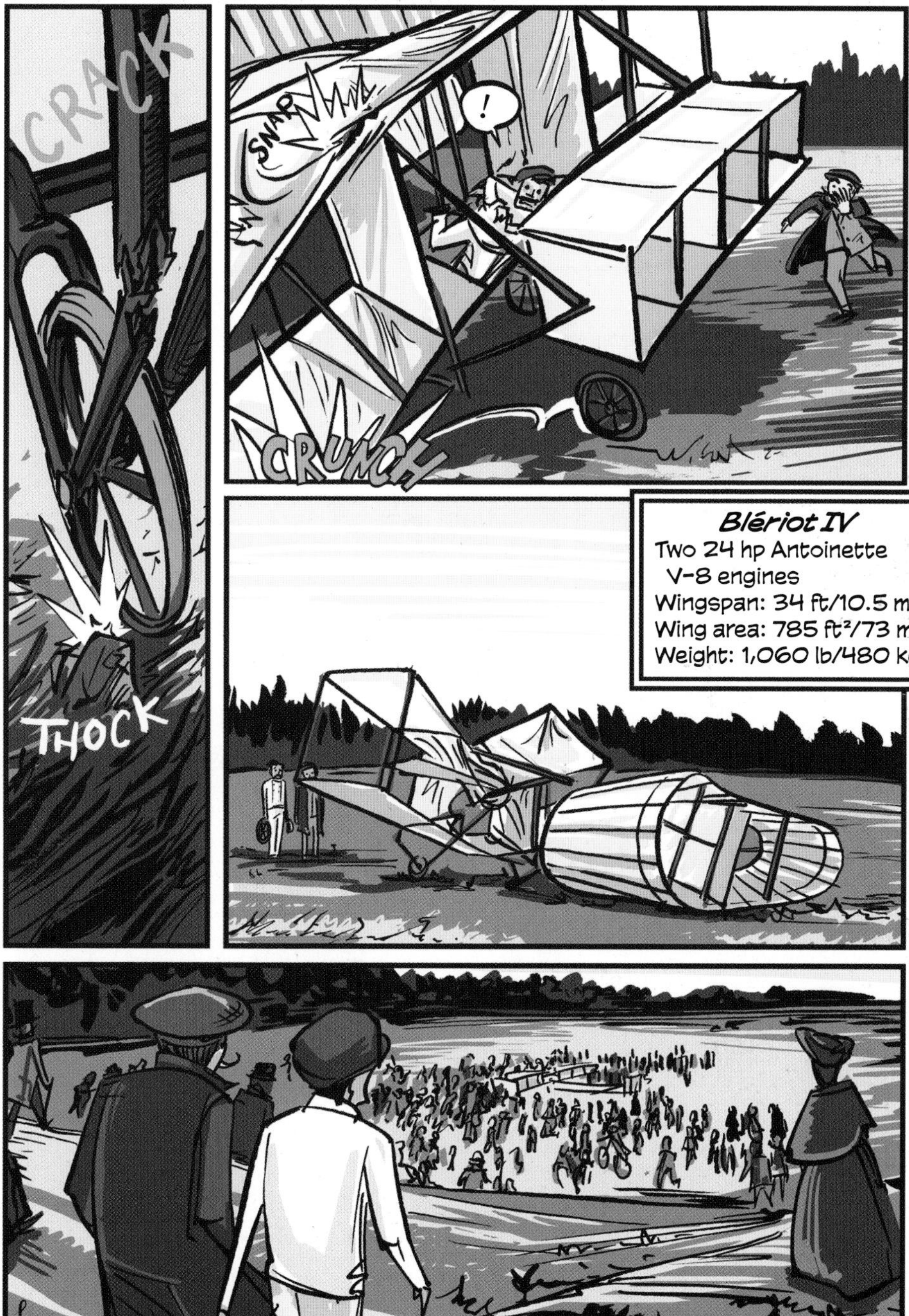
CRACK
SNAP
!
CRUNCH
Blériot IV
Two 24 hp Antoinette
V-8 engines
Wingspan: 34 ft/10.5 m
Wing area: 785 ft²/73 m²
Weight: 1,060 lb/480 kg
THOCK

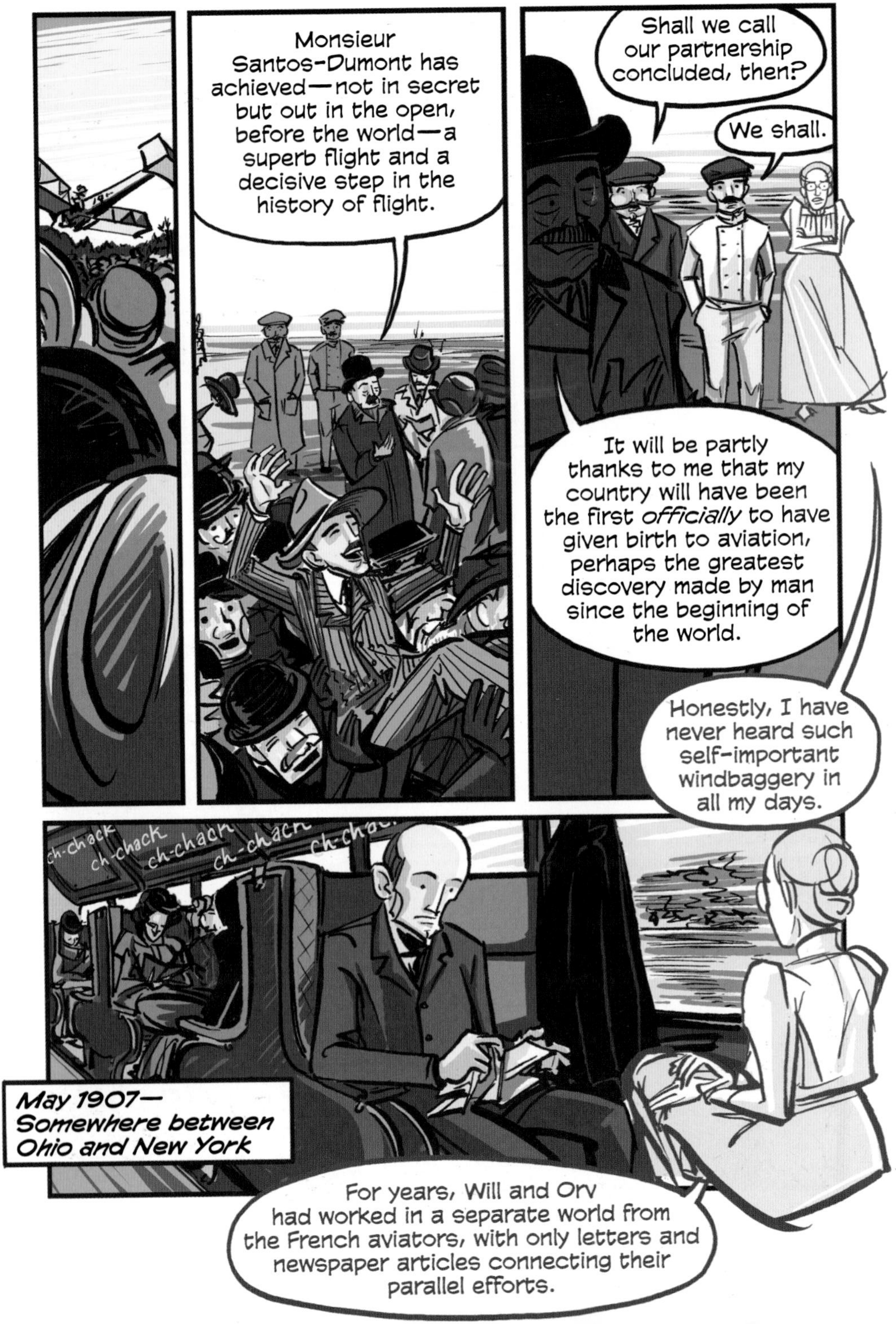
Monsieur Santos-Dumont has achieved—not in secret but out in the open, before the world—a superb flight and a decisive step in the history of flight.
Shall we call our partnership concluded, then?
We shall.
It will be partly thanks to me that my country will have been the first *officially* to have given birth to aviation, perhaps the greatest discovery made by man since the beginning of the world.
Honestly, I have never heard such self-important windbaggery in all my days.
ch-chack
ch-chack
May 1907— Somewhere between Ohio and New York
For years, Will and Orv had worked in a separate world from the French aviators, with only letters and newspaper articles connecting their parallel efforts.

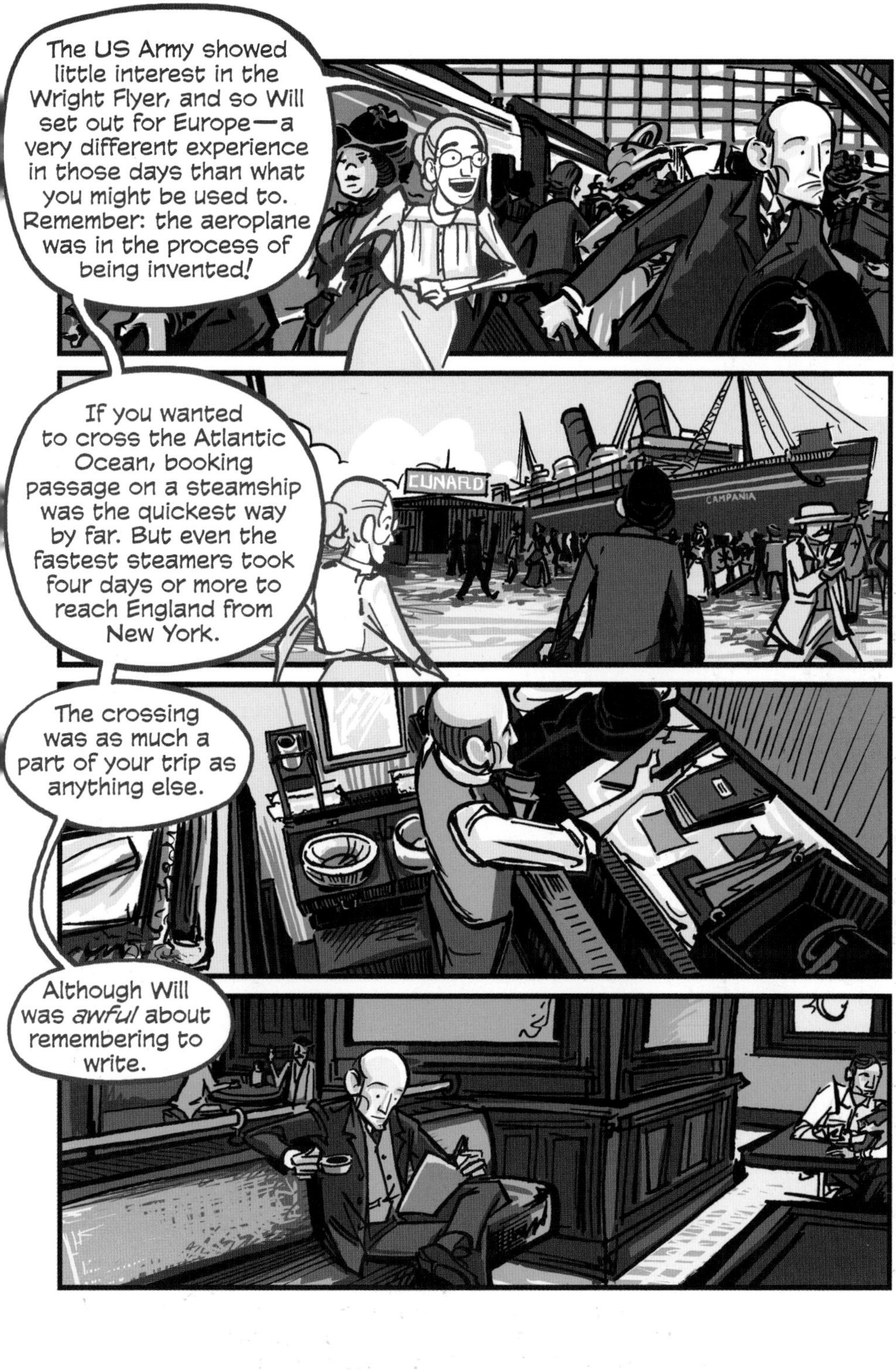
The US Army showed little interest in the Wright Flyer, and so Will set out for Europe—a very different experience in those days than what you might be used to. Remember: the aeroplane was in the process of being invented!
If you wanted to cross the Atlantic Ocean, booking passage on a steamship was the quickest way by far. But even the fastest steamers took four days or more to reach England from New York.
CUNARD
CAMPANIA
The crossing was as much a part of your trip as anything else.
Although Will was *awful* about remembering to write.

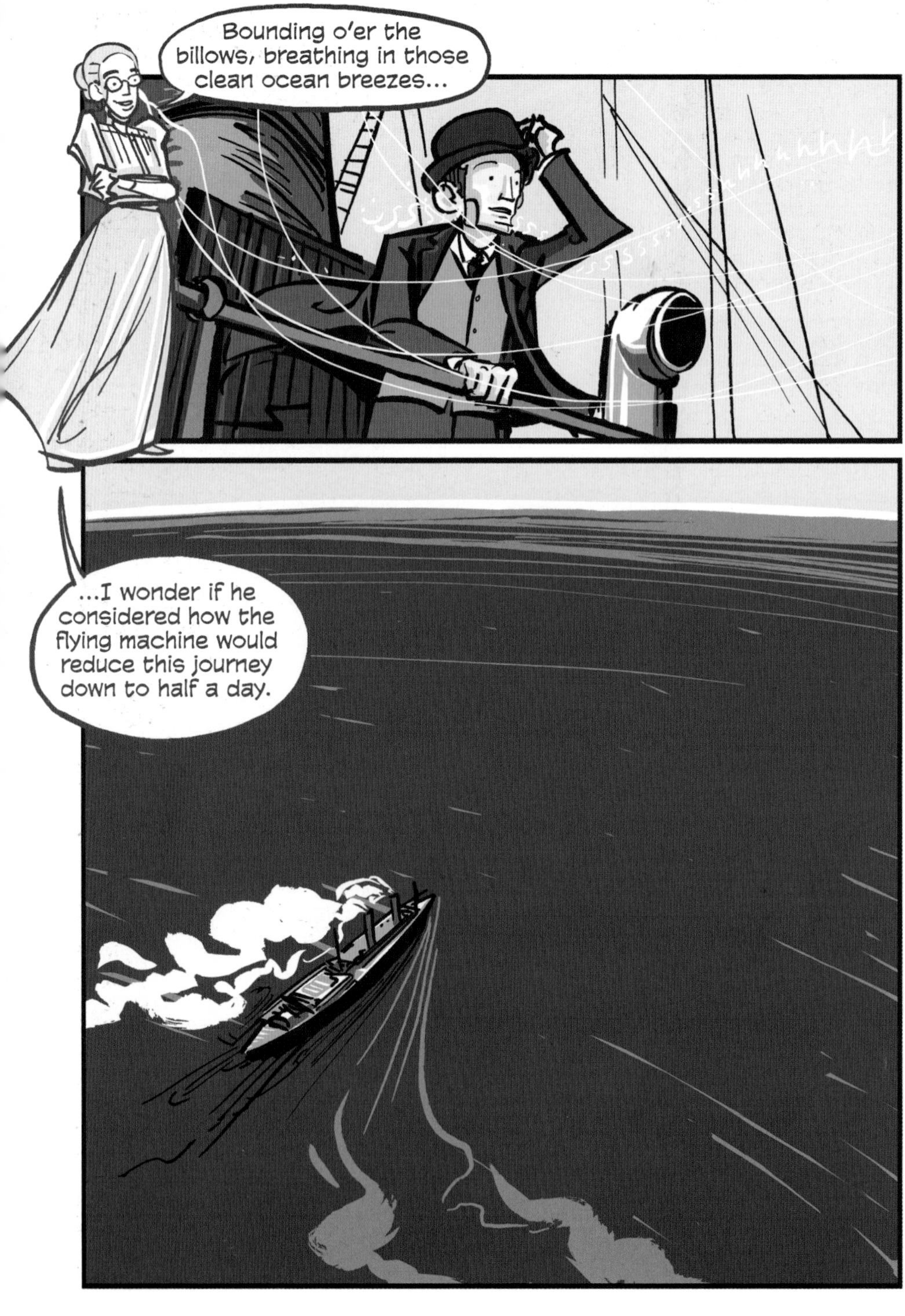
Bounding o'er the billows, breathing in those clean ocean breezes...
...I wonder if he considered how the flying machine would reduce this journey down to half a day.

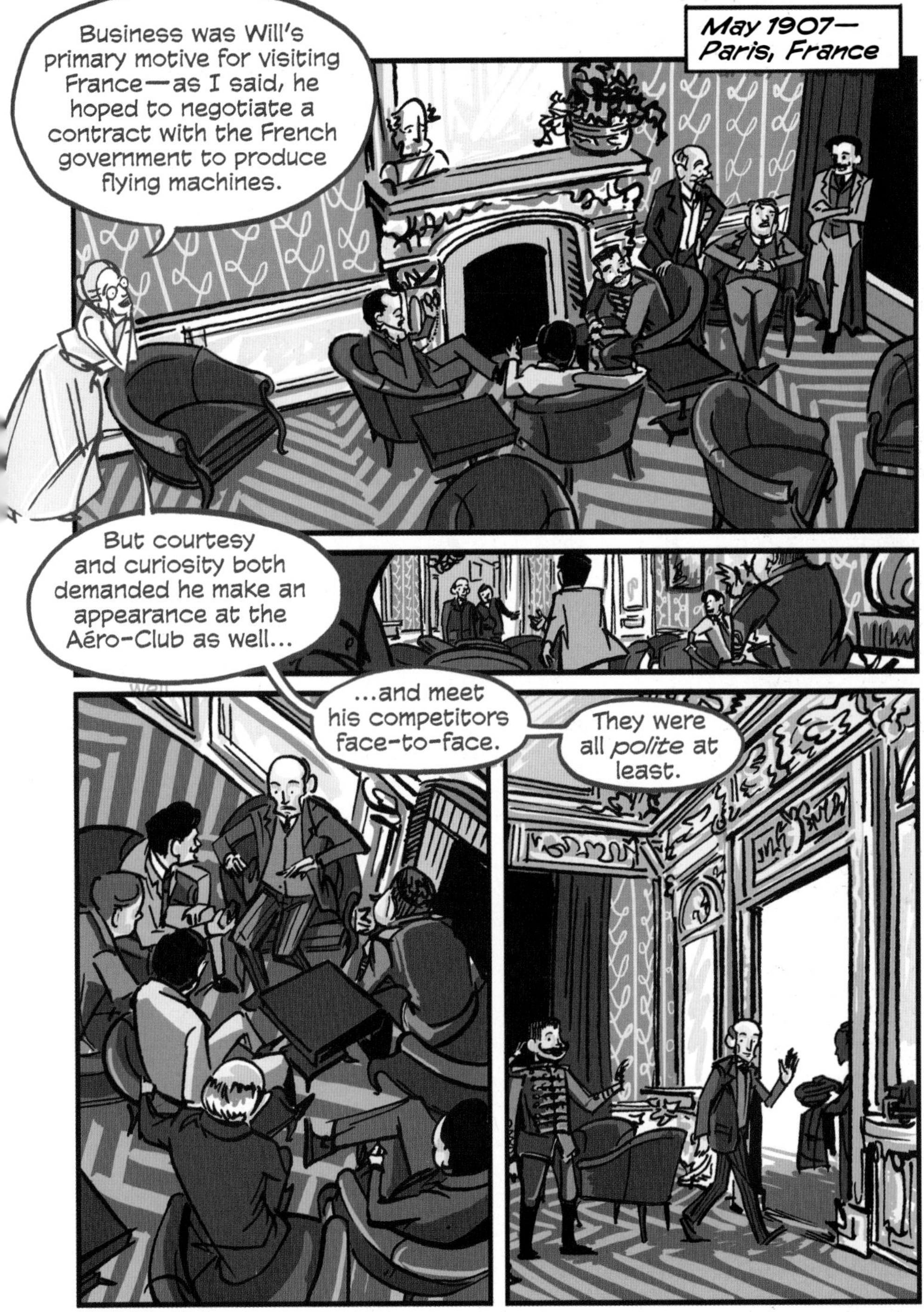
May 1907—Paris, France
Business was Will's primary motive for visiting France—as I said, he hoped to negotiate a contract with the French government to produce flying machines.
But courtesy and curiosity both demanded he make an appearance at the Aéro-Club as well...
...and meet his competitors face-to-face.
They were all *polite* at least.

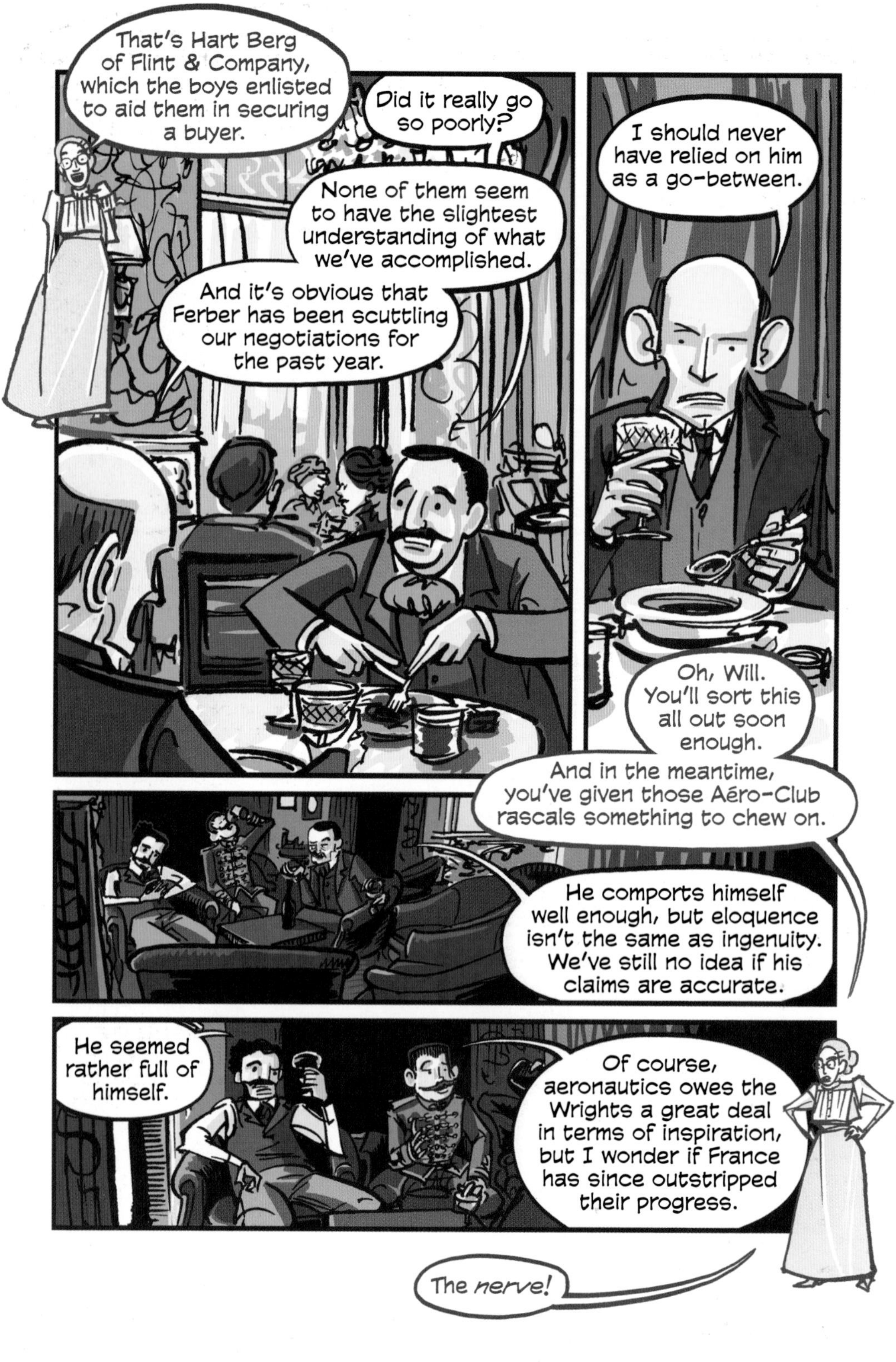
That's Hart Berg of Flint & Company, which the boys enlisted to aid them in securing a buyer.
Did it really go so poorly?
None of them seem to have the slightest understanding of what we've accomplished.
And it's obvious that Ferber has been scuttling our negotiations for the past year.
I should never have relied on him as a go-between.
Oh, Will. You'll sort this all out soon enough.
And in the meantime, you've given those Aéro-Club rascals something to chew on.
He comports himself well enough, but eloquence isn't the same as ingenuity. We've still no idea if his claims are accurate.
He seemed rather full of himself.
Of course, aeronautics owes the Wrights a great deal in terms of inspiration, but I wonder if France has since outstripped their progress.
The *nerve!*

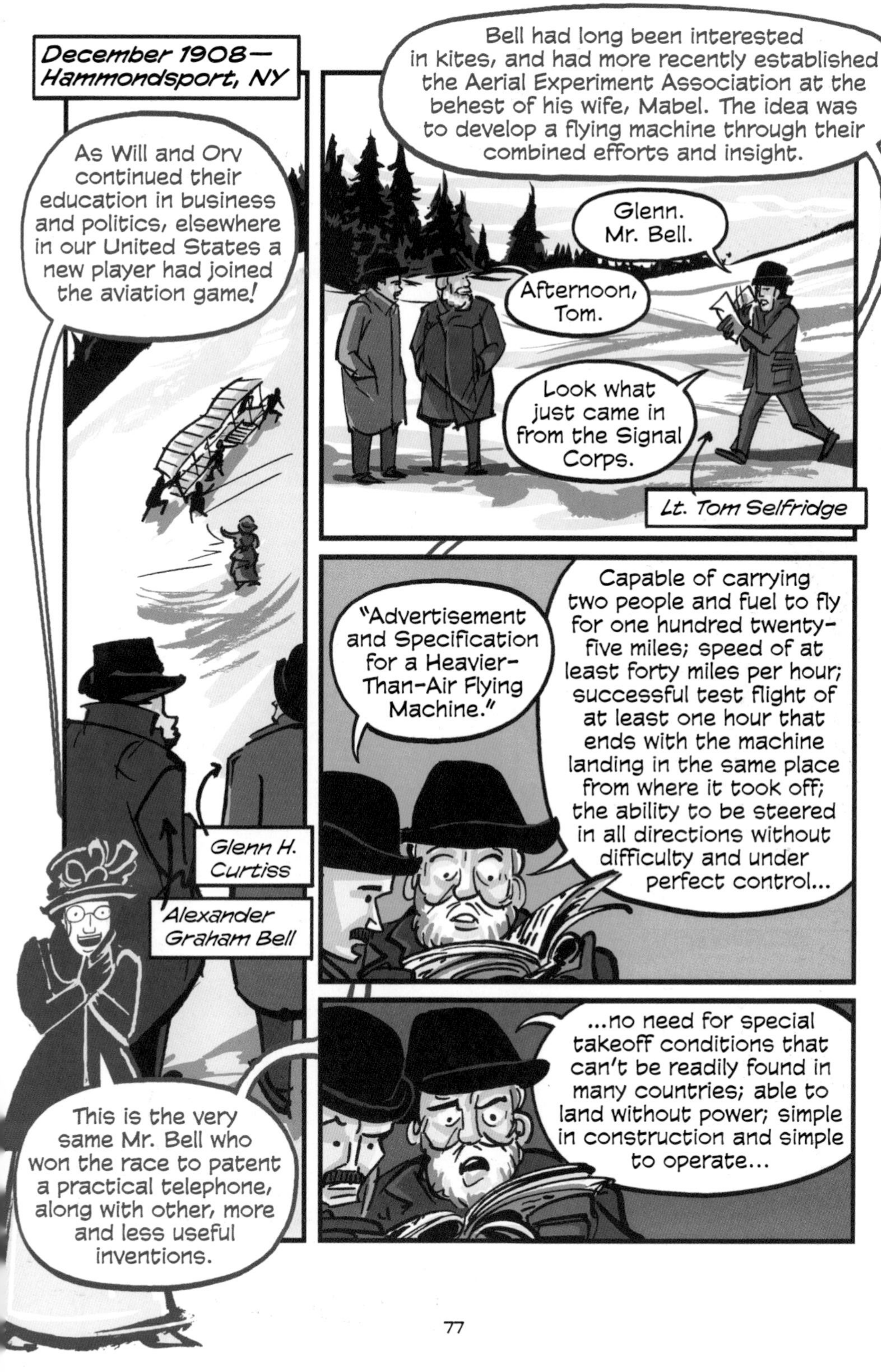
December 1908—Hammondsport, NY
As Will and Orv continued their education in business and politics, elsewhere in our United States a new player had joined the aviation game!
Glenn H. Curtiss
Alexander Graham Bell
This is the very same Mr. Bell who won the race to patent a practical telephone, along with other, more and less useful inventions.
Bell had long been interested in kites, and had more recently established the Aerial Experiment Association at the behest of his wife, Mabel. The idea was to develop a flying machine through their combined efforts and insight.
Glenn. Mr. Bell.
Afternoon, Tom.
Look what just came in from the Signal Corps.
Lt. Tom Selfridge
"Advertisement and Specification for a Heavier-Than-Air Flying Machine."
Capable of carrying two people and fuel to fly for one hundred twenty-five miles; speed of at least forty miles per hour; successful test flight of at least one hour that ends with the machine landing in the same place from where it took off; the ability to be steered in all directions without difficulty and under perfect control...
...no need for special takeoff conditions that can't be readily found in many countries; able to land without power; simple in construction and simple to operate...

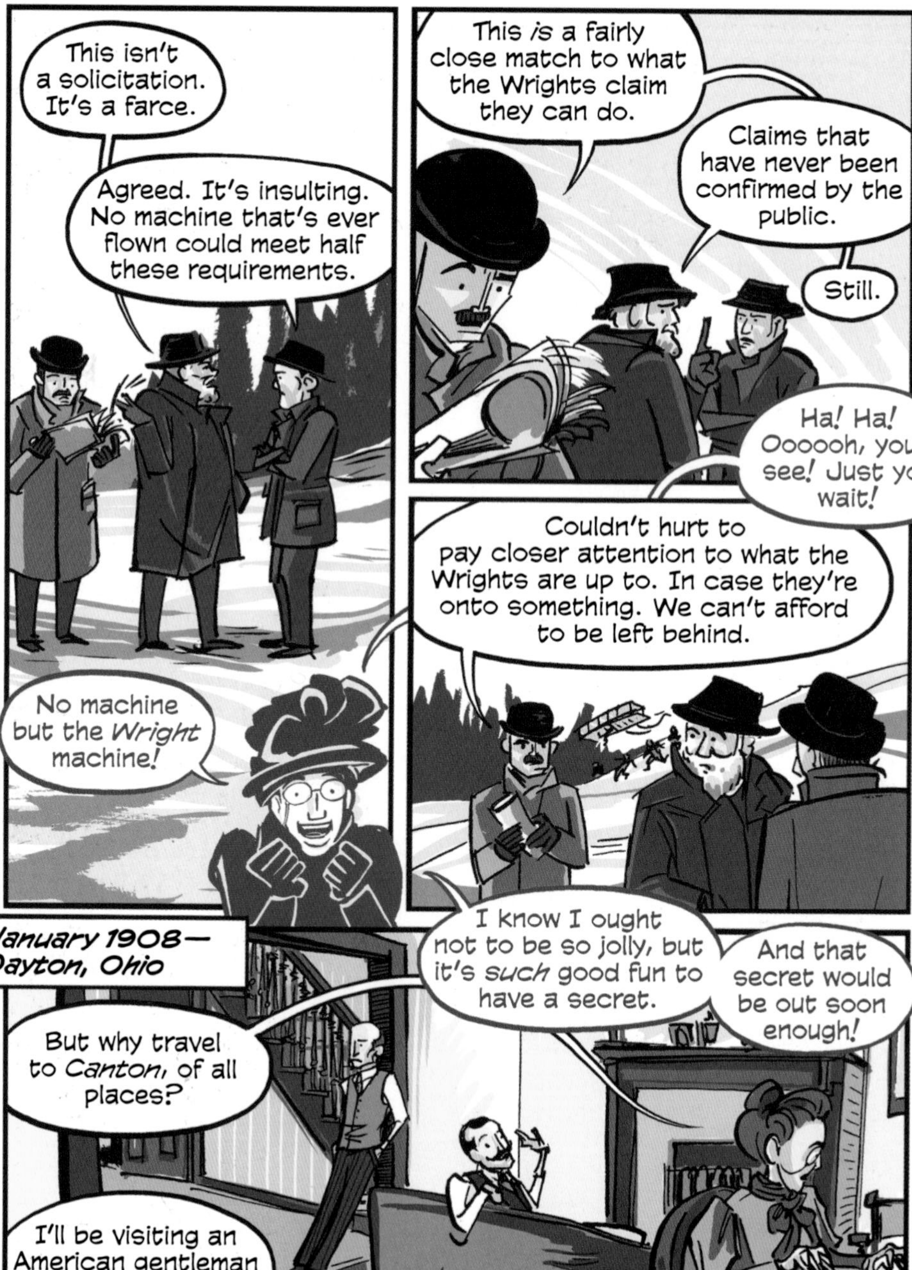
This isn't a solicitation. It's a farce.
Agreed. It's insulting. No machine that's ever flown could meet half these requirements.
No machine but the *Wright* machine!
This *is* a fairly close match to what the Wrights claim they can do.
Claims that have never been confirmed by the public.
Still.
Ha! Ha! Oooooh, you'll see! Just you wait!
Couldn't hurt to pay closer attention to what the Wrights are up to. In case they're onto something. We can't afford to be left behind.
January 1908— Dayton, Ohio
I know I ought not to be so jolly, but it's *such* good fun to have a secret.
And that secret would be out soon enough!
But why travel to *Canton*, of all places?
I'll be visiting an American gentleman we met in France. A Lt. Frank Lahm.

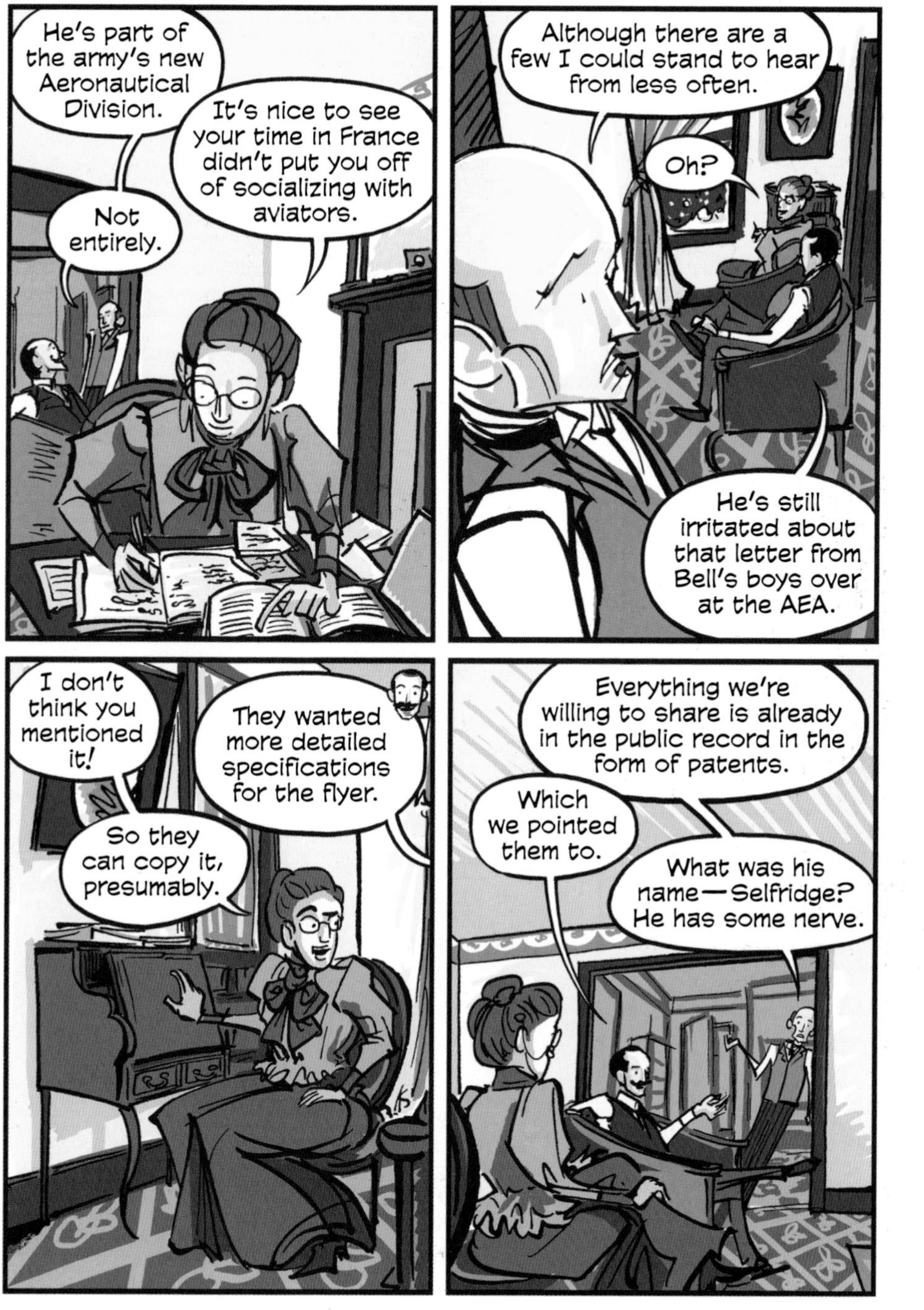
He's part of the army's new Aeronautical Division.
Not entirely.
It's nice to see your time in France didn't put you off of socializing with aviators.
Although there are a few I could stand to hear from less often.
Oh?
He's still irritated about that letter from Bell's boys over at the AEA.
I don't think you mentioned it!
They wanted more detailed specifications for the flyer.
So they can copy it, presumably.
Everything we're willing to share is already in the public record in the form of patents.
Which we pointed them to.
What was his name—Selfridge? He has some nerve.

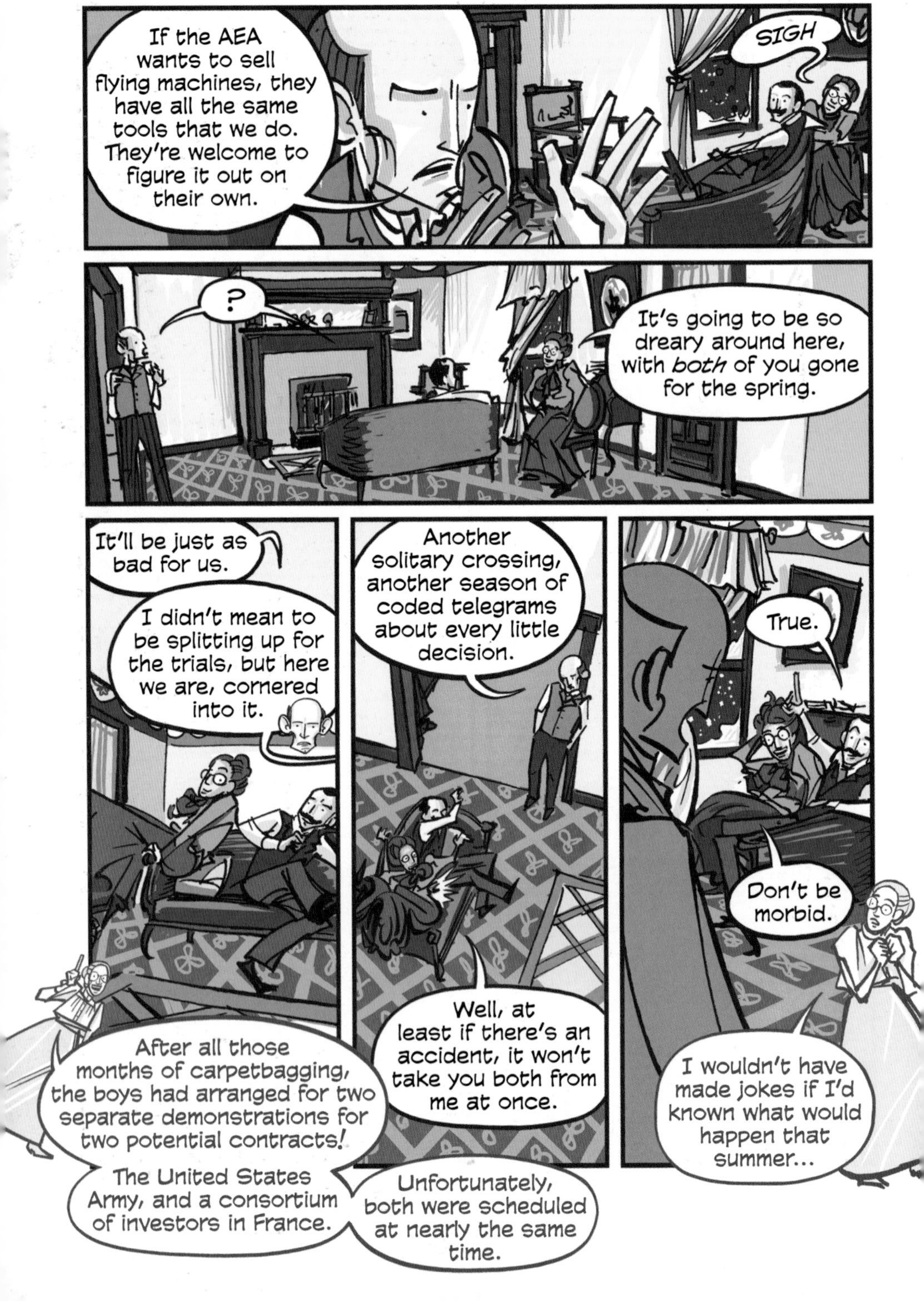
If the AEA wants to sell flying machines, they have all the same tools that we do. They're welcome to figure it out on their own.
SIGH
?
It's going to be so dreary around here, with *both* of you gone for the spring.
It'll be just as bad for us.
I didn't mean to be splitting up for the trials, but here we are, cornered into it.
Another solitary crossing, another season of coded telegrams about every little decision.
True.
Don't be morbid.
After all those months of carpetbagging, the boys had arranged for two separate demonstrations for two potential contracts!
The United States Army, and a consortium of investors in France.
Well, at least if there's an accident, it won't take you both from me at once.
Unfortunately, both were scheduled at nearly the same time.
I wouldn't have made jokes if I'd known what would happen that summer...

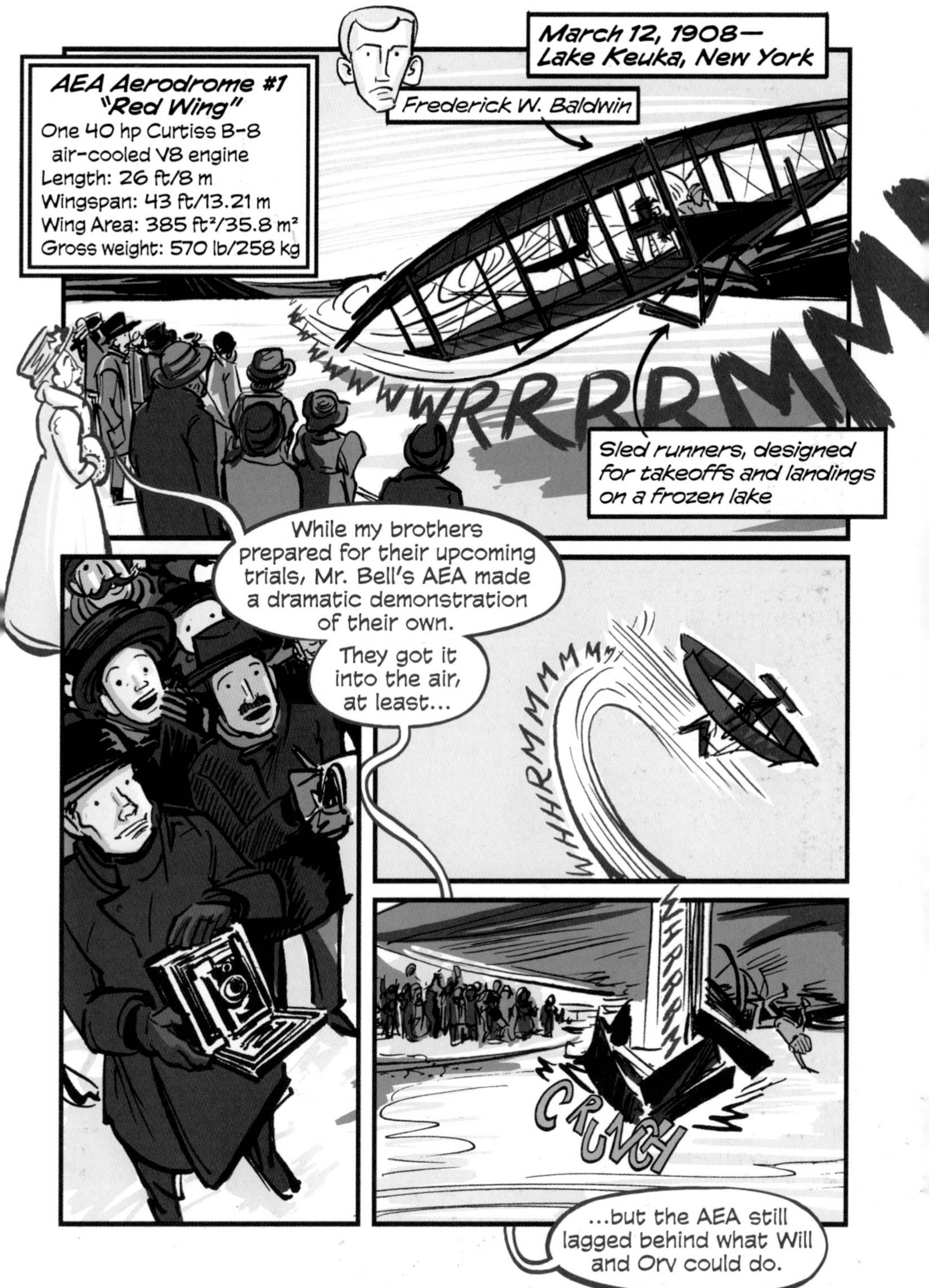

AEA Aerodrome #1 "Red Wing"
One 40 hp Curtiss B-8 air-cooled V8 engine
Length: 26 ft/8 m
Wingspan: 43 ft/13.21 m
Wing Area: 385 ft²/35.8 m²
Gross weight: 570 lb/258 kg
March 12, 1908— Lake Keuka, New York
Frederick W. Baldwin
WWWWWWWRRRRRMMM
Sled runners, designed for takeoffs and landings on a frozen lake
While my brothers prepared for their upcoming trials, Mr. Bell's AEA made a dramatic demonstration of their own.
They got it into the air, at least...
WHHRMMMMMMM
WHRRRM
CRUNCH
...but the AEA still lagged behind what Will and Orv could do.

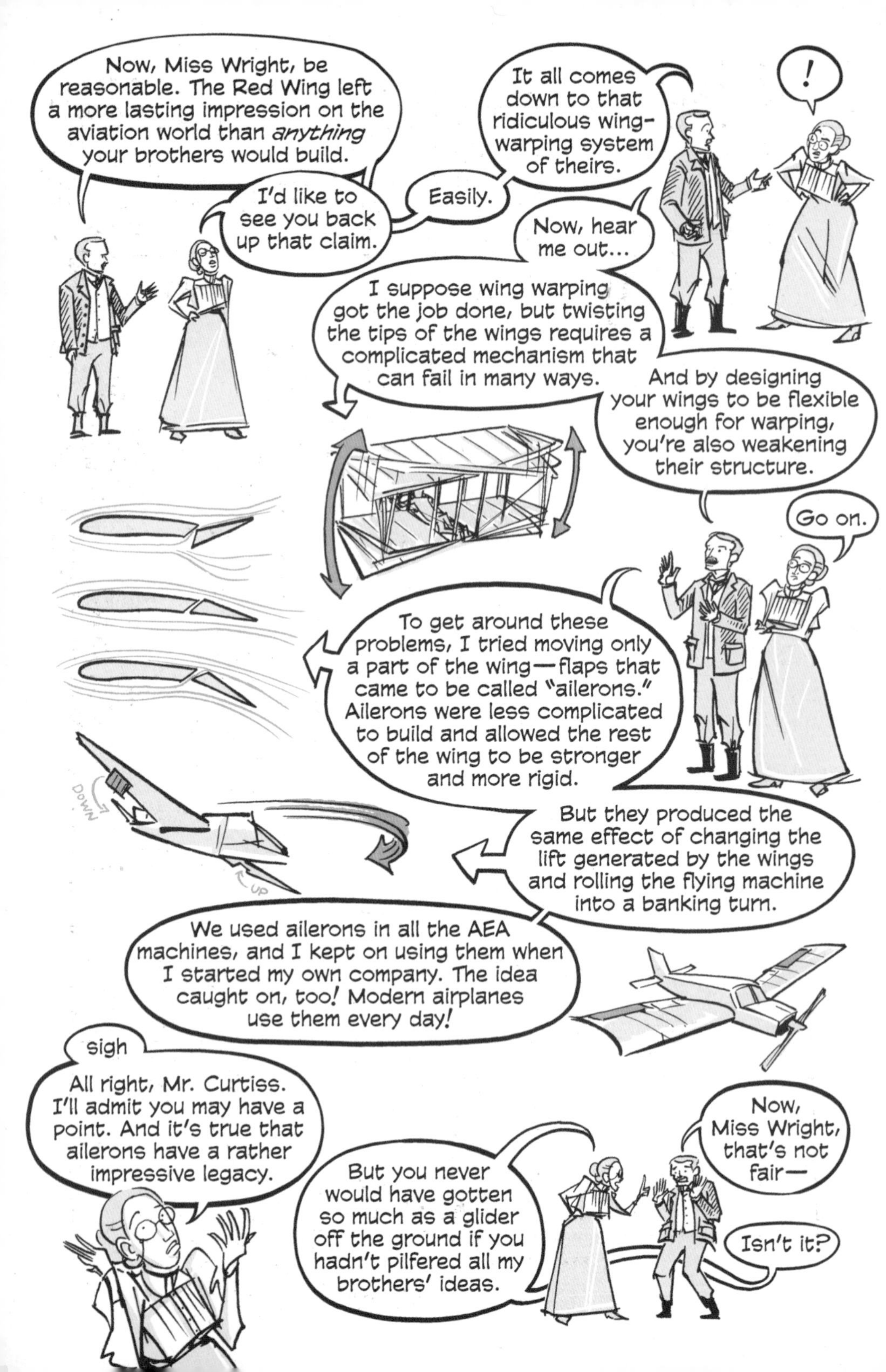

Now, Miss Wright, be reasonable. The Red Wing left a more lasting impression on the aviation world than *anything* your brothers would build.
I'd like to see you back up that claim.
Easily.
It all comes down to that ridiculous wing-warping system of theirs.
!
Now, hear me out...
I suppose wing warping got the job done, but twisting the tips of the wings requires a complicated mechanism that can fail in many ways.
And by designing your wings to be flexible enough for warping, you're also weakening their structure.
Go on.
To get around these problems, I tried moving only a part of the wing—flaps that came to be called "ailerons." Ailerons were less complicated to build and allowed the rest of the wing to be stronger and more rigid.
DOWN
UP
But they produced the same effect of changing the lift generated by the wings and rolling the flying machine into a banking turn.
We used ailerons in all the AEA machines, and I kept on using them when I started my own company. The idea caught on, too! Modern airplanes use them every day!
sigh
All right, Mr. Curtiss. I'll admit you may have a point. And it's true that ailerons have a rather impressive legacy.
But you never would have gotten so much as a glider off the ground if you hadn't pilfered all my brothers' ideas.
Now, Miss Wright, that's not fair—
Isn't it?

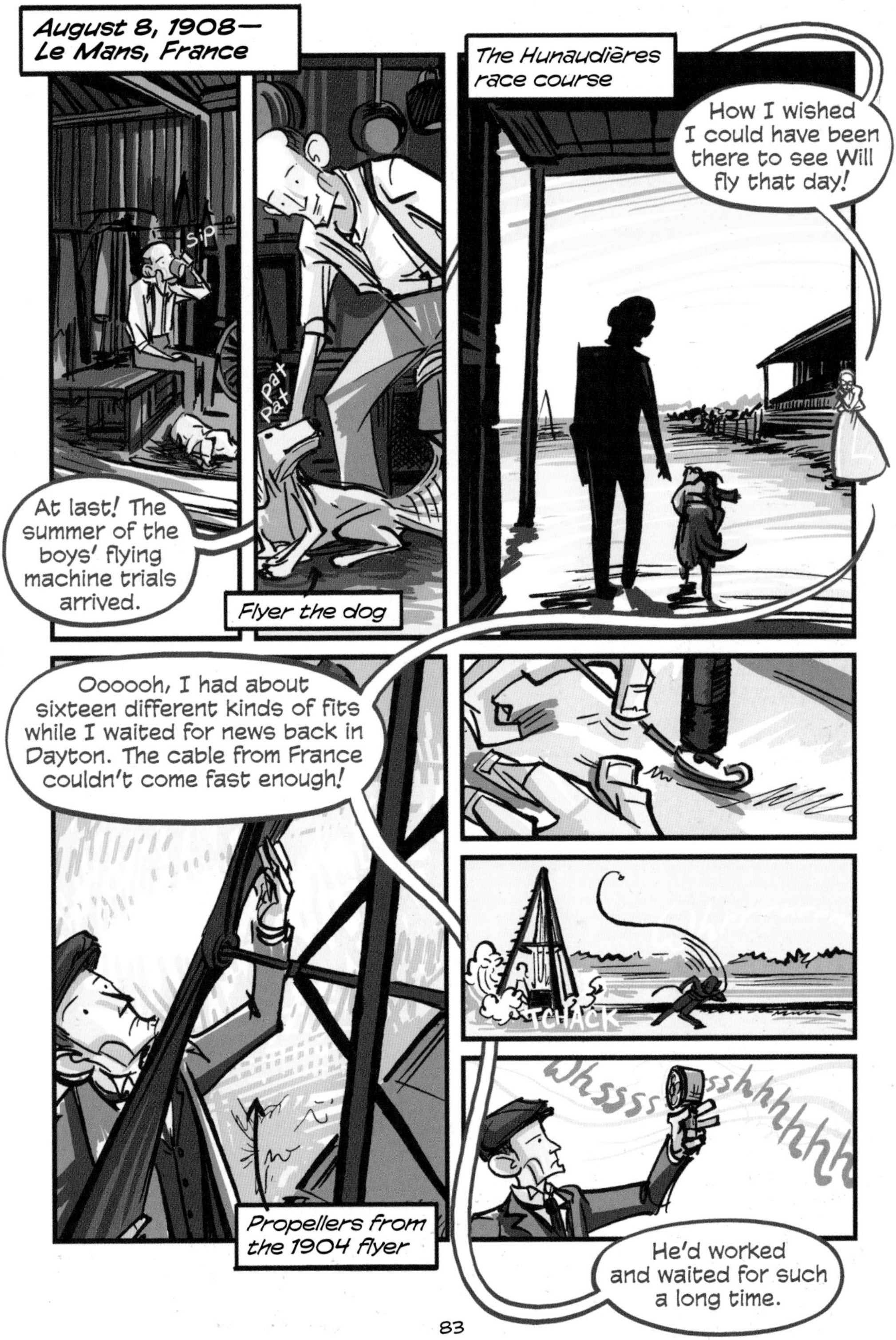
August 8, 1908—
Le Mans, France
Sip
Pat pat
At last! The summer of the boys' flying machine trials arrived.
Flyer the dog
The Hunaudières race course
How I wished I could have been there to see Will fly that day!
Oooooh, I had about sixteen different kinds of fits while I waited for news back in Dayton. The cable from France couldn't come fast enough!
Propellers from the 1904 flyer
TCHACK
Whssss sshhhhhh
He'd worked and waited for such a long time.

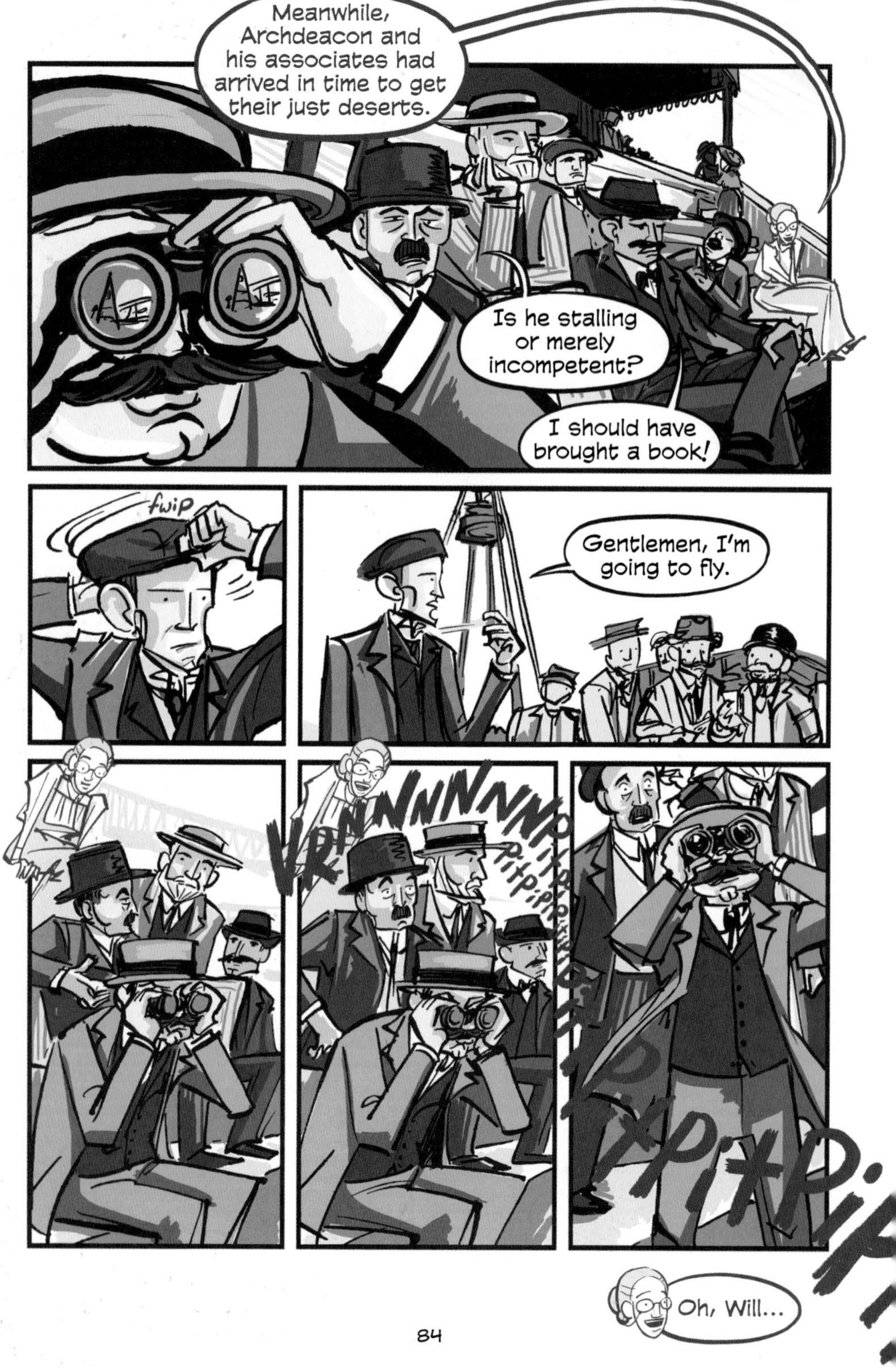
Meanwhile, Archdeacon and his associates had arrived in time to get their just deserts.
Is he stalling or merely incompetent?
I should have brought a book!
fwip
Gentlemen, I'm going to fly.
Oh, Will...

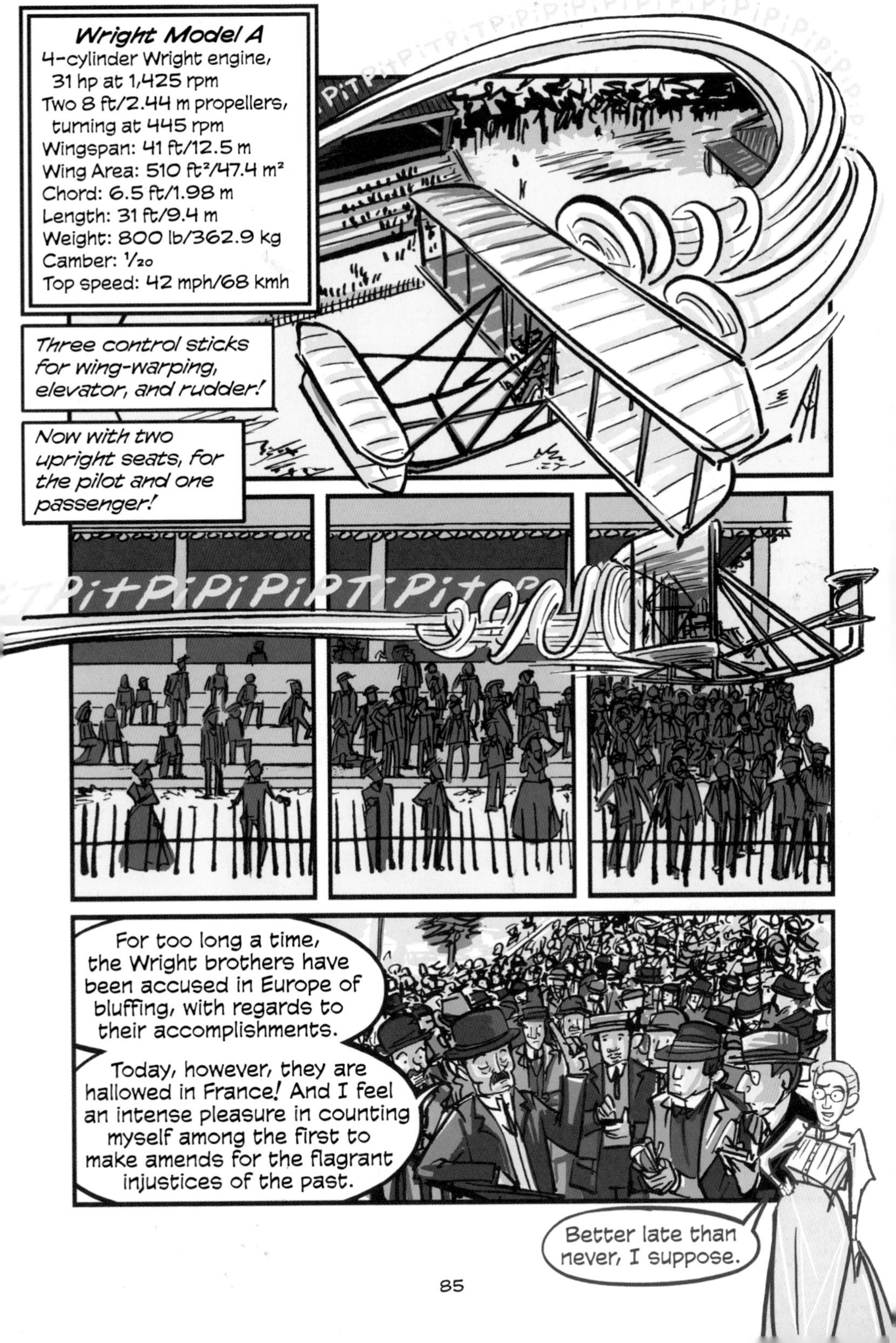
Wright Model A
4-cylinder Wright engine, 31 hp at 1,425 rpm
Two 8 ft/2.44 m propellers, turning at 445 rpm
Wingspan: 41 ft/12.5 m
Wing Area: 510 ft²/47.4 m²
Chord: 6.5 ft/1.98 m
Length: 31 ft/9.4 m
Weight: 800 lb/362.9 kg
Camber: 1/20
Top speed: 42 mph/68 kmh
PiTPiTPiPiPiPiPiPiPi
Three control sticks for wing-warping, elevator, and rudder!
Now with two upright seats, for the pilot and one passenger!
PiTPiPiPiPiTPiT
For too long a time, the Wright brothers have been accused in Europe of bluffing, with regards to their accomplishments.
Today, however, they are hallowed in France! And I feel an intense pleasure in counting myself among the first to make amends for the flagrant injustices of the past.
Better late than never, I suppose.

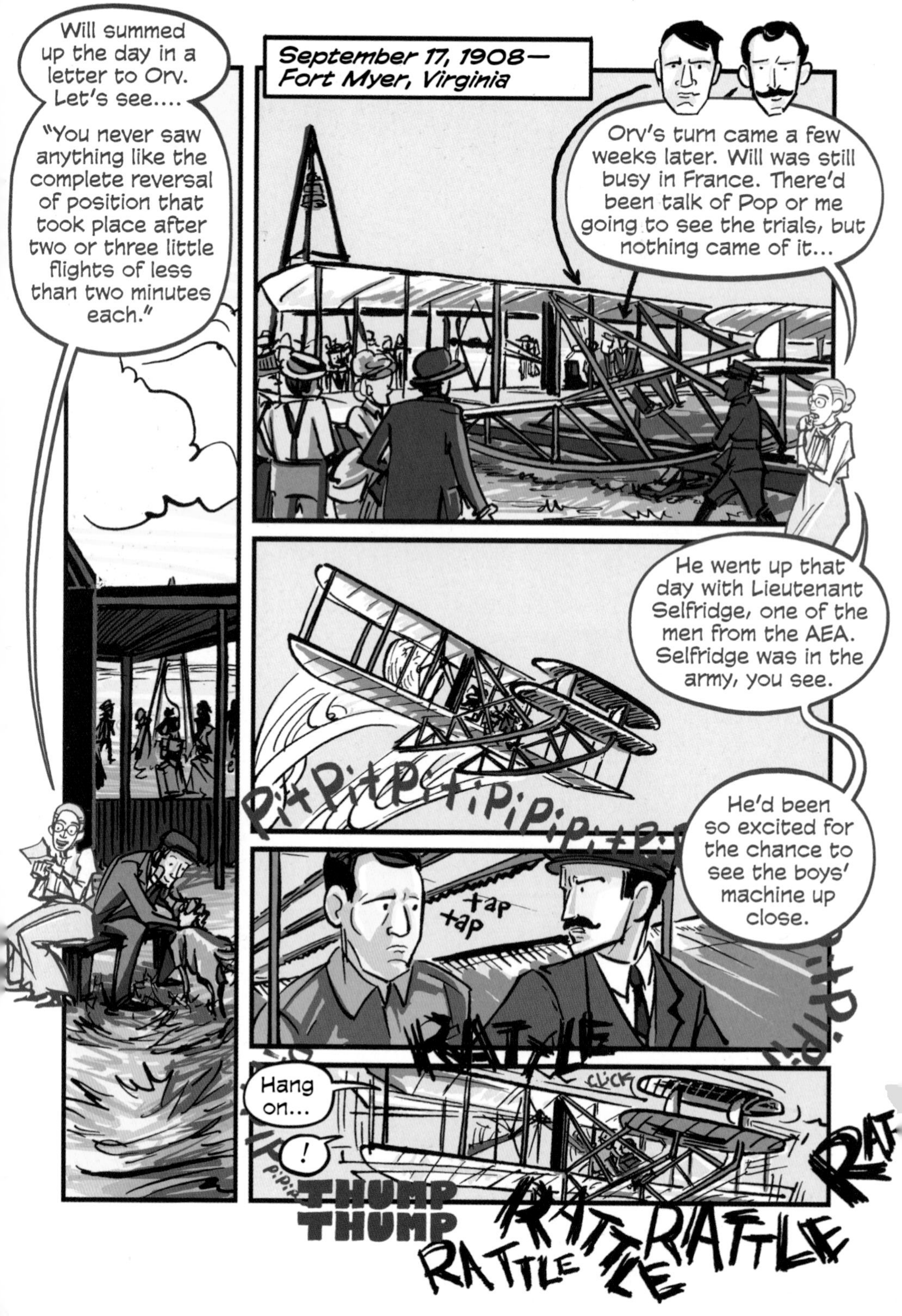

Will summed up the day in a letter to Orv. Let's see....
"You never saw anything like the complete reversal of position that took place after two or three little flights of less than two minutes each."
September 17, 1908— Fort Myer, Virginia
Orv's turn came a few weeks later. Will was still busy in France. There'd been talk of Pop or me going to see the trials, but nothing came of it...
He went up that day with Lieutenant Selfridge, one of the men from the AEA. Selfridge was in the army, you see.
PitPitPitPitPiPiPiPitPiPi
He'd been so excited for the chance to see the boys' machine up close.
tap tap
RATTLE
Hang on...
CLICK
!
THUMP THUMP
RATTLE RATTLE RATTLE RATTLE RAT

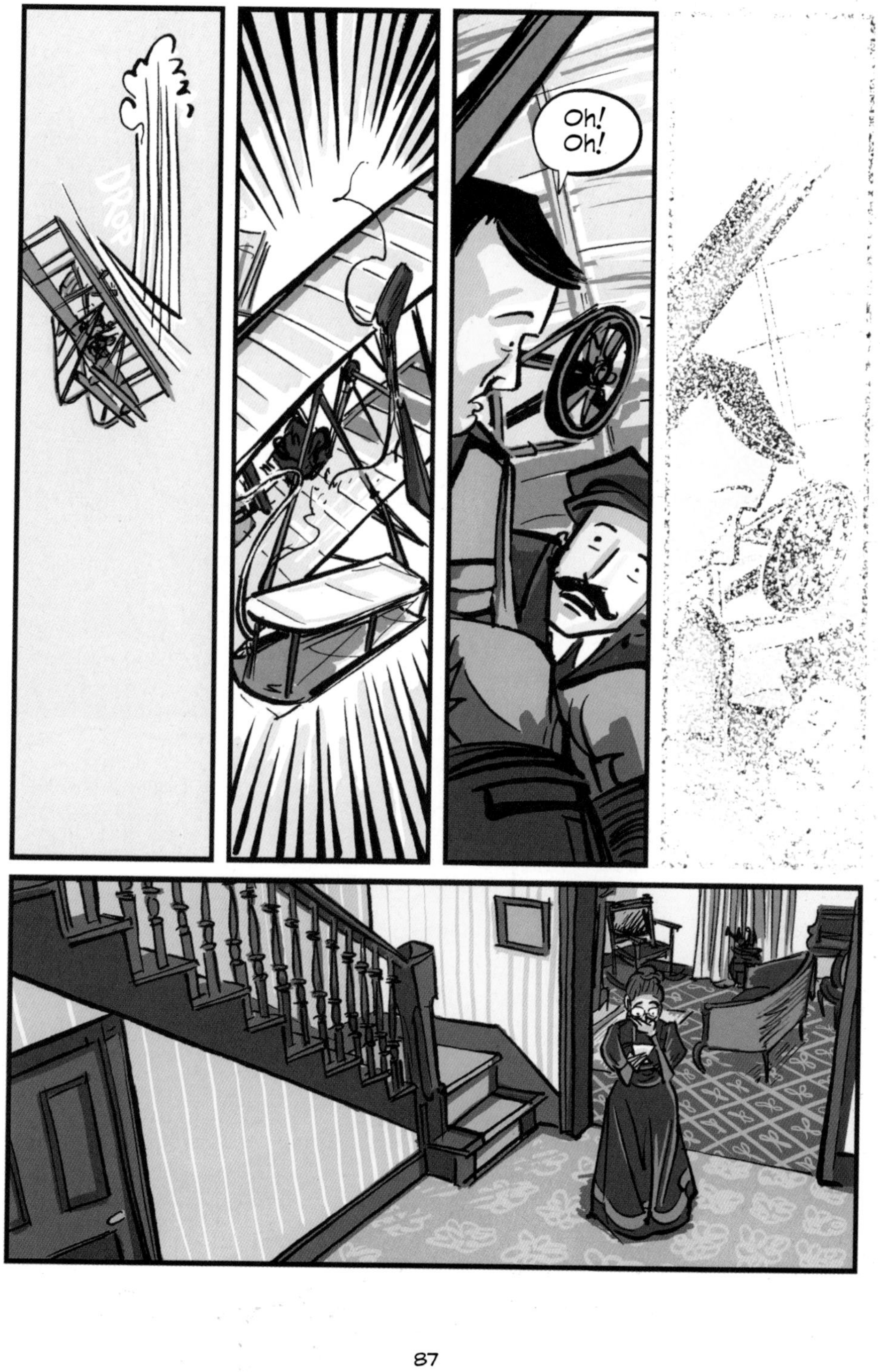
DROP
Oh!
Oh!

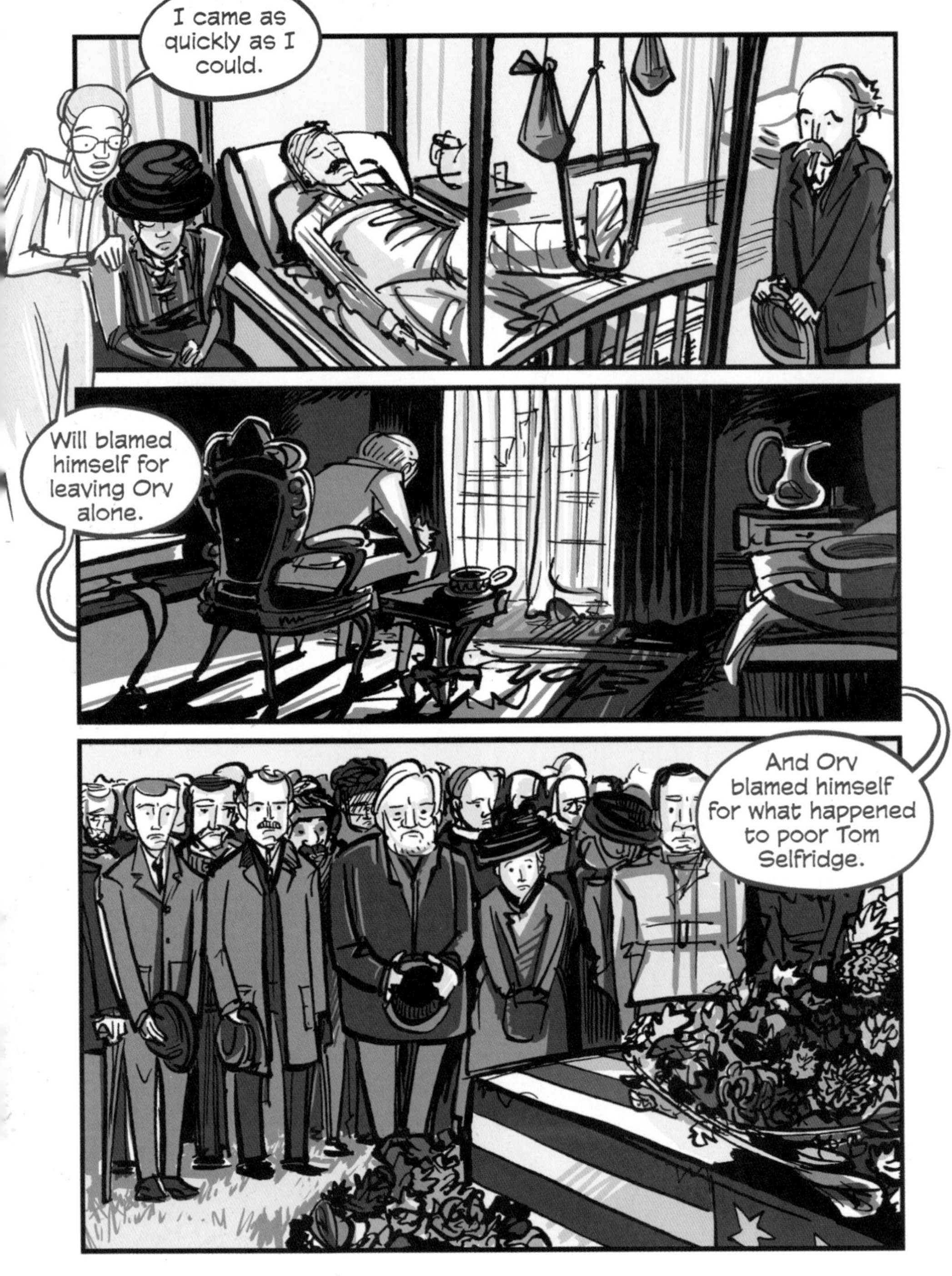
I came as quickly as I could.
Will blamed himself for leaving Orv alone.
And Orv blamed himself for what happened to poor Tom Selfridge.

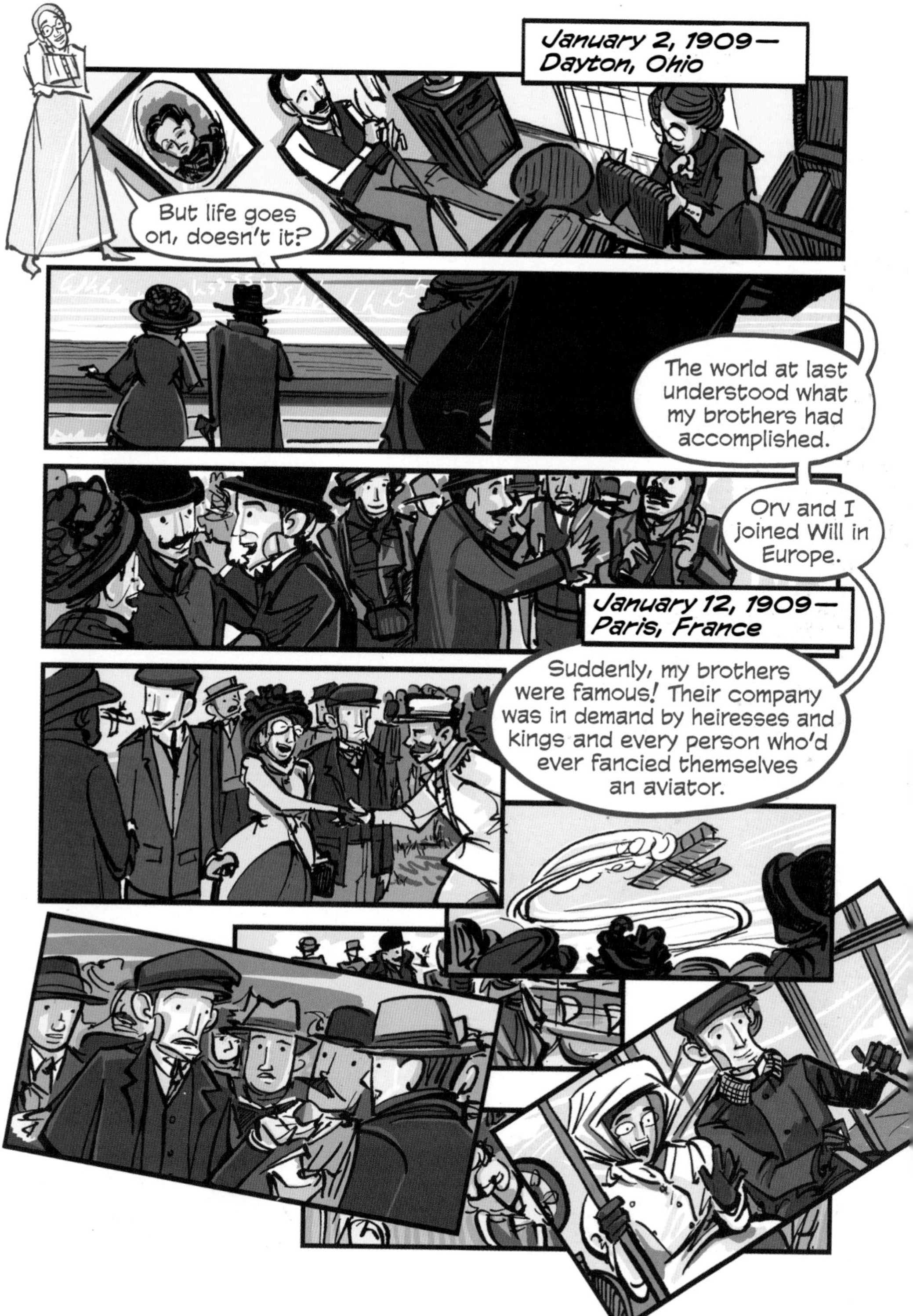
January 2, 1909—
Dayton, Ohio
But life goes on, doesn't it?
The world at last understood what my brothers had accomplished.
Orv and I joined Will in Europe.
January 12, 1909—
Paris, France
Suddenly, my brothers were famous! Their company was in demand by heiresses and kings and every person who'd ever fancied themselves an aviator.

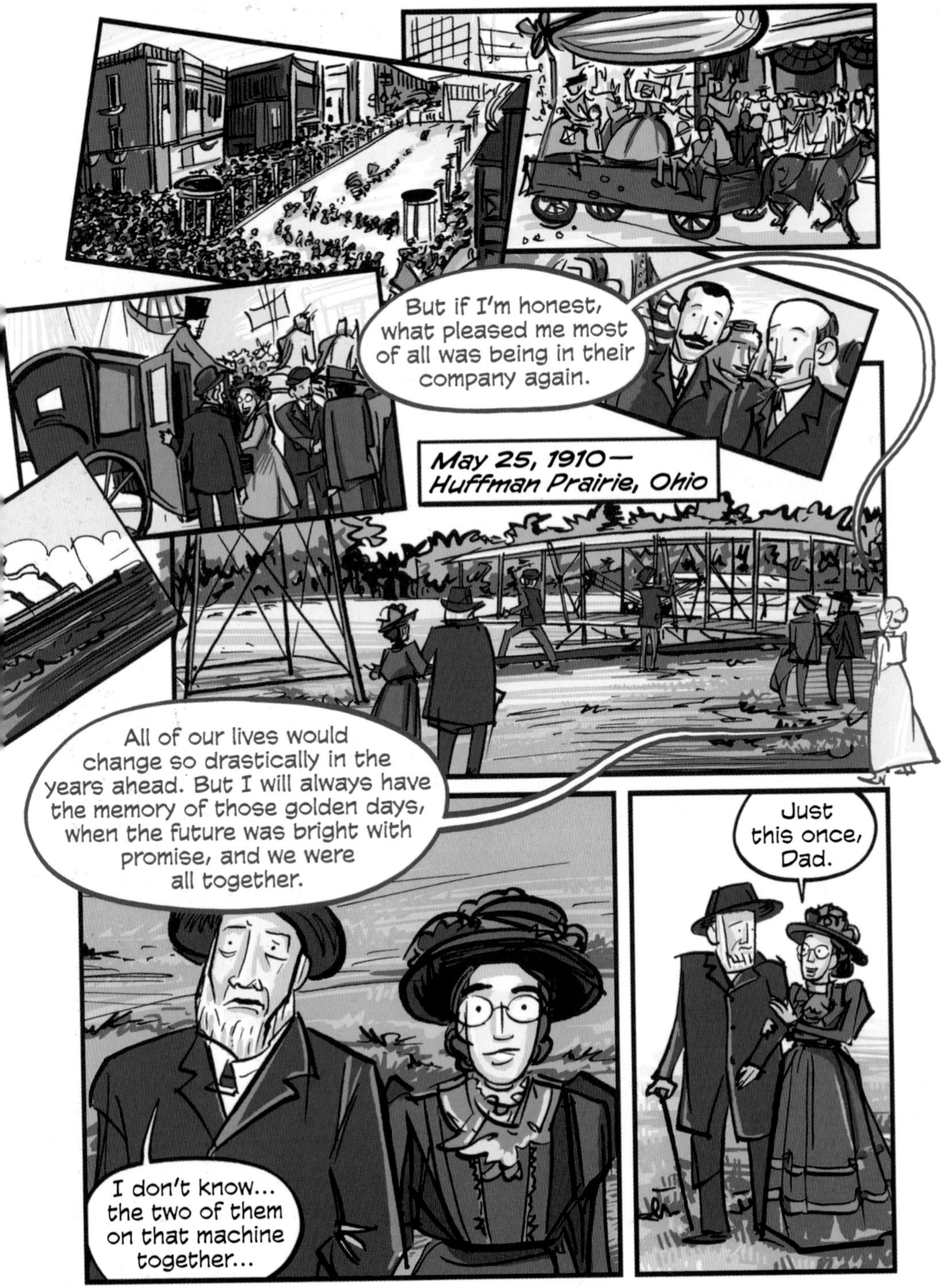
But if I'm honest, what pleased me most of all was being in their company again.
May 25, 1910— Huffman Prairie, Ohio
All of our lives would change so drastically in the years ahead. But I will always have the memory of those golden days, when the future was bright with promise, and we were all together.
I don't know... the two of them on that machine together...
Just this once, Dad.

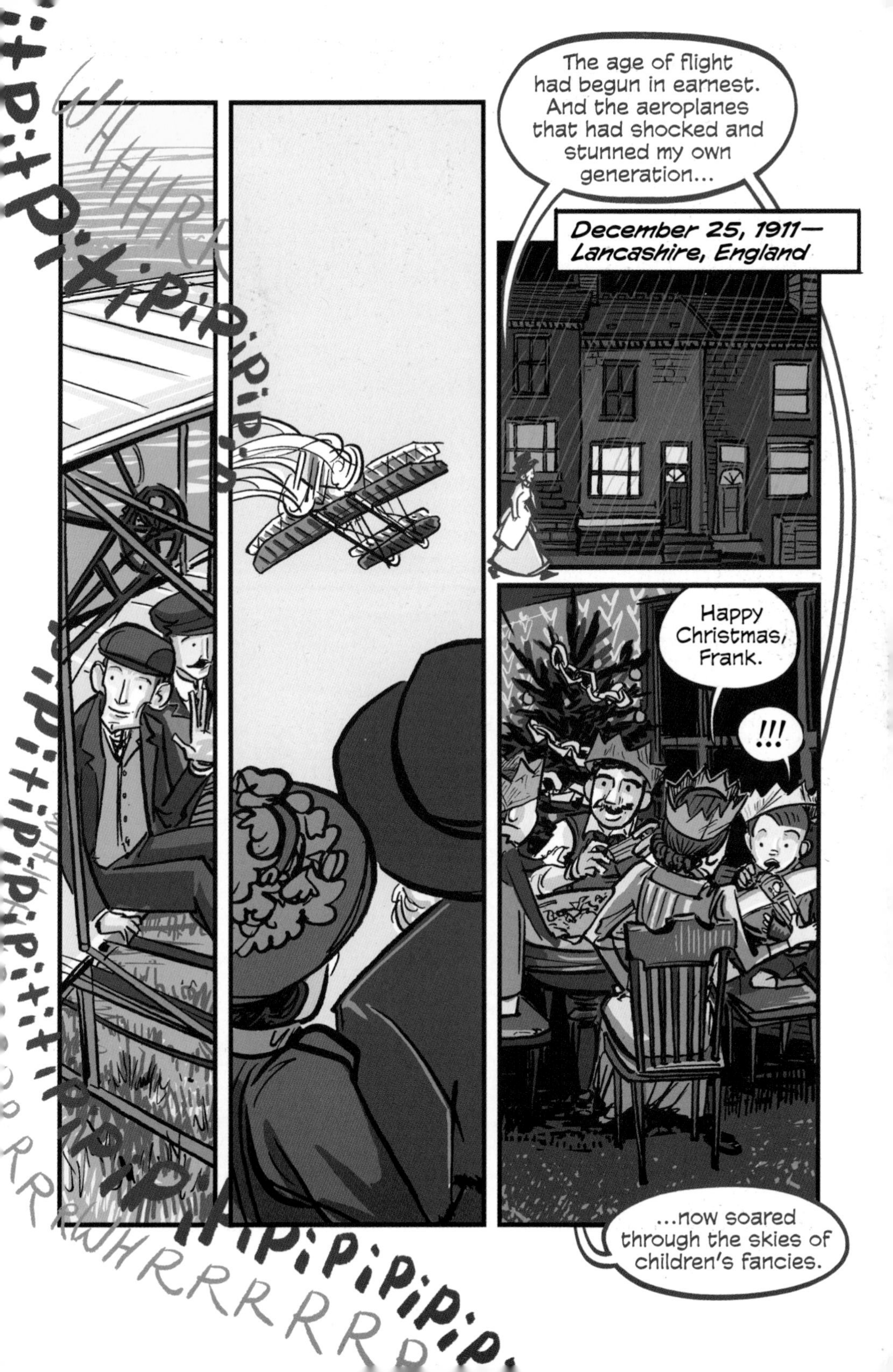
WHHHRRR
PiPiPiPiPiPiPi
The age of flight had begun in earnest. And the aeroplanes that had shocked and stunned my own generation...
December 25, 1911—Lancashire, England
Happy Christmas, Frank.
!!!
...now soared through the skies of children's fancies.
WHHRRRRRR
PiPiPiPiPiPiPi

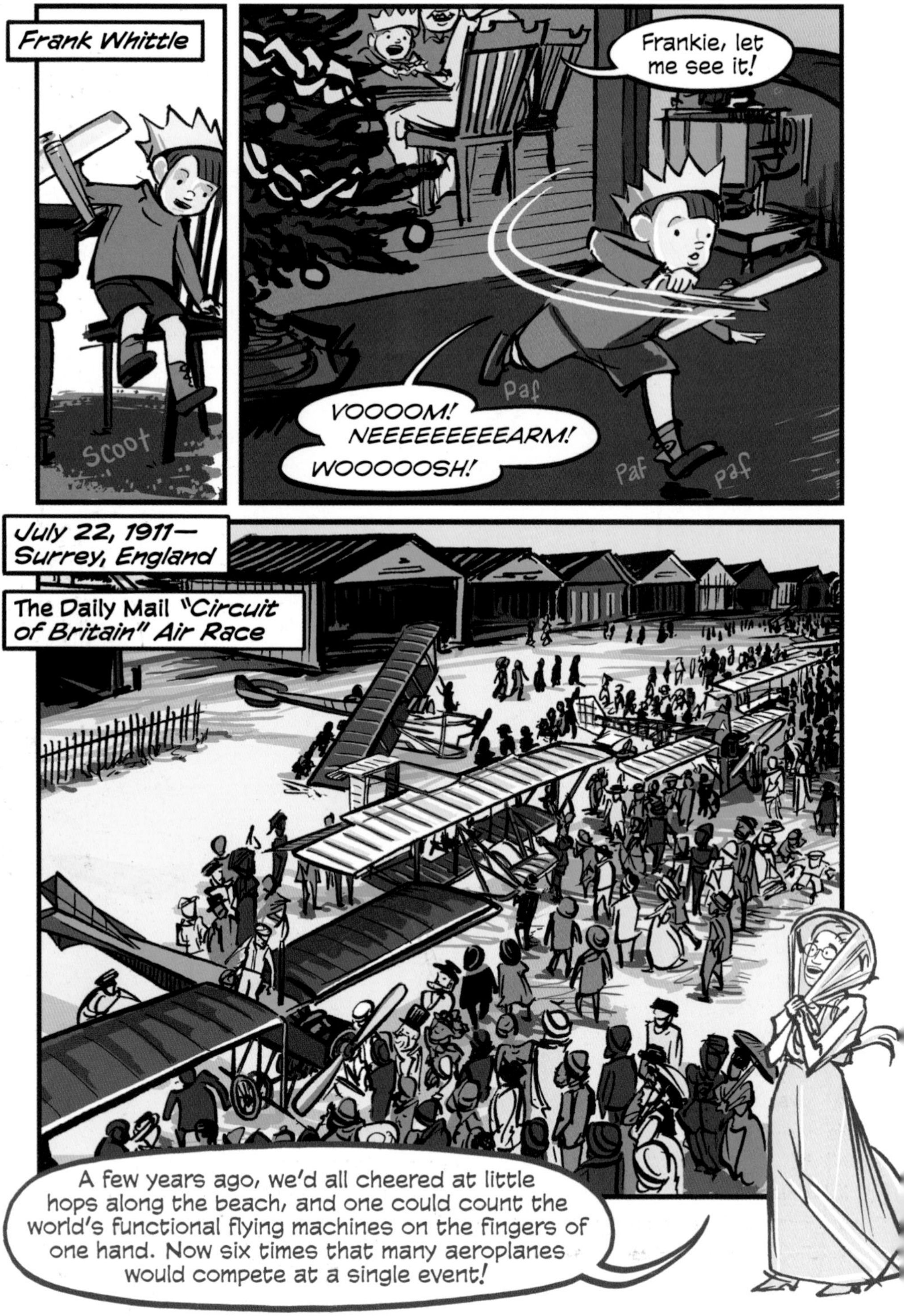

Frank Whittle
scoot
Frankie, let me see it!
VOOOOM! NEEEEEEEEEARM! WOOOOOSH!
paf
Paf
paf
July 22, 1911— Surrey, England
The Daily Mail "Circuit of Britain" Air Race
A few years ago, we'd all cheered at little hops along the beach, and one could count the world's functional flying machines on the fingers of one hand. Now six times that many aeroplanes would compete at a single event!

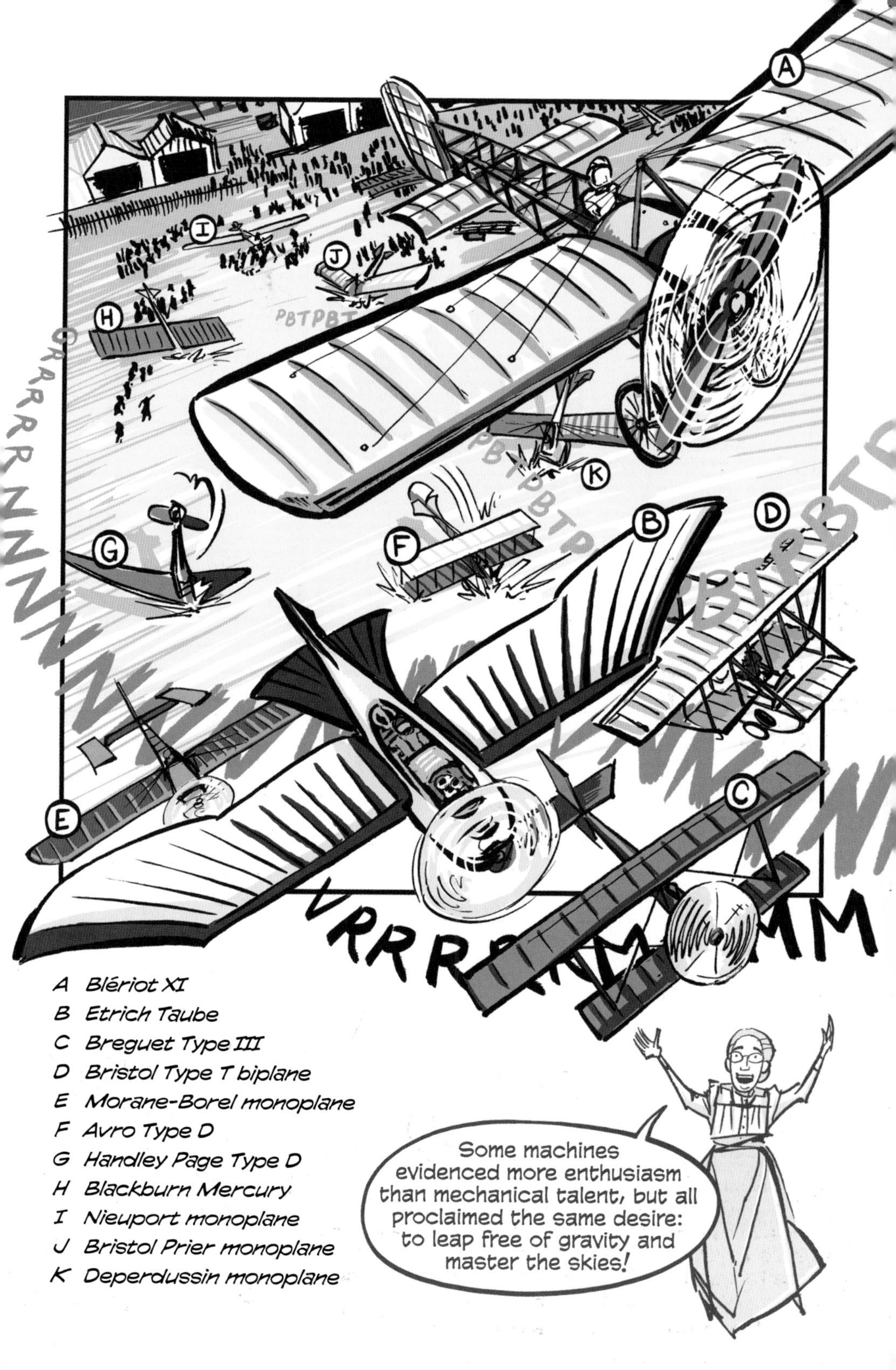
A
I
J
H
PBTPBT
K
G
F
B
D
E
C
A Blériot XI
B Etrich Taube
C Breguet Type III
D Bristol Type T biplane
E Morane-Borel monoplane
F Avro Type D
G Handley Page Type D
H Blackburn Mercury
I Nieuport monoplane
J Bristol Prier monoplane
K Deperdussin monoplane
Some machines evidenced more enthusiasm than mechanical talent, but all proclaimed the same desire: to leap free of gravity and master the skies!

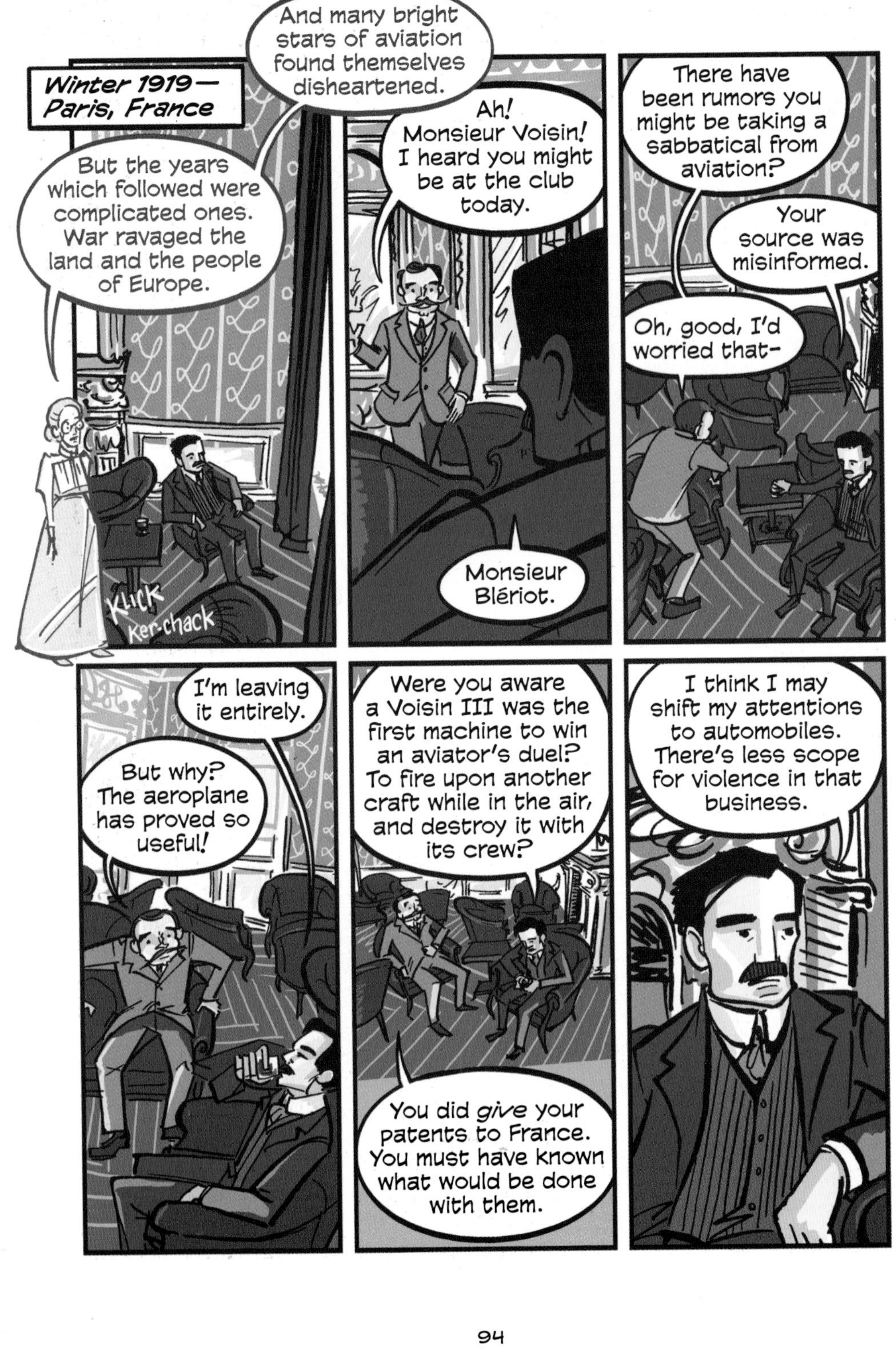
Winter 1919— Paris, France
But the years which followed were complicated ones. War ravaged the land and the people of Europe.
And many bright stars of aviation found themselves disheartened.
KLICK
Ker-chack
Ah! Monsieur Voisin! I heard you might be at the club today.
Monsieur Blériot.
There have been rumors you might be taking a sabbatical from aviation?
Your source was misinformed.
Oh, good, I'd worried that-
I'm leaving it entirely.
But why? The aeroplane has proved so useful!
Were you aware a Voisin III was the first machine to win an aviator's duel? To fire upon another craft while in the air, and destroy it with its crew?
You did *give* your patents to France. You must have known what would be done with them.
I think I may shift my attentions to automobiles. There's less scope for violence in that business.

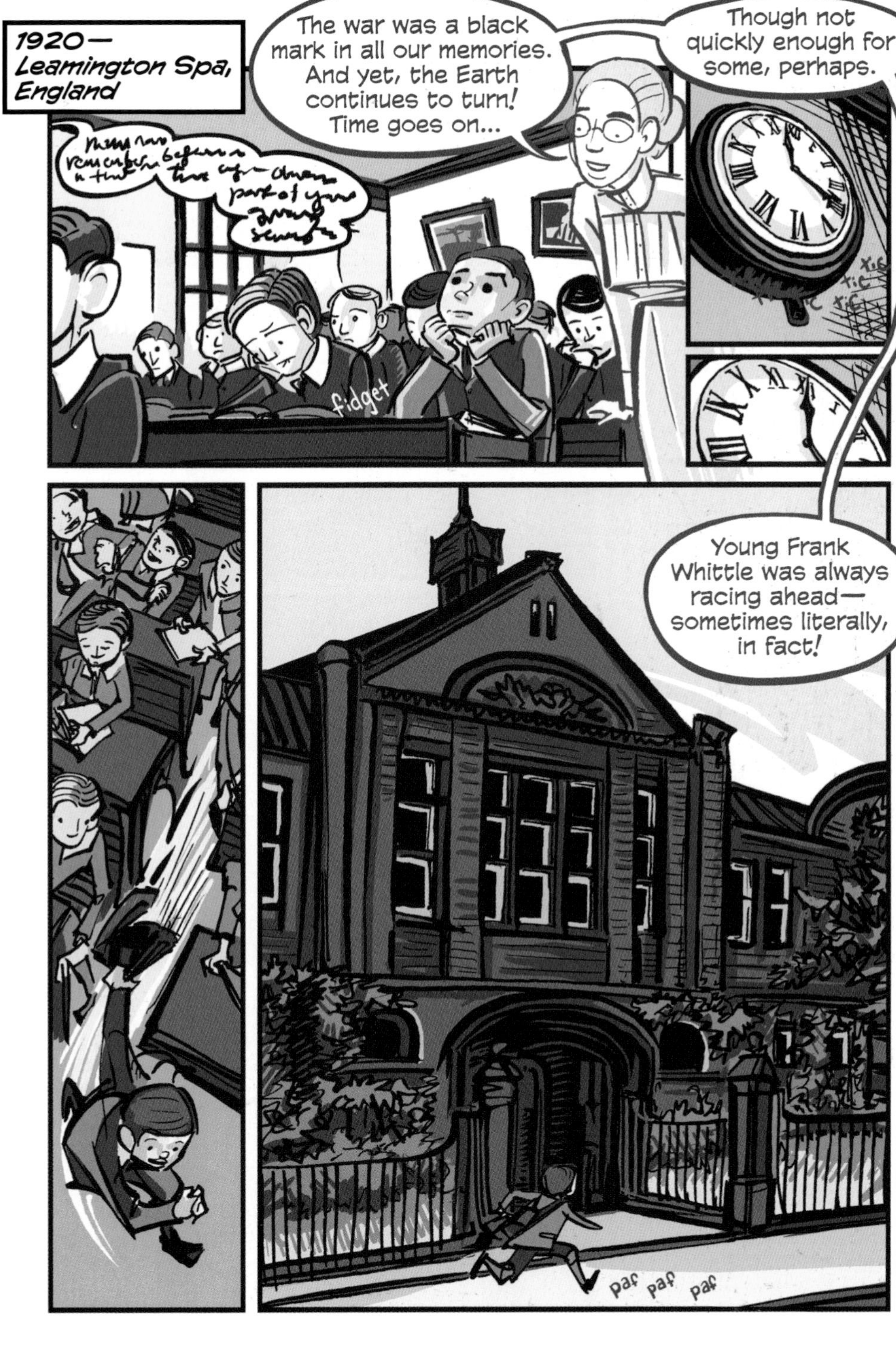
1920—
Leamington Spa, England
The war was a black mark in all our memories. And yet, the Earth continues to turn! Time goes on...
fidget
Though not quickly enough for some, perhaps.
Young Frank Whittle was always racing ahead— sometimes literally, in fact!
paf paf paf

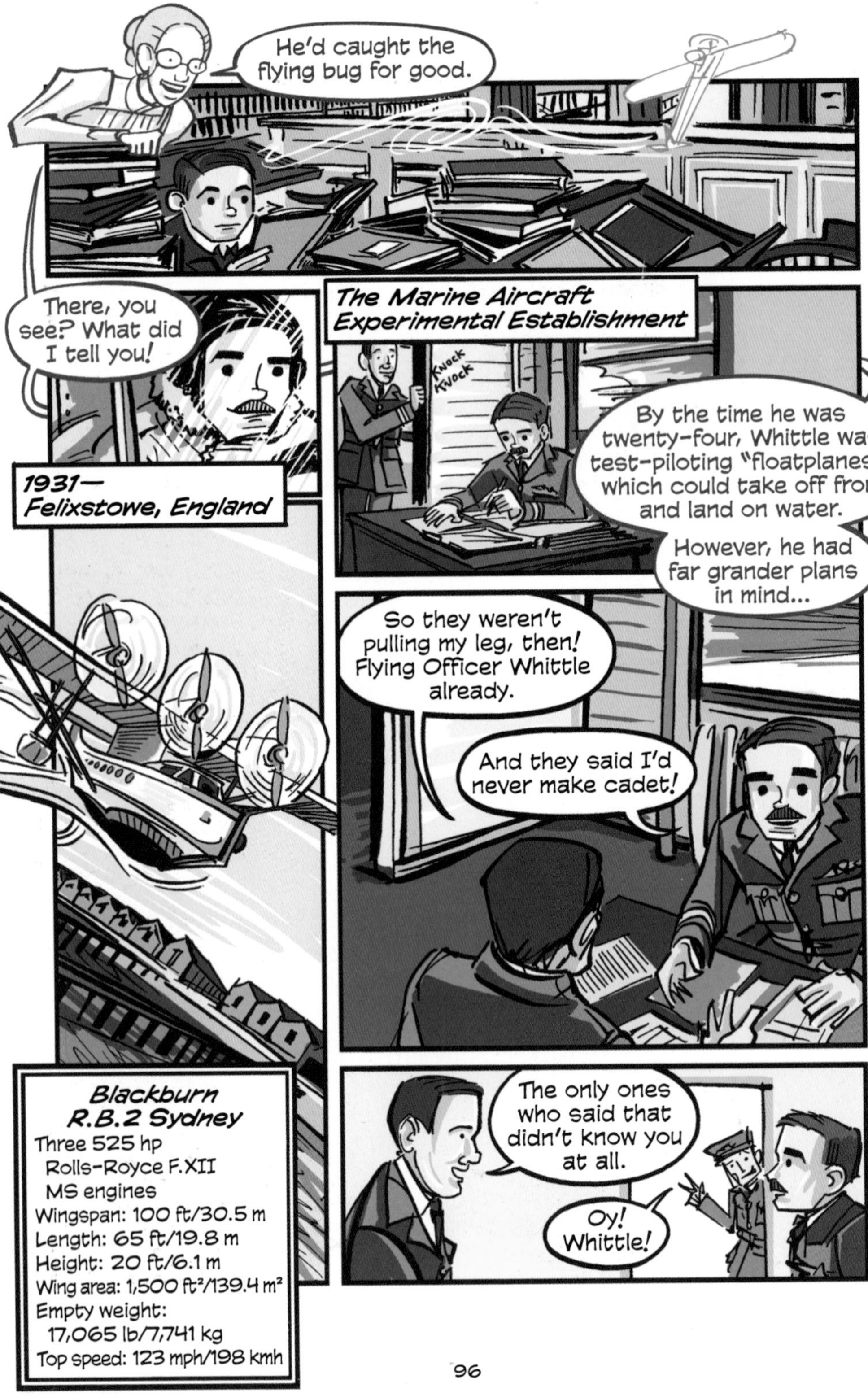
He'd caught the flying bug for good.
There, you see? What did I tell you!
The Marine Aircraft Experimental Establishment
Knock Knock
1931—Felixstowe, England
By the time he was twenty-four, Whittle was test-piloting "floatplanes," which could take off from and land on water.
However, he had far grander plans in mind...
So they weren't pulling my leg, then! Flying Officer Whittle already.
And they said I'd never make cadet!
Blackburn R.B.2 Sydney
Three 525 hp Rolls-Royce F.XII MS engines
Wingspan: 100 ft/30.5 m
Length: 65 ft/19.8 m
Height: 20 ft/6.1 m
Wing area: 1,500 ft²/139.4 m²
Empty weight: 17,065 lb/7,741 kg
Top speed: 123 mph/198 kmh
The only ones who said that didn't know you at all.
Oy! Whittle!

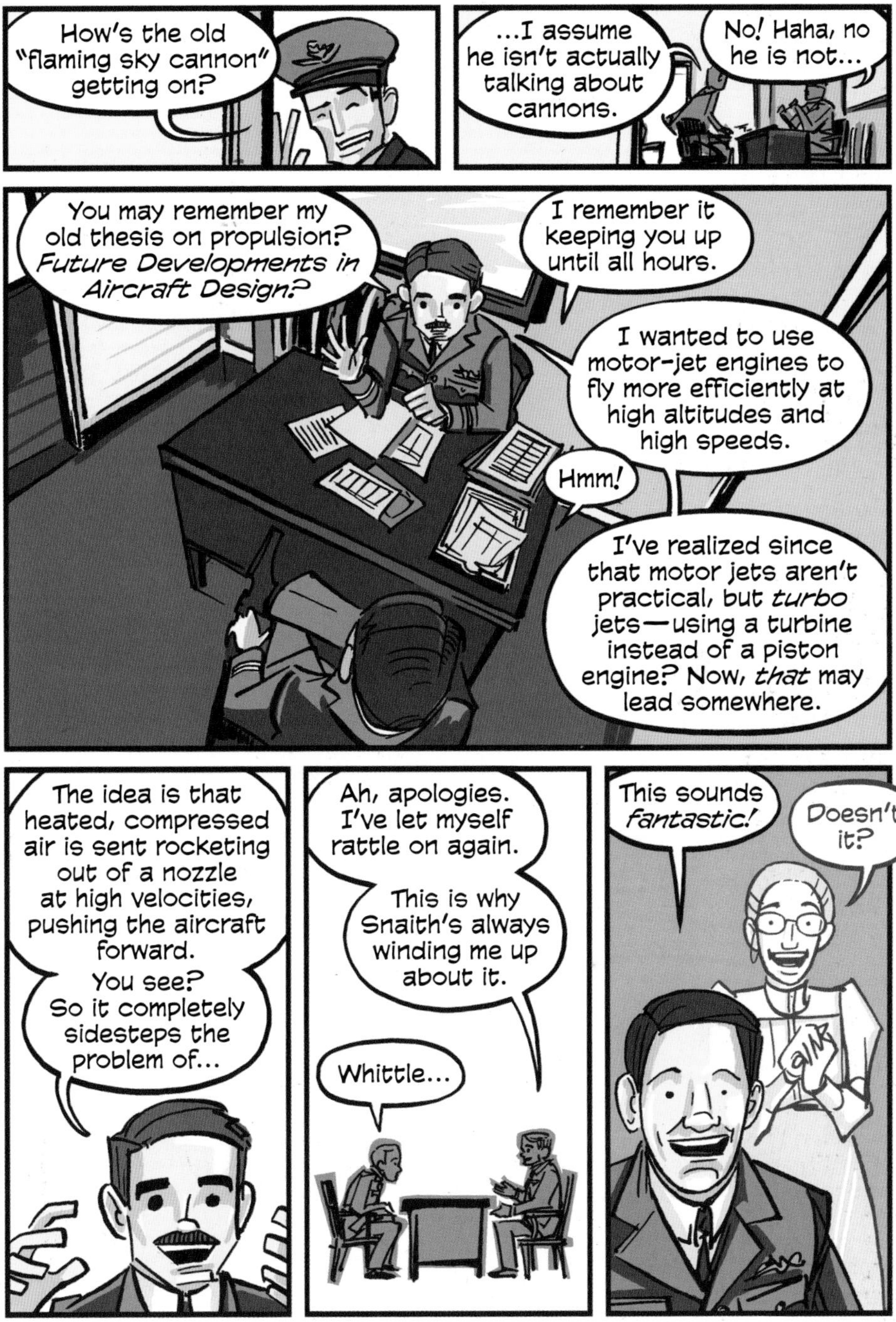
How's the old "flaming sky cannon" getting on?
...I assume he isn't actually talking about cannons.
No! Haha, no he is not...
You may remember my old thesis on propulsion? *Future Developments in Aircraft Design?*
I remember it keeping you up until all hours.
I wanted to use motor-jet engines to fly more efficiently at high altitudes and high speeds.
Hmm!
I've realized since that motor jets aren't practical, but *turbo* jets—using a turbine instead of a piston engine? Now, *that* may lead somewhere.
The idea is that heated, compressed air is sent rocketing out of a nozzle at high velocities, pushing the aircraft forward.
You see? So it completely sidesteps the problem of...
Ah, apologies. I've let myself rattle on again.
This is why Snaith's always winding me up about it.
Whittle...
This sounds *fantastic!*
Doesn't it?

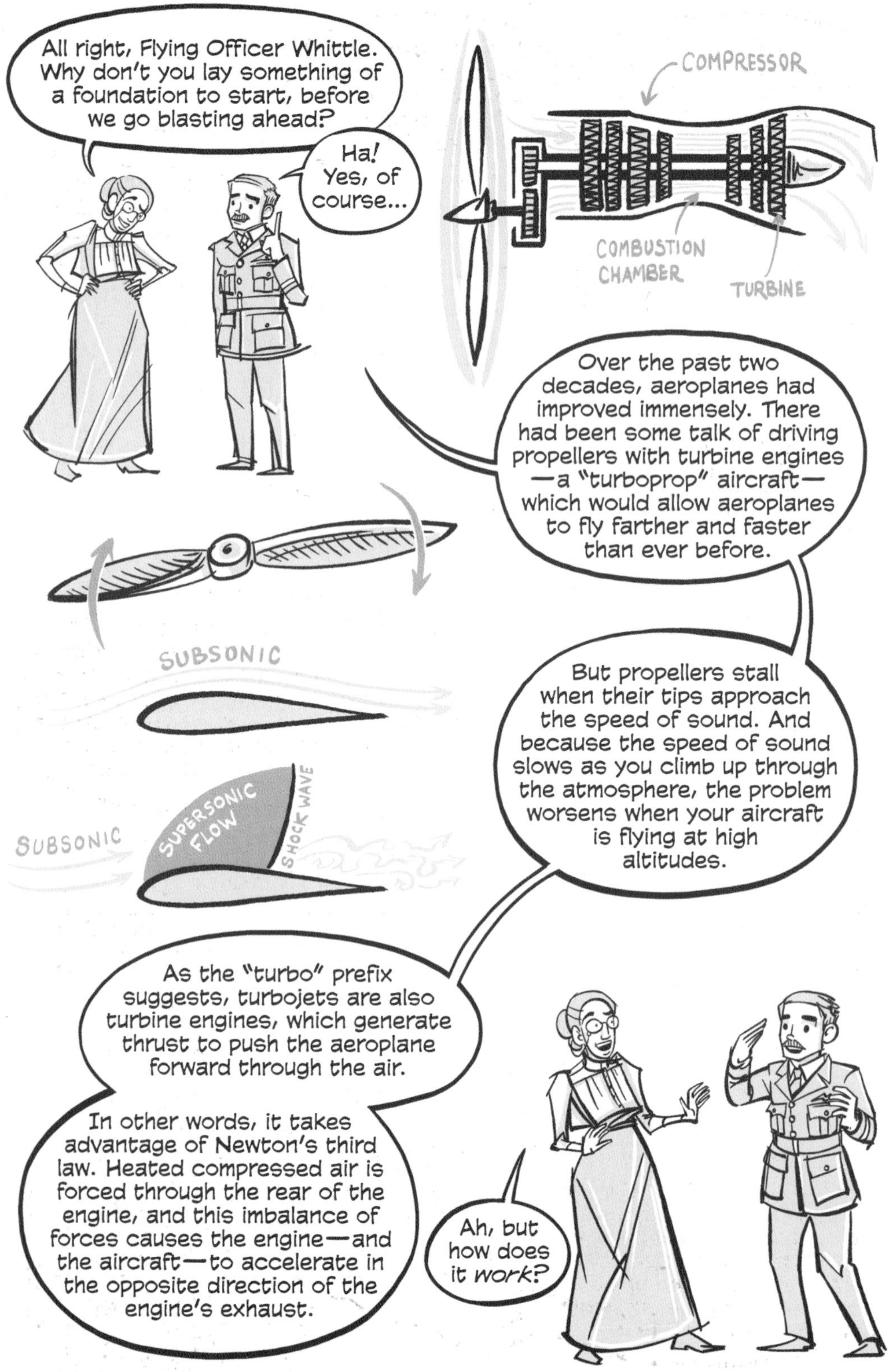

All right, Flying Officer Whittle. Why don't you lay something of a foundation to start, before we go blasting ahead?
Ha! Yes, of course...
COMPRESSOR
COMBUSTION CHAMBER
TURBINE
Over the past two decades, aeroplanes had improved immensely. There had been some talk of driving propellers with turbine engines —a "turboprop" aircraft— which would allow aeroplanes to fly farther and faster than ever before.
SUBSONIC
SUPERSONIC FLOW
SHOCK WAVE
SUBSONIC
But propellers stall when their tips approach the speed of sound. And because the speed of sound slows as you climb up through the atmosphere, the problem worsens when your aircraft is flying at high altitudes.
As the "turbo" prefix suggests, turbojets are also turbine engines, which generate thrust to push the aeroplane forward through the air.
In other words, it takes advantage of Newton's third law. Heated compressed air is forced through the rear of the engine, and this imbalance of forces causes the engine—and the aircraft—to accelerate in the opposite direction of the engine's exhaust.
Ah, but how does it *work*?

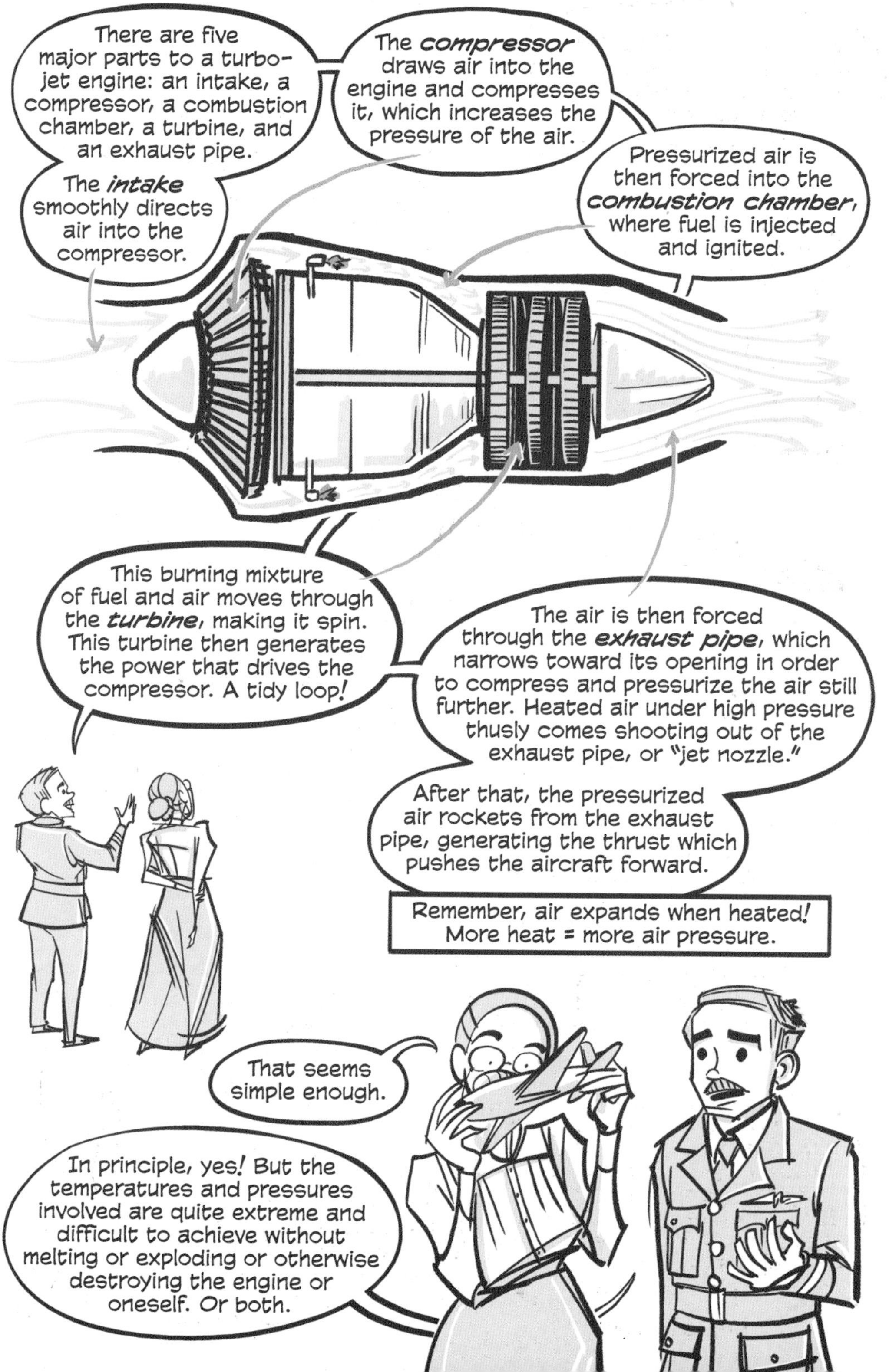
There are five major parts to a turbo-jet engine: an intake, a compressor, a combustion chamber, a turbine, and an exhaust pipe.
The compressor draws air into the engine and compresses it, which increases the pressure of the air.
The intake smoothly directs air into the compressor.
Pressurized air is then forced into the combustion chamber, where fuel is injected and ignited.
This burning mixture of fuel and air moves through the turbine, making it spin. This turbine then generates the power that drives the compressor. A tidy loop!
The air is then forced through the exhaust pipe, which narrows toward its opening in order to compress and pressurize the air still further. Heated air under high pressure thusly comes shooting out of the exhaust pipe, or "jet nozzle."
After that, the pressurized air rockets from the exhaust pipe, generating the thrust which pushes the aircraft forward.
Remember, air expands when heated! More heat = more air pressure.
That seems simple enough.
In principle, yes! But the temperatures and pressures involved are quite extreme and difficult to achieve without melting or exploding or otherwise destroying the engine or oneself. Or both.

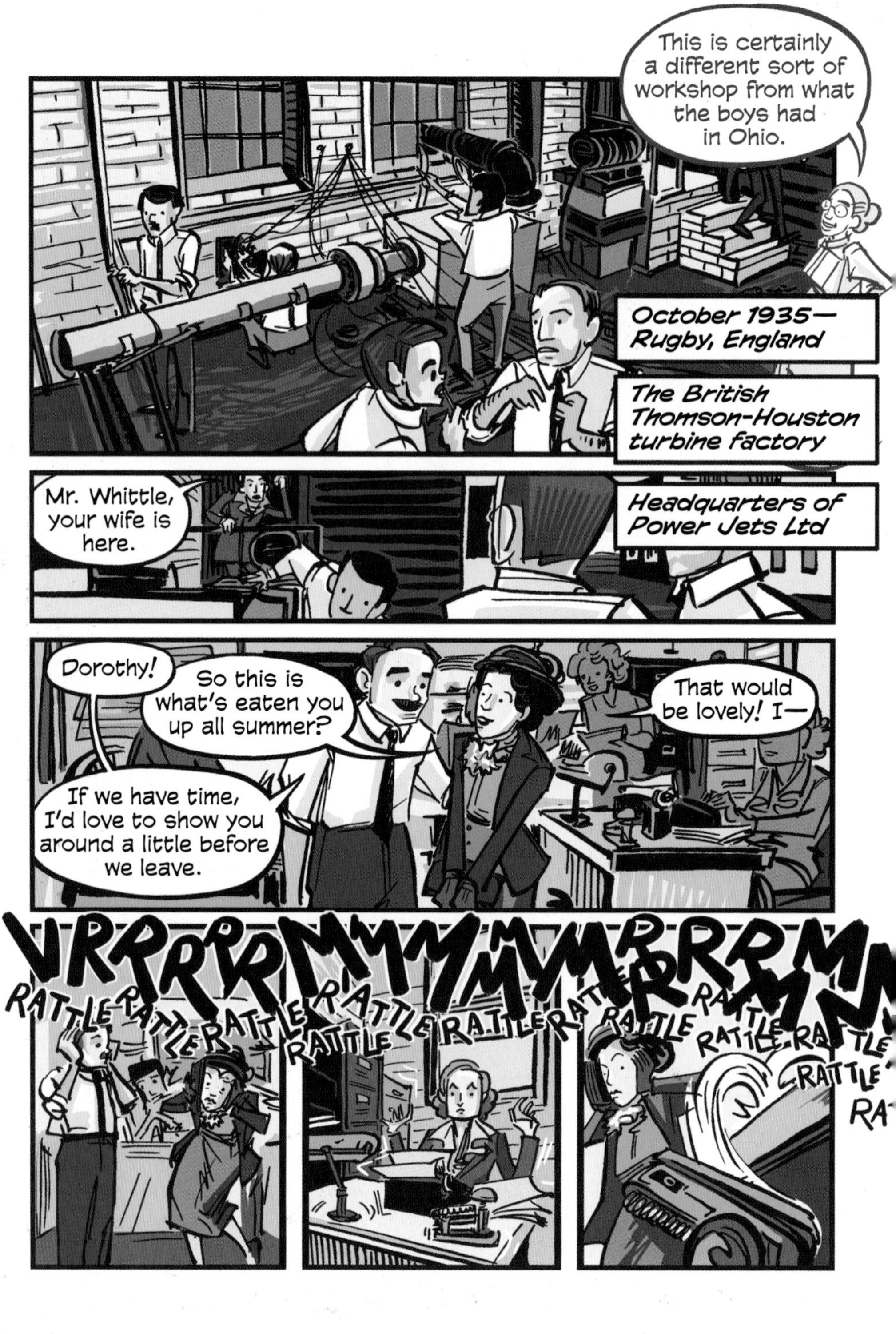
This is certainly a different sort of workshop from what the boys had in Ohio.
October 1935— Rugby, England
The British Thomson-Houston turbine factory
Mr. Whittle, your wife is here.
Headquarters of Power Jets Ltd
Dorothy!
So this is what's eaten you up all summer?
If we have time, I'd love to show you around a little before we leave.
That would be lovely! I—
VRRRRRMMMMMMMRRRRMM
RATTLE RATTLE RATTLE RATTLE RATTLE RATTLE RATTLE RATTLE RATTLE RATTLE RATTLE RATTLE RA

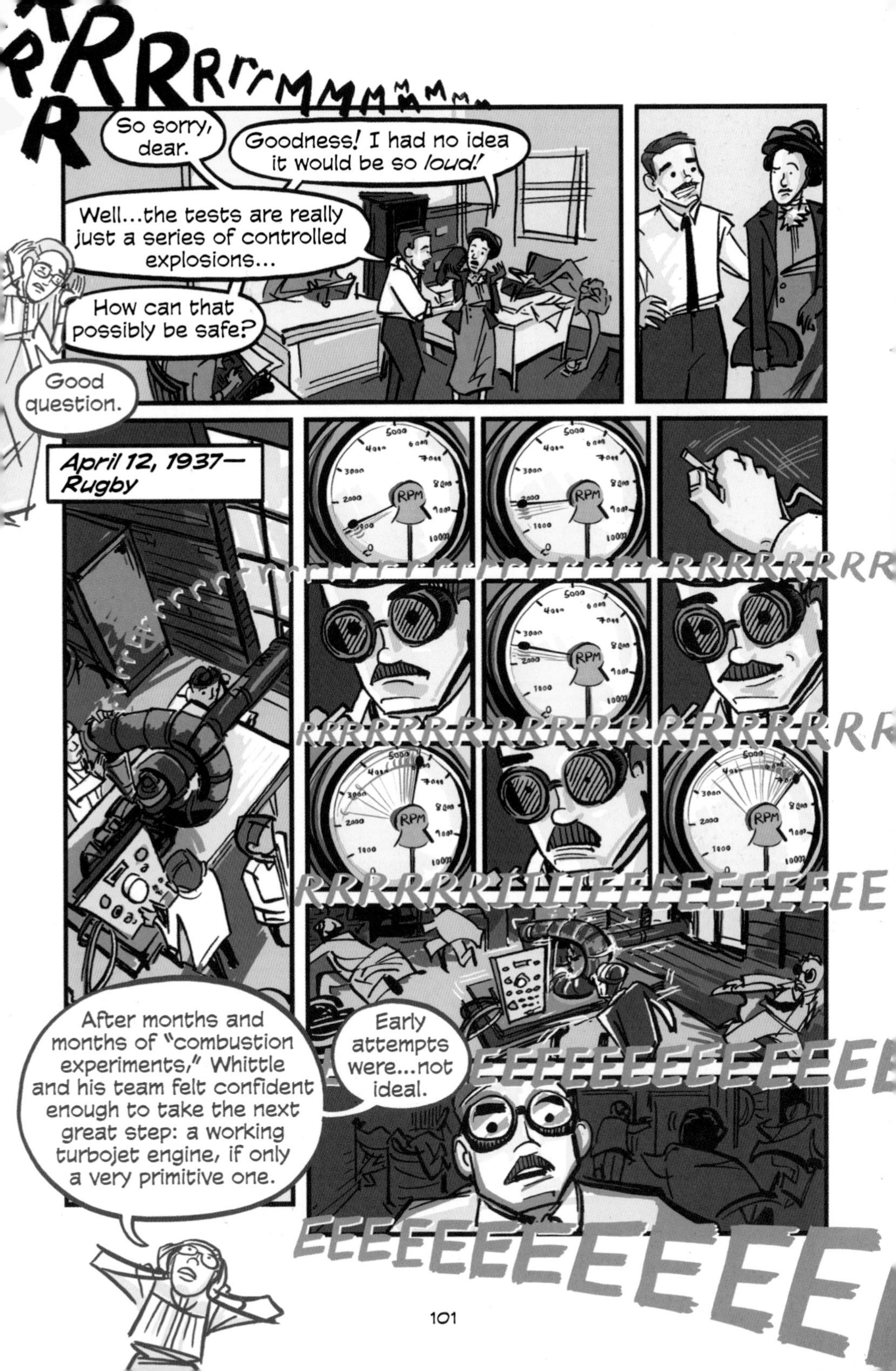
RRRRRrrrMMMMMMMM...
So sorry, dear.
Goodness! I had no idea it would be so *loud!*
Well...the tests are really just a series of controlled explosions...
How can that possibly be safe?
Good question.
April 12, 1937— Rugby
RPM
RRRRRRRRRR
RRRRRRRRRRRRRRRRRRRRRRRR
RRRRRRRIIIIEEEEEEEEEEEE
After months and months of "combustion experiments," Whittle and his team felt confident enough to take the next great step: a working turbojet engine, if only a very primitive one.
Early attempts were...not ideal.
EEEEEEEEEEEEEEE
EEEEEEEEEEEEE

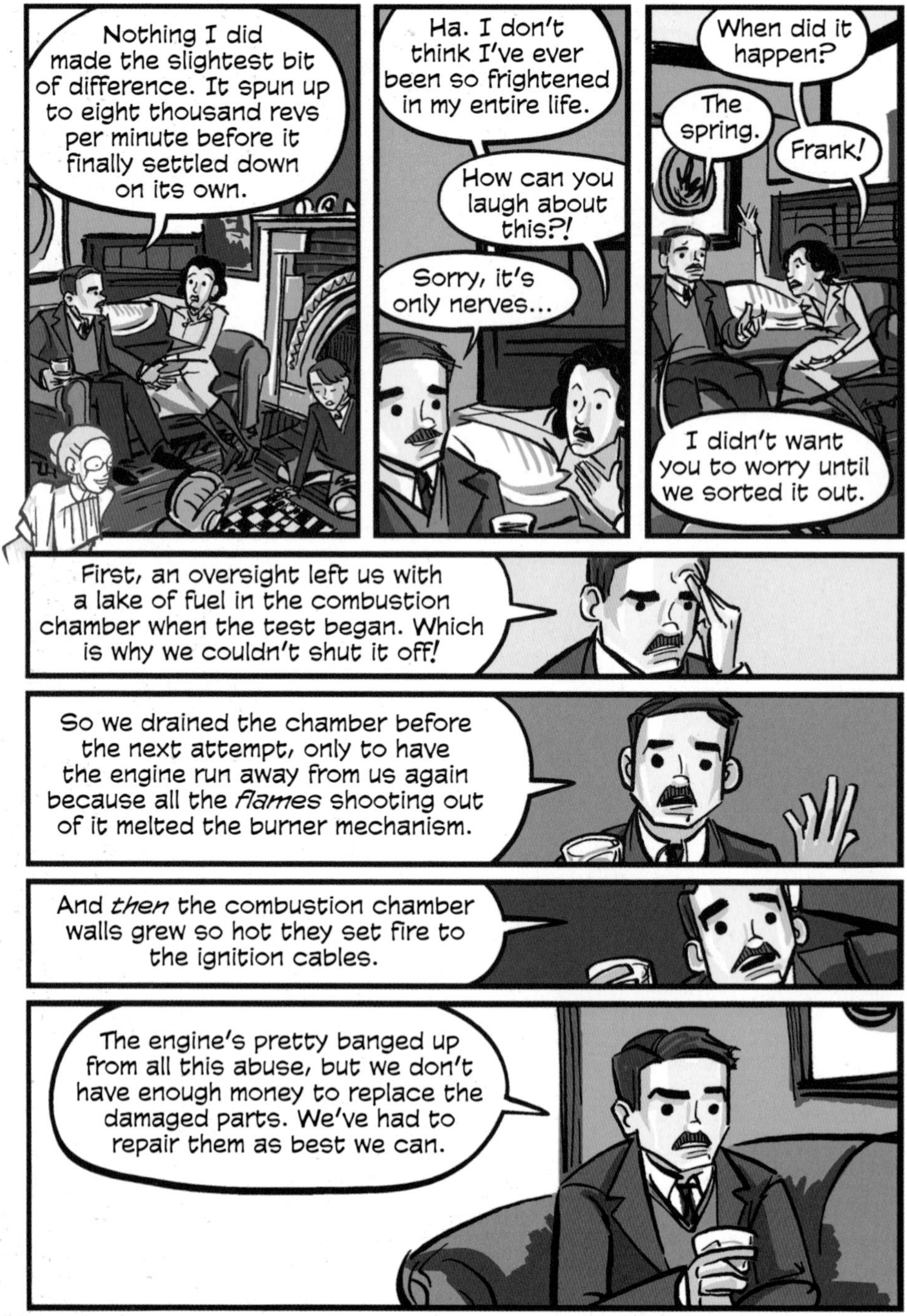
Nothing I did made the slightest bit of difference. It spun up to eight thousand revs per minute before it finally settled down on its own.
Ha. I don't think I've ever been so frightened in my entire life.
How can you laugh about this?!
Sorry, it's only nerves...
When did it happen?
The spring.
Frank!
I didn't want you to worry until we sorted it out.
First, an oversight left us with a lake of fuel in the combustion chamber when the test began. Which is why we couldn't shut it off!
So we drained the chamber before the next attempt, only to have the engine run away from us again because all the *flames* shooting out of it melted the burner mechanism.
And *then* the combustion chamber walls grew so hot they set fire to the ignition cables.
The engine's pretty banged up from all this abuse, but we don't have enough money to replace the damaged parts. We've had to repair them as best we can.

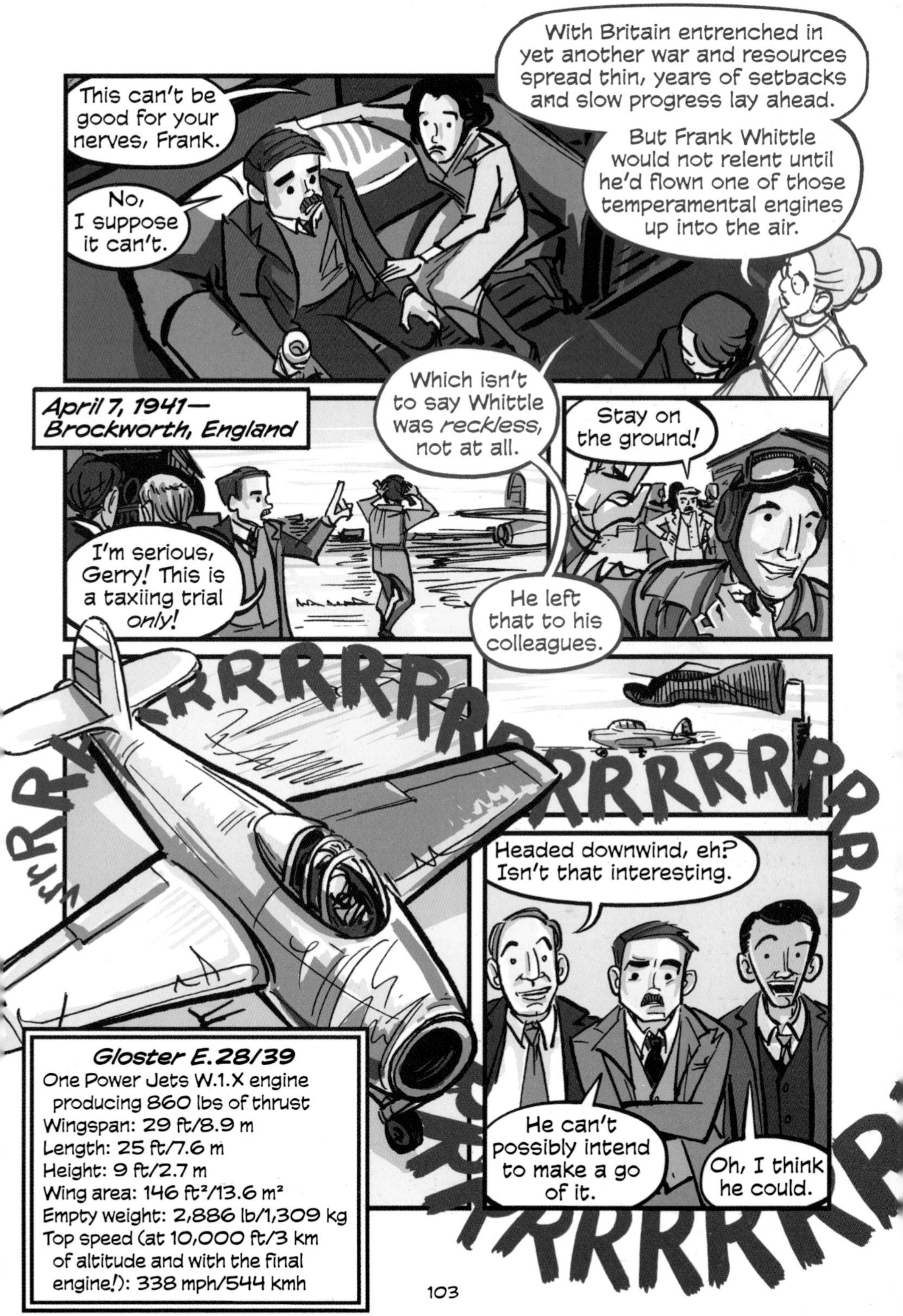
This can't be good for your nerves, Frank.
No, I suppose it can't.
With Britain entrenched in yet another war and resources spread thin, years of setbacks and slow progress lay ahead.
But Frank Whittle would not relent until he'd flown one of those temperamental engines up into the air.
April 7, 1941— Brockworth, England
Which isn't to say Whittle was *reckless*, not at all.
He left that to his colleagues.
I'm serious, Gerry! This is a taxiing trial *only*!
Stay on the ground!
Headed downwind, eh? Isn't that interesting.
He can't possibly intend to make a go of it.
Oh, I think he could.
Gloster E.28/39
One Power Jets W.1.X engine producing 860 lbs of thrust
Wingspan: 29 ft/8.9 m
Length: 25 ft/7.6 m
Height: 9 ft/2.7 m
Wing area: 146 ft²/13.6 m²
Empty weight: 2,886 lb/1,309 kg
Top speed (at 10,000 ft/3 km of altitude and with the final engine!): 338 mph/544 kmh

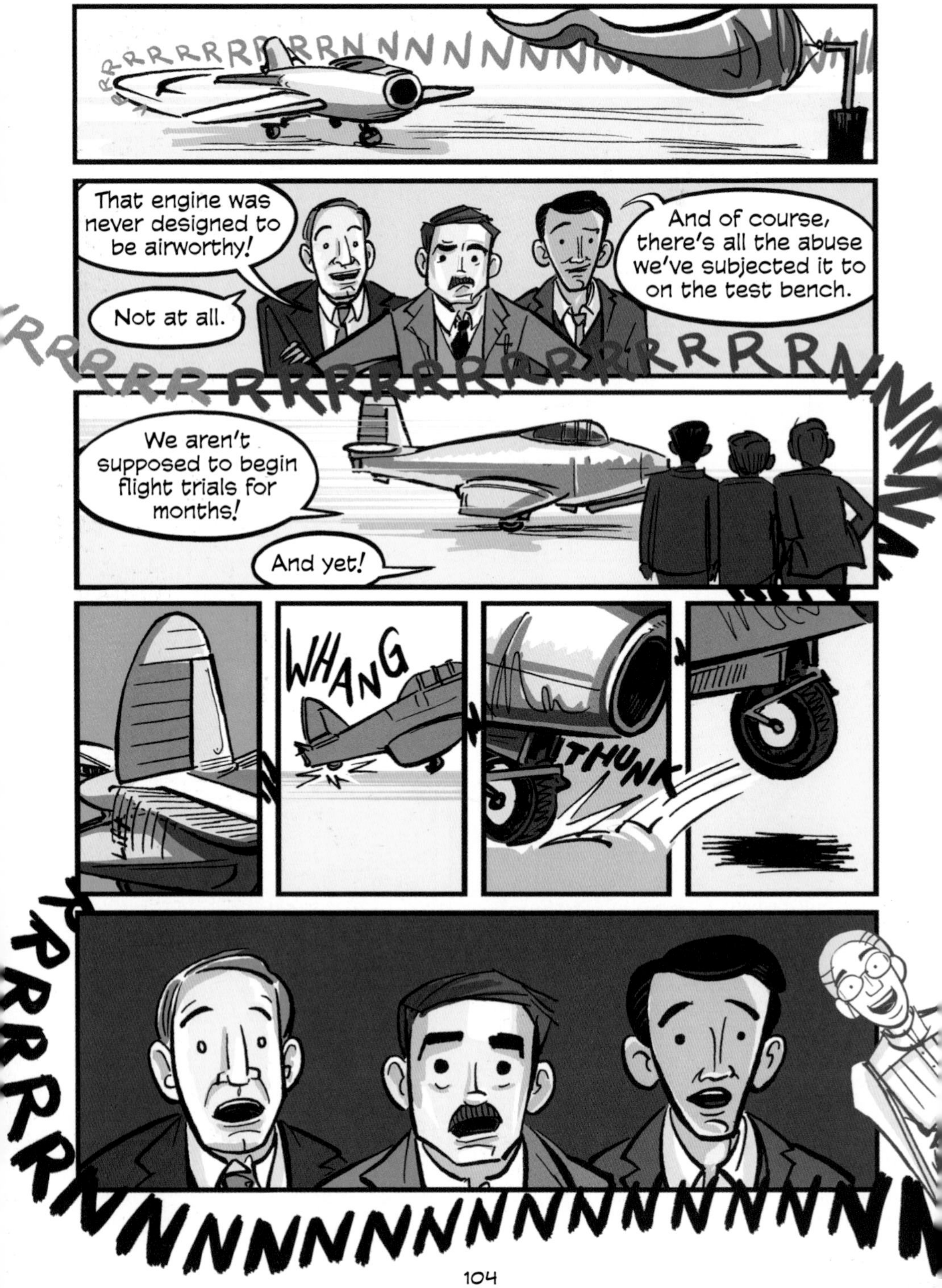
RRRRRRRRRRRRRNNNNNNNNNNN
That engine was never designed to be airworthy!
Not at all.
And of course, there's all the abuse we've subjected it to on the test bench.
RRRRRRRRRRRRRRRRRRRRRRRNNNNNN
We aren't supposed to begin flight trials for months!
And yet!
WHANG
THUNK
RRRRRRRNNNNNNNNNNNNNNNNNNNNN

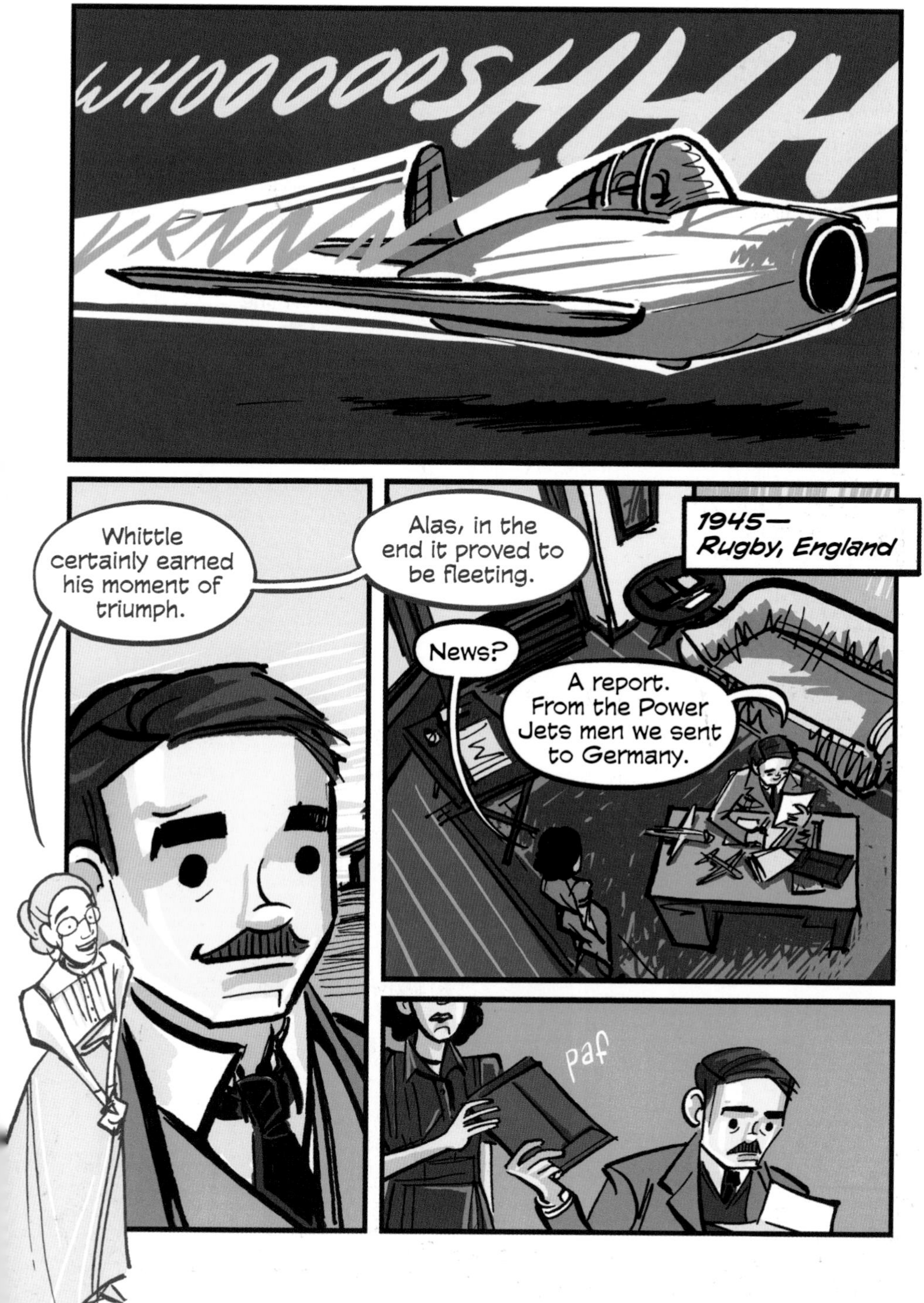
WHOOOOOSHHH
VRNNN
Whittle certainly earned his moment of triumph.
Alas, in the end it proved to be fleeting.
1945— Rugby, England
News?
A report. From the Power Jets men we sent to Germany.
paf

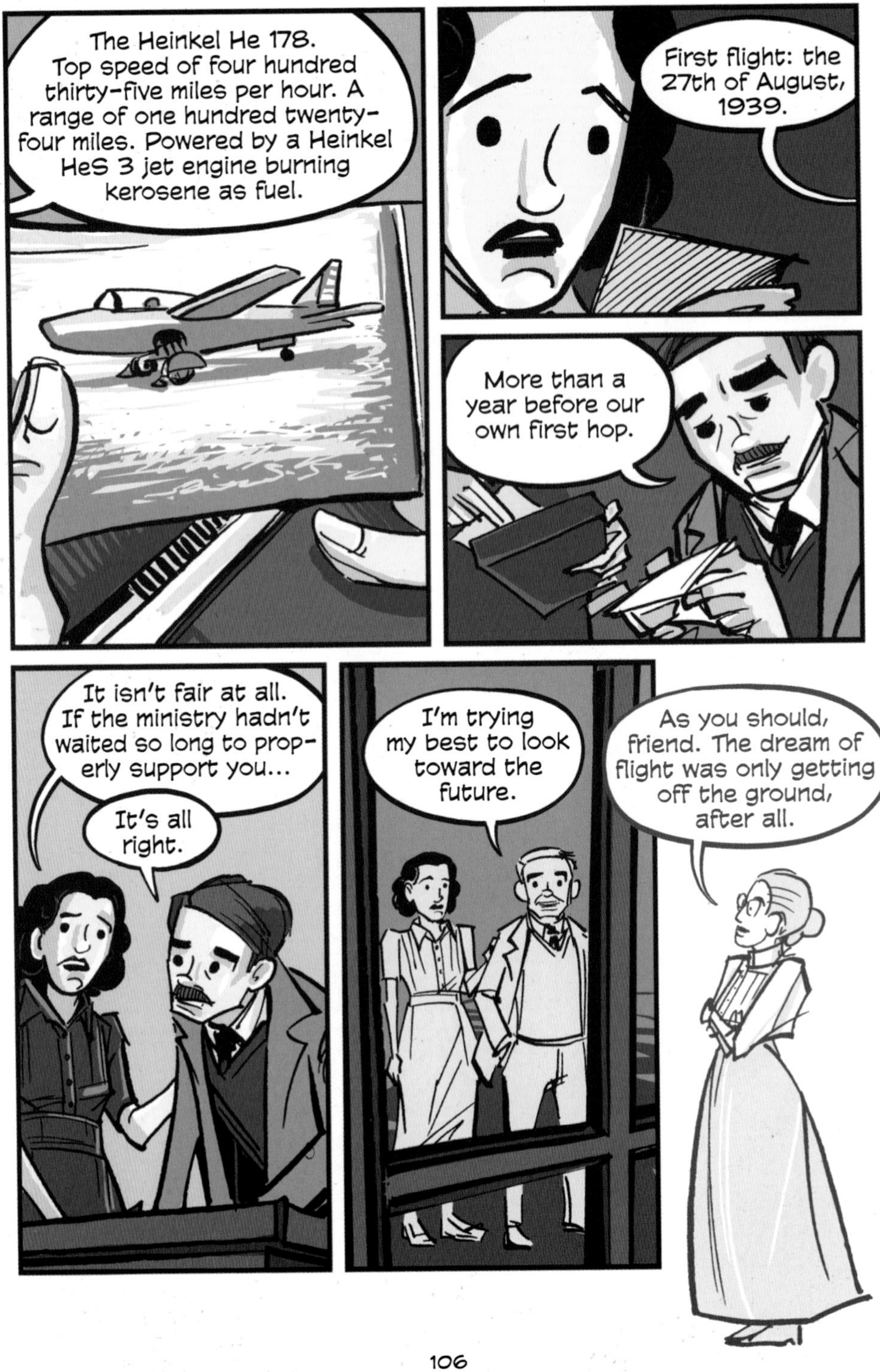
The Heinkel He 178. Top speed of four hundred thirty-five miles per hour. A range of one hundred twenty-four miles. Powered by a Heinkel HeS 3 jet engine burning kerosene as fuel.
First flight: the 27th of August, 1939.
More than a year before our own first hop.
It isn't fair at all. If the ministry hadn't waited so long to properly support you...
It's all right.
I'm trying my best to look toward the future.
As you should, friend. The dream of flight was only getting off the ground, after all.

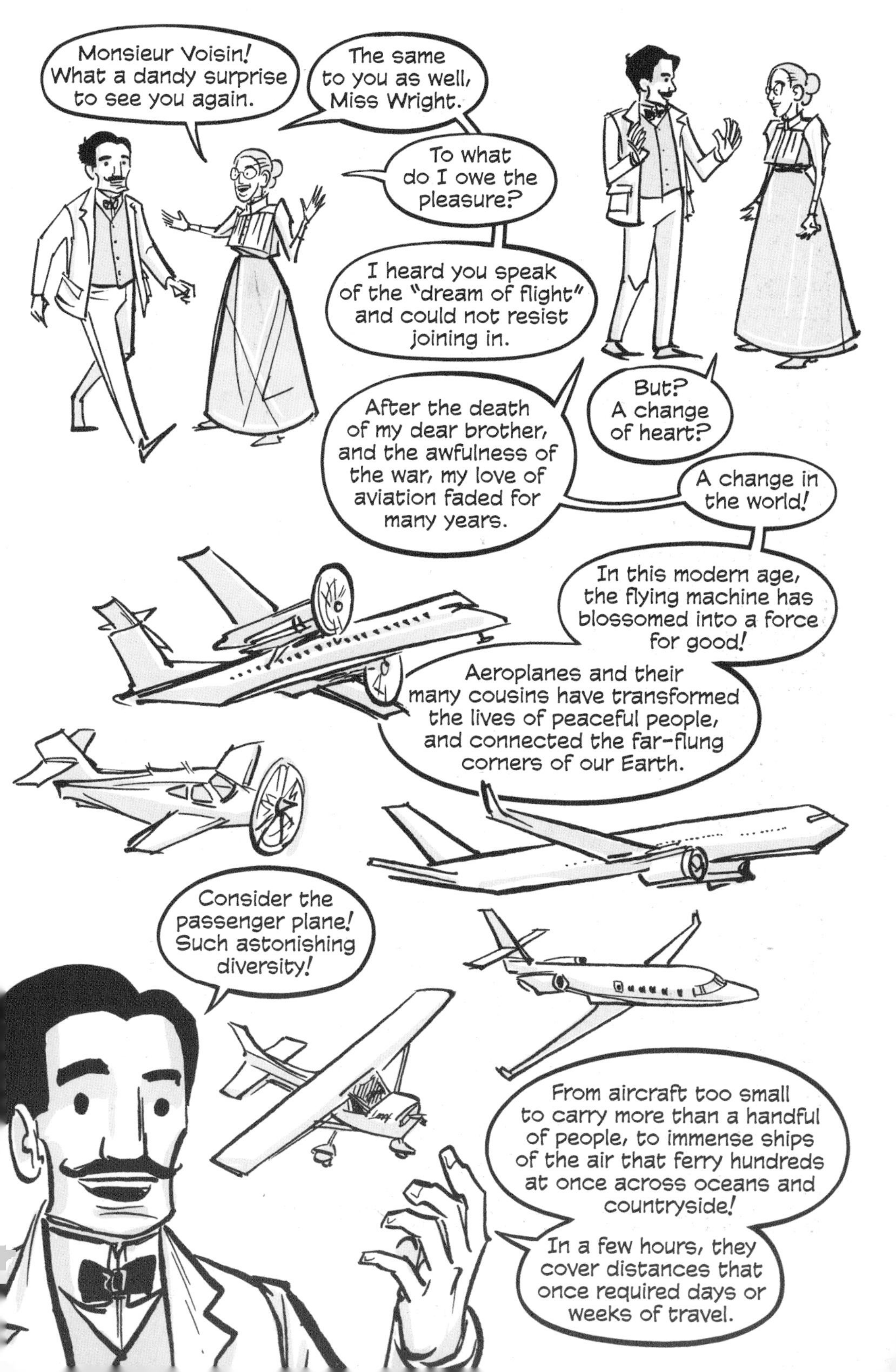
Monsieur Voisin! What a dandy surprise to see you again.
The same to you as well, Miss Wright.
To what do I owe the pleasure?
I heard you speak of the "dream of flight" and could not resist joining in.
After the death of my dear brother, and the awfulness of the war, my love of aviation faded for many years.
But? A change of heart?
A change in the world!
In this modern age, the flying machine has blossomed into a force for good!
Aeroplanes and their many cousins have transformed the lives of peaceful people, and connected the far-flung corners of our Earth.
Consider the passenger plane! Such astonishing diversity!
From aircraft too small to carry more than a handful of people, to immense ships of the air that ferry hundreds at once across oceans and countryside!
In a few hours, they cover distances that once required days or weeks of travel.

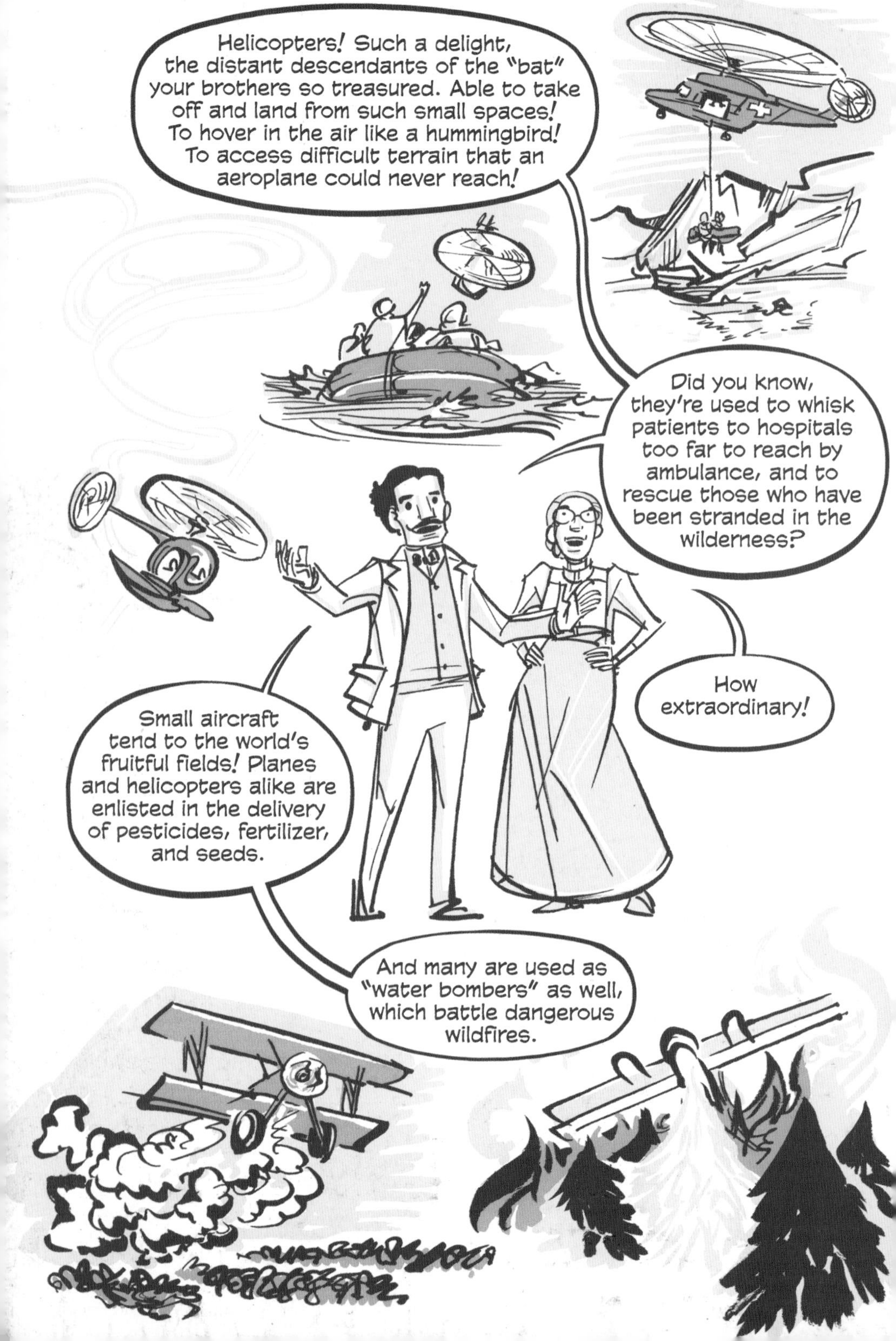
Helicopters! Such a delight, the distant descendants of the "bat" your brothers so treasured. Able to take off and land from such small spaces! To hover in the air like a hummingbird! To access difficult terrain that an aeroplane could never reach!
Did you know, they're used to whisk patients to hospitals too far to reach by ambulance, and to rescue those who have been stranded in the wilderness?
How extraordinary!
Small aircraft tend to the world's fruitful fields! Planes and helicopters alike are enlisted in the delivery of pesticides, fertilizer, and seeds.
And many are used as "water bombers" as well, which battle dangerous wildfires.

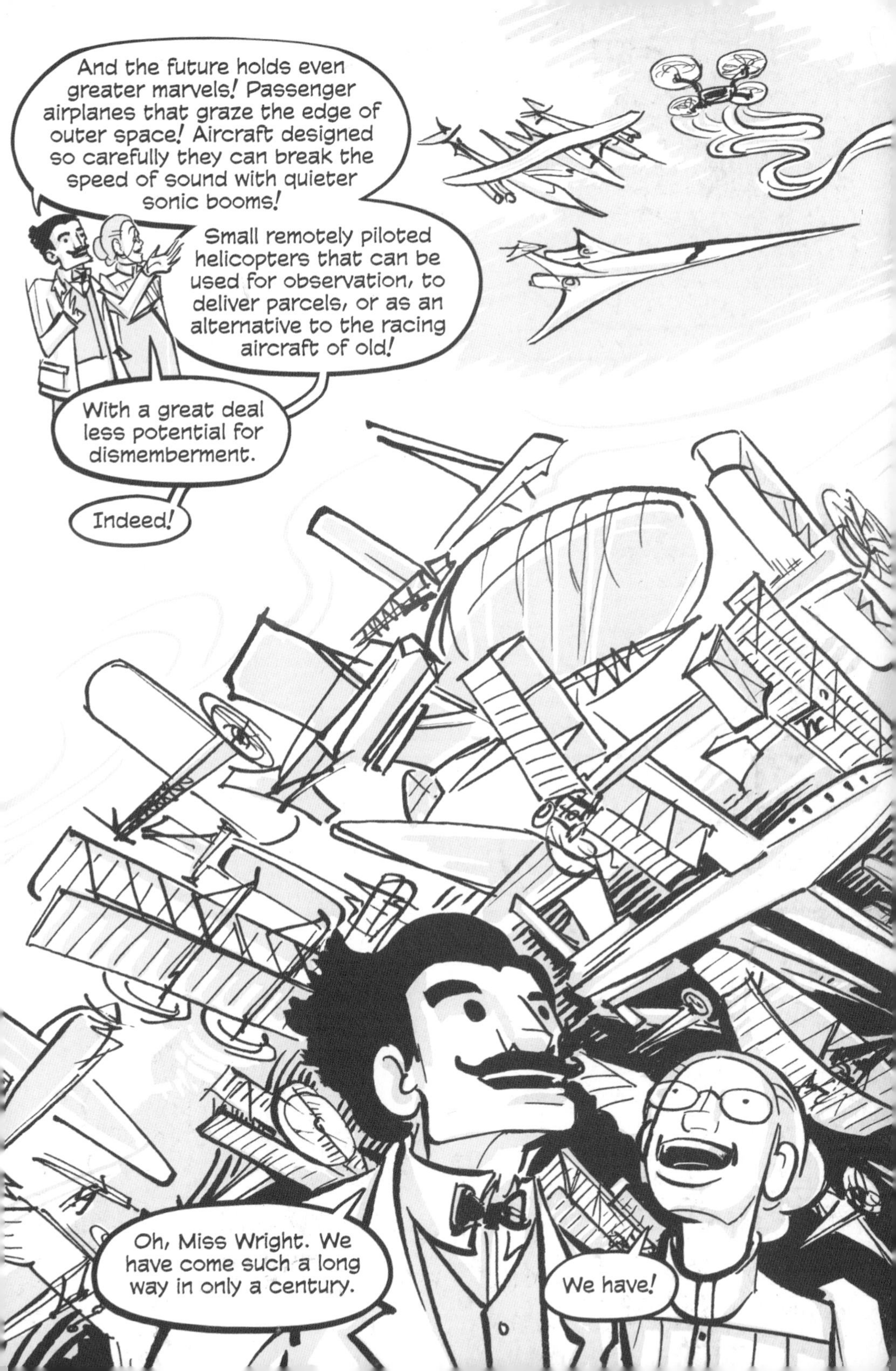

And the future holds even greater marvels! Passenger airplanes that graze the edge of outer space! Aircraft designed so carefully they can break the speed of sound with quieter sonic booms!
Small remotely piloted helicopters that can be used for observation, to deliver parcels, or as an alternative to the racing aircraft of old!
With a great deal less potential for dismemberment.
Indeed!
Oh, Miss Wright. We have come such a long way in only a century.
We have!

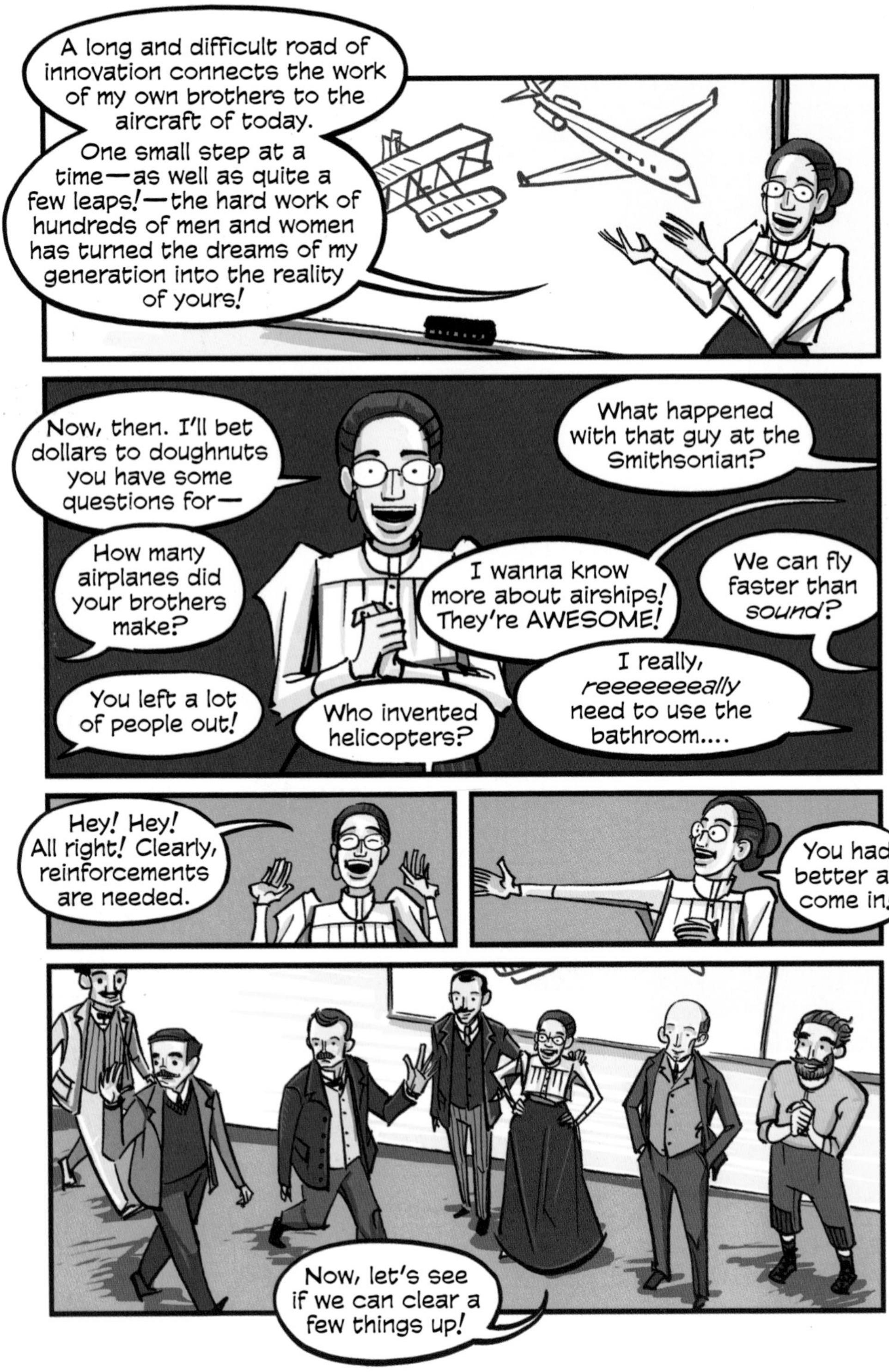
A long and difficult road of innovation connects the work of my own brothers to the aircraft of today.
One small step at a time—as well as quite a few leaps!—the hard work of hundreds of men and women has turned the dreams of my generation into the reality of yours!
Now, then. I'll bet dollars to doughnuts you have some questions for—
What happened with that guy at the Smithsonian?
How many airplanes did your brothers make?
I wanna know more about airships! They're AWESOME!
We can fly faster than *sound*?
I really, *reeeeeeeally* need to use the bathroom....
You left a lot of people out!
Who invented helicopters?
Hey! Hey! All right! Clearly, reinforcements are needed.
You had better all come in!
Now, let's see if we can clear a few things up!

—OTHER AVIATION PIONEERS—

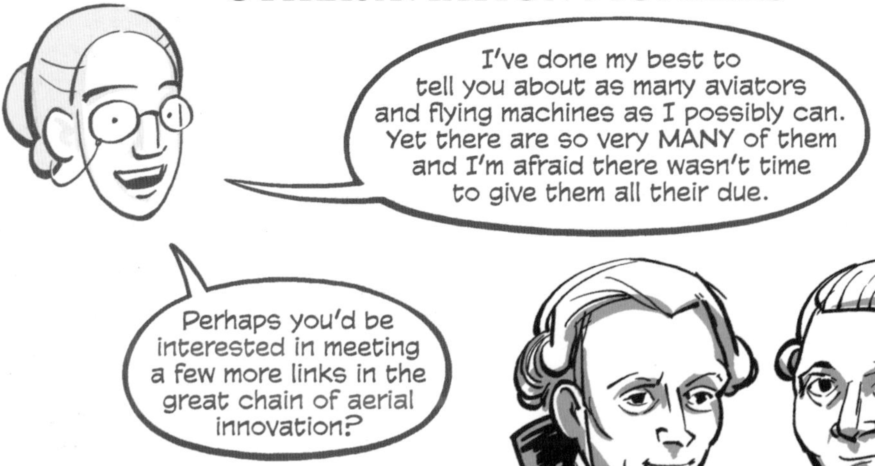
I've done my best to tell you about as many aviators and flying machines as I possibly can. Yet there are so very MANY of them and I'm afraid there wasn't time to give them all their due.
Perhaps you'd be interested in meeting a few more links in the great chain of aerial innovation?

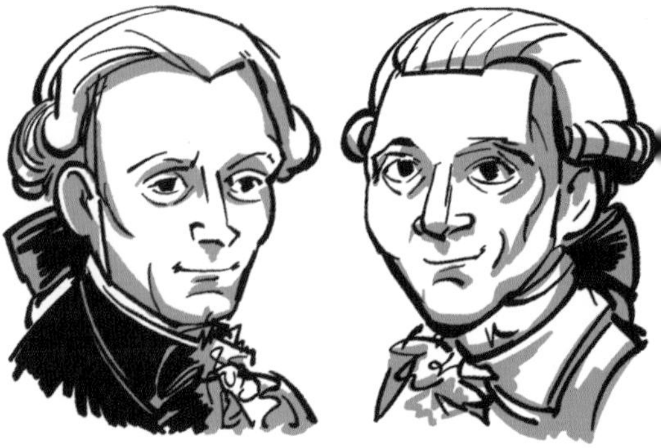

Joseph-Michel and Jacques-Étienne Montgolfier

In 1782, Joseph Montgolfier builds a 3' x 4' box out of wood and taffeta and lights a flame under an opening in the bottom—when the box fills with hot air, it lifts off of his worktable and bumps into the ceiling. This is the first of many experiments Joseph conducts with progressively larger and more ambitious hot-air balloons, and in November 1783, a balloon designed by Joseph and his brother, Étienne, lifts off from the western outskirts of Paris with two passengers on board.

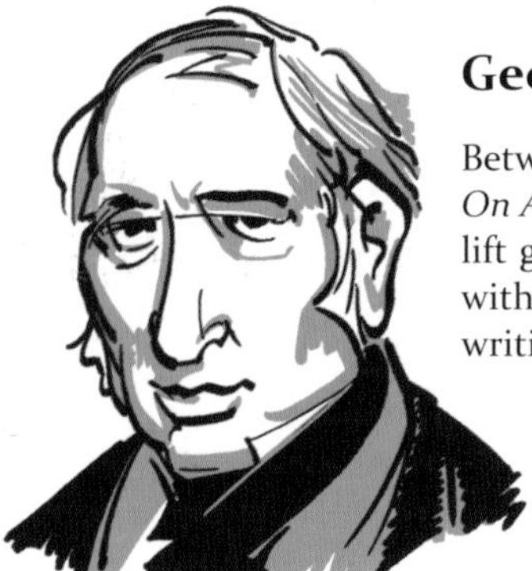

George Cayley

Between 1809 and 1810, British aviator George Cayley publishes *On Aerial Navigation* in three parts, which describes how the lift generated by a bird's cambered wing allows her to glide without flapping once she's reached a certain velocity. His writings are a major influence on later aviators.

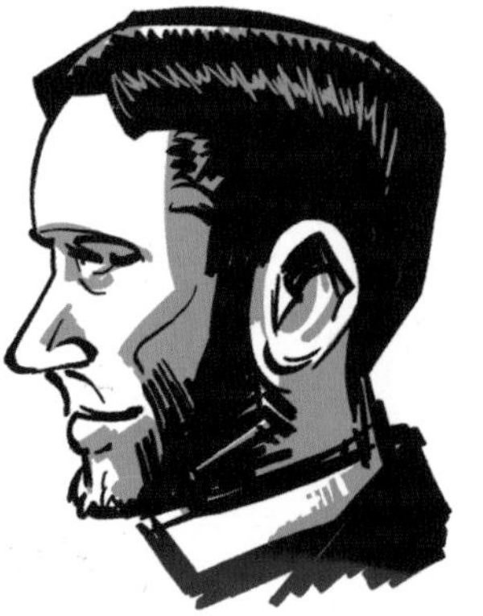

Alphonse Pénaud

In the early 1870s, French aviator Alphonse Pénaud designs and builds a variety of small flying machines powered by rubber bands, including a little helicopter made of bamboo and cork which will one day inspire the Wright brothers' "bat."

Samuel Pierpont Langley

In 1887, inspired in part by Alphonse Pénaud, Smithsonian Institute Director Samuel Pierpont Langley begins to build his own model flying machines with rubber band–driven propellers. His work culminates in two steam-powered "aerodromes," piloted by Charles Manley and launched off the roof of a house boat moored in the Potomac River. However, neither of these flights are successful, and the aerodromes plummet into the water.

Lawrence Hargrave

In 1893, Australian aviator Laurence Hargrave invents the box kite, or cellular kite. He eventually uses a chain of four box kites to lift himself off of the ground. Hargrave believes in the open exchange of ideas, and never patents any of his work. Many future flying machines, including Alberto Santos-Dumont's 14-*bis*, will use box kites as wings.

Octave Chanute

After a successful career as a civil engineer in Chicago, Octave Chanute elects to spend his retirement investigating the world of heavier-than-air flight, eventually collecting his thoughts and findings into a book, *Progress in Flying Machines*, in 1894. Chanute's interest in fostering innovation leads to a friendship with the Wright family, and in addition to introducing the Wrights to other aviators, he also joins Wilbur and Orville in Kill Devil Hills for some of their experiments.

—BIOGRAPHY OF KATHARINE WRIGHT—

Katharine Wright, born on August 19, 1874, was the youngest child and only daughter of Susan and Milton Wright. Her oldest brothers, Lorin and Reuchlin, were already twelve and thirteen when she was born, and so little Katie was much better friends with Wilbur, seven years older than her, and Orville, who was only three when she was born and even shared her birthday.

Their mother, Susan Wright, died when Katharine was only fourteen, and Katharine saw no choice but to step into the role of managing the Wright household. A string of family emergencies kept her from graduating high school, but Katharine was set on her own education, and in September 1893 she boarded the train which would take her to Oberlin College, one of the new "coeducational" schools where women and men studied together in the same classes. Her roommates at the Oberlin boarding house became her friends for life.

About a year after graduating in 1898, Katharine had managed to snatch up a substitute teaching job at Dayton's Steele High School, and as the new century began, she was a full-time instructor of Latin, a professional woman being paid a fair wage, and the only one of her siblings to graduate from college.
Katharine taught for eight years, dividing her spare time between her family and her many friends. But as Will and Orv's notoriety increased, she took over the task of answering the queries of other aviators and enthusiasts, particularly when her brothers were away at Kill Devil Hills, and later, traveling the US and Europe.

When Orv was injured in the Wright Flyer crash at Fort Myer, Katharine left her classes in the care of a substitute and rushed down to Virginia. She stayed for the many weeks of his recovery, and afterward, she and Orv joined Will for his grand tour of Europe.

Katharine was a charming and gracious woman, and grew to be nearly as famous as her brothers. She met the kings of Spain and England, was introduced to President Taft, and was invited to the exclusive Cosmos Club in DC despite its usual prohibition against women visitors. But by the time she returned to Dayton, her position at Steele had been released to someone else, and her career as a teacher had ended.

Will died of typhoid fever, quite young and very suddenly, in May 1912. Orv sold the Wright Company in 1915. Milton lived a few years longer, but after his death in 1917, Orv and Katharine lived in their new Dayton house, "Hawthorn Hill," by themselves.

Aside from a brief engagement, Katharine had never been in anything like a romantic relationship. But as it turned out, one of her old college chums had admired her from afar: a man named Harry Haskell who now worked as a reporter in Chicago. After the death of his first wife, he and Katharine renewed their old friendship and eventually fell in love. Although Orville took the news of his sister's engagement extremely hard, the rest of the surviving Wright family were thrilled, and in November 1926, Harry and Katharine were wed at the home of a friend near Oberlin College.

Katherine Wright first saw the Wright Flyer in the air in August 1905, at Huffman Prairie, watching in amazement as first Will and then Orv lifted off the launch rail. Her own first flight came at Pau in France, with Wilbur in the pilot seat. She was a woman who brimmed with friendliness, wit, and generosity of spirit. There's no doubt that without her years of hard work in support of her brothers, we wouldn't be talking about the Wright Flyer today.

—GLOSSARY—

Acceleration
    The rate at which an object's velocity is changing. In other words, acceleration is a measure of how an object's speed is changing over time.

Aerodrome
    Any one of the series of powered, propeller-driven flying machines designed and built by Samuel Pierpont Langley. More recently, the word is also used to describe a location from which aircraft take off and land.

Aerofoil
    The cross-section of an object—such as a wing—that generates lift as it moves forward through the air. The word may also describe the lift-generating surface as a whole. More commonly written as "airfoil" in modern American English.

Aeronautics
    The scientific study of flight. When describing a scientist or engineer or other investigator who is working within this field, the adjective "aeronautical" is used. As in, "aeronautical engineer."

Ailerons
    A movable surface, usually located at the trailing edge of a wing, which a pilot can swing up and down in order to control the amount of lift each wing generates. This allows the pilot to roll or turn the aircraft while in flight.

Air pressure
    The force with which air is pressing against an object in the air.

Aircraft
    A vehicle designed for flight, which is capable of moving through the air without touching the ground.

A glider invented by Octave Chanute

Airship

A balloon or system of connected balloons with a gondola or cabin for carrying passengers, as well as a propulsion and control system that allow it to be piloted intentionally. In modern times, helium is more commonly used than hydrogen to inflate the balloons.

Altitude

In aviation, this describes the vertical distance of an aircraft from either the ground below (absolute altitude) or sea level (true altitude.)

Angle of attack

The angle at which an aerofoil—or wing—hits the oncoming flow of air in front of it. This angle impacts the amount of lift an aerofoil generates.

Aviator

A person who pilots an aircraft.

Axis of control

The three directions in which a pilot can control the rotation of an aircraft. These are pitch (rotating forward and back, with the front or rear of the aircraft rising or falling), yaw (rotating side to side, with the aircraft staying "flat" on the same horizontal plane), and roll (rotating such that the aircraft rolls in one direction or the other, around a line drawn between the front and rear of the aircraft).

Biplane

An aircraft with two pairs of wings, one pair stacked on top of the other. The Wright flying machines were all biplanes.

A hot-air balloon invented by the Montgolfier brothers

Camber

The difference between the top and bottom surfaces of an aerofoil, or wing. A cambered wing is one for which the upper and lower surfaces have differently shaped curves; in most cases, the upper surface has a larger curve than the lower surface. An aerofoil's camber is defined by a "camber line," a curve drawn halfway between the upper and lower surfaces.

Chord

The distance between the leading and trailing edges of an aerofoil, or wing. A layman might describe this distance as the "width" of the wing.

Dirigible

Another word for "airship."

Elevator

A movable surface or surfaces that can be controlled by the pilot, and which cause the aircraft to pitch up or down as it flies. In modern aircraft, the elevator or elevators are usually in the rear of the machine and form part of the tail.

Flying Machine

A term used in the early days of aviation to describe a device built to move through the air unsupported—in particular, a vehicle which can fly while carrying a human being.

Force

An interaction that, if unopposed, will change the motion of an object.

Glider

A winged aircraft without an engine or propellers.

Model flying machines invented by Alphonse Pénaud

HP

Short for "horsepower," a unit which measures the power output of an engine.

Lift

The force exerted on an object that causes it to move toward an area of lower air pressure. Lift is often generated by air moving over an aerofoil, and is what allows an aircraft to rise up off the ground and fly.

Mass

The amount of matter that is in an object. On Earth under normal conditions, when we measure the mass of an object we're describing how much it weighs.

Monoplane

An aircraft with a single pair of wings. Most modern airplanes are monoplanes.

Parabolic

In the shape of a parabola, which is a U-shaped curve.

Powered flight

When an aircraft is pushed or pulled through the air with the aid of an engine, which in turn drives propellers or turbines.

Propeller

Two or more aerofoils arranged around a central hub, which are spun around that hub to generate lift in the direction of flight. This lifting force pulls or pushes the aircraft forward through the air, and is often referred to as "thrust."

Rudder

A movable surface, perpendicular to the wings and elevators, which the pilot can use to control the yaw, or side-to-side rotation, of an aircraft in flight. When used with the ailerons, this allows the aircraft to turn.

A glider invented by George Cayley

Smeaton Coefficient

A number used by the Wright brothers in their early calculations of the lift they expected an aerofoil to generate. This number, 0.005 lb, was supposedly equivalent to the drag that a plate measuring one square foot would generate when moving at one mile per hour flat-side-first through the air. The Wrights later corrected this number to 0.0033 lb after conducting their own wind tunnel experiments.

Stall

When the angle of attack becomes too steep, and the smooth flow of air over the wings is disrupted. The amount of lift generated by the aerofoil decreases, which causes the aircraft to lose altitude suddenly and quickly.

Streamline

A path traced by an imaginary particle with no mass as it moves with the flow of air. Drawing many of these paths above and below an object allows us to visualize the flow of air over that object, and to show changes in air pressure based on how close the streamlines are to each other.

Wind tunnel

A device that generates artificial wind at a controllable speed, which an engineer or scientist can use in experiments to test aerofoils and other aircraft components and see how they interact with moving air.

Wing warping

A system for controlling an airplane in flight, which twists the wings in order to change their angle of attack. This also changes the amount of lift each wing generates, and allows the pilot to turn the airplane. Wing-warping systems are rarely used in modern aircraft, and have been replaced by ailerons.

Pierpont Langley's failed aerodrome

—FURTHER READING—

Crouch, Tom D. *The Bishop's Boys: A Life of Wilbur and Orville Wright*. W. W. Norton & Company, 2003.

Gillispie, Charles Coulston. *The Montgolfier Brothers and the Invention of Aviation 1783–1784: With a Word on the Importance of Ballooning for the Science of Heat and the Art of Building Railroads*. Princeton Legacy Library, 2014.

Grant, R.G. *Flight: The Complete History*. DK Publishing, 2007.

Jenkins, Garry. *Colonel Cody and the Flying Cathedral: The Adventures of the Cowboy Who Conquered Britain's Skies*. Touchstone, 2000.

Maurer, Richard. *The Wright Sister: Katharine Wright and Her Famous Brothers*. Roaring Brook Press, 2003.

McCollough, David. *The Wright Brothers*. Simon & Schuster, 2015.

Tobin, James. *To Conquer the Air: The Wright Brothers and the Great Race for Flight*. Free Press, 2004.

Whittle, Frank. *Jet: The Story of a Pioneer*. Frederick Muller Ltd., 1953.

A hot-air balloon invented by Jacques Alexandre César Charles

Thanks to Clio, MK, Kari, Scott, Paul,
and Mom for the sympathy and for the
excellent advice. Thanks also and especially
to Molly, whose thorough research and
impeccable style made this book shine.
—Alison

Special thanks to Nick Engler at the Wright Brothers
Aeroplane Company for answering a technical question
super quickly and thoroughly when I was first auditioning
for this book, and to the history nerds of the internet
who shared personal photos and footage of historic
aviation sites I was unable to visit in person.
—Molly

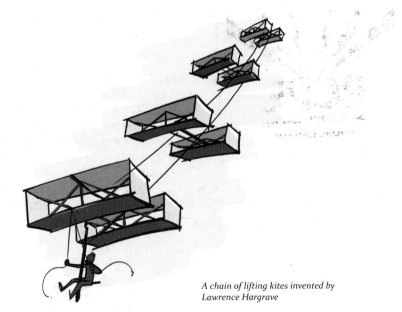

A chain of lifting kites invented by Lawrence Hargrave